Coping with Survivors and Surviving

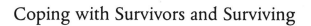

of related interest

Managing Child Sexual Abuse Cases
Brian Corby
ISBN 1 85302 593 3

Boys: Sexual Abuse and Treatment
Anders Nyman and Börje Svensson
ISBN 1 85302 491 0

Sexual Abuse
The Child's Voice – Poppies on the Rubbish Heap
Madge Bray
Introduction by Sarah Boyle
ISBN 1 85302 487 2

Psychodynamic Perspectives on Abuse
The Cost of Fear
Edited by Una McCluskey and Carol-Ann Hooper
ISBN 1 85302 687 7 pb
ISBN 1 85302 685 9 hb

Coping with Survivors and Surviving

Julie Skinner

Jessica Kingsley Publishers
London and Philadelphia

The right of Julie Skinner to be identified as author of this work has been asserted by her in accordance with the Copyright, Designs and Patents Act 1988.
First published in the United Kingdom in 2000 by
Jessica Kingsley Publishers Ltd
116 Pentonville Road
London N1 9JB, England
and
325 Chestnut Street
Philadelphia, PA 19106, USA

www.jkp.com

© Copyright 2000 Julie Skinner

Library of Congress Cataloging in Publication Data
A CIP catalog record for this book is available from the Library of Congress

British Library Cataloguing in Publication Data
A CIP catalogue record for this book is available from the British Library

ISBN 1 85302 822 3

Printed and Bound in Great Britain by
Athenaeum Press, Gateshead, Tyne and Wear

Contents

List of Figures

List of Tables

Acknowledgements

I would like to thank all those who have enabled me to complete this book. The first group deserving of my gratitude consists of all those who have given so freely of their time and their emotions in sharing with me the stories of their experiences.

The second group includes the friends and colleagues who buoyed me up during the process of research and writing. In particular, my thanks go to Dr Carol-Ann Hooper for her knowledge and direction, to Dr Chris Kyriacou for his empowerment and support whilst the original study was being carried out, to Linda Barkas for her promptings, and to Dr Andrew Hodges for checking and commenting on the manuscript as it neared completion.

My thanks are also due to Helen Parry of Jessica Kingsley Publishers for her assistance and motivation whilst turning my original study into this book.

Finally, I am indebted to Jeremy, Justin, Emma, Helen and Joanna for their continuing love, forbearance and tolerance.

Introduction

Background to the study

The study upon which this book is based aimed to explore how survivors of child sexual abuse, and mothers and teachers of such survivors, coped in the aftermath of the abuse. In my initial research, I had hoped to be able to contact respondents from each of these three groups who were connected with the same cases but I was unable to do so. However, I did receive interest from unconnected individuals from all of the groups mentioned. Their stories looked interesting and they had taken the time to contact me. I had originally assumed that the findings of the study would provide useful background material for teachers. I now feel that they have wider implications, and that they may also provide a useful text for social workers, healthcare professionals and others involved in dealing with survivors. The third element of the study – the effects on teachers – came from a conversation with a friend. She remarked that, in her own dealings with abused children within the school context, she had been provided with training about signs, symptoms and procedures, but had been told nothing about how dealing with abuse might affect *her*. This theme of feeling personally unprepared has relevance for all of the groups I have mentioned.

My search of the literature revealed that much of what was written about child sexual abuse only dealt with the experiences of particular groupings. For example, there was a body of writing which sought to explain the effects on, or treatment of, victims. Another body dealt with why abusers offended. A further strand dealt with the problem families that spawned such problems. These often, overtly or otherwise, blamed the inadequate mothers. Largely, such literature was based on medical models which prescribed treatment and predicted outcomes. It was reassuring, towards the end of writing up the original research, to read that 'the wider context in which sexual abuse takes place and the complex interaction between the inner and outer worlds of the survivor is now being addressed' (Christo 1997, p.208).

Just as current research is beginning to acknowledge complexities and differences between those who are affected by abuse, there are also developments which have the potential for promoting changes in practice. The Crime and Disorder Act 1998 embodies a statutory requirement for interagency co-operation to tackle crime; this will have implications for the issues involved in child protection.

In this book, I intend to address some of the complexities and differences which my research uncovered and to make some suggestions for future practice. Perceptions of child sexual abuse, and of its causes and effects, are changing. When I began researching in 1993, there was a small literature dealing sympathetically with mothers whose children had been abused and conceptualising them as survivors themselves. Until 1991, there had been little official distinction between an abusing and a non-abusing mother. Indeed, the stance in treatment had tended to assume family collusion. The literature, which was focused towards the educational sector, emphasised the implementation of procedures and the provision of suitable guidelines for staff.

As a background to this, various child protection inquiries in the 1980s, arguably peaking with the report of Cleveland inquiry (Butler-Sloss 1988), had drawn public attention to the shortfalls of existing provision. The Children Act 1989 was an active attempt to change practice. Whereas before the Act children were routinely removed from abusive situations, measures now focused on the child's individual needs. Similarly, at the commence- ment of the study, *Working Together* (Department of Health 1991) was beginning to have an impact on practice, both in social services provision and in schools.

The Department of Education and Science Circular No. 4/88 (Hancock 1988) required local education authorities and individual schools to nominate and train staff to be responsible for child protection issues. This circular, which noted the importance of teachers in monitoring children for signs of abuse, outlined the need for tighter procedures, although it concluded with the telling sentence: 'The recommendations should not have significant additional financial or manpower consequences.' The role of the nominated person involved training, but in some schools, perhaps, this provision restricted training opportunities for other staff members, unless staff training days were used to cascade information gained by the nominated person. Another source of information for teachers was the teaching unions. But whether a teacher would request such information unless actually dealing with abuse is debatable. The material provided by unions (e.g. Sage 1993) was, like the DES circular, concerned with procedures and contained no reference to how dealing with an abused child, or the child's family, might affect the teacher involved. Indeed, there seemed to be little acknowledgement of the effects on teachers and, where this did exist (e.g. Maher 1988), it coexisted with the mother-blaming tendencies to be found in theories dealing with causation. One theme which particularly concerned me was that training for those involved in dealing with survivors was not always as current as research thinking, and that it often failed to address the unexplored assumptions which might be held by teachers or health professionals.

I wanted to examine the effects on some of those involved in dealing with the aftermath of child sexual abuse and to look at how interaction between them might impact upon practice. Hence my study, which was a qualitative enquiry, sought to interview a small sample of survivors and mothers of survivors, who were self-selected in that they responded to a letter in local newspapers, and a sample of teachers who had knowingly dealt with child abuse survivors, and who represented different sectors of educational provision. The respondents were all interviewed using a storytelling style which allowed them to have control over what details they included. The main aim of the study was to explore how the three different groups were affected by, and responded to, dealing with child sexual abuse; what they perceived as their difficulties; how they coped; and how they felt they were supported. It was predicted that whilst there would probably be areas of difference in such responses across the groups, there may also be areas of similarity between their experiences. I also wanted to explore what more they thought could have been done to help and support them and how they thought provision could be improved for others. I used an interview schedule with all respondents. I found that this usually meant just letting them talk, perhaps asking one or two questions towards the end about points which had not been mentioned. Interestingly, the members of the first two groups, once they had made the decision to talk to me, were very open and gave me information that I would not have attempted to elicit by using structured questions.

The teacher group had a similar willingness to contribute information, and I was often surprised by their reactions. I wanted to interview only teachers who had knowingly dealt with sexual abuse survivors so that they could comment on the realities of that situation as they had experienced it. What I found was that when I approached people who I thought might be willing to be involved, I sometimes received phone calls from friends or colleagues of theirs who had dealt with abused children, perhaps on only one occasion some years earlier, and who really wanted to talk about their experiences. I seemed to have uncovered a need. I had anticipated that dealing with survivors and mothers of survivors might have elements of a counselling encounter, where permissions were given for people to talk about personal or taboo issues. I had not assumed that teachers would have a similarly acute need to talk. The perception that teachers were often adversely affected by dealing with abused children allowed connections to be drawn between aspects of their experience and of the other two groups in the study. It seemed that there was potential for teachers to be viewed as secondary survivors in some instances. I have written about how research may have elements of a counselling encounter elsewhere (Skinner 1998). I was aware that in some instances respondents were using the research interview as an opportunity to revisit their own stories and reactions.

Decisions about definitions

Whilst researching the background literature on child sexual abuse, it became apparent that definitions were an important issue for any study in this area. Kelly (1988) argues that definitions prescribe meaning and allow people to judge whether their particular experience fits into a general category. Just as a definition can allow some phenomena to become visible, so it can ensure that others remain invisible. The power to name something for what it is is not available to every group. Herman (1992) notes that in the past 'women did not have a name for the tyranny of private life' (p.28). My research provided some indications that the inability to acknowledge events for what they are can prevent people from coming to terms with an experience. A further problem with definitions is that they are used differently by various groups engaged in dealing with the phenomenon concerned – thus the purpose of a definition may have an impact on the definition itself. Researchers, workers and survivors will approach the question of the meaning of sexual abuse from different perspectives. Hence, to assume shared understanding of the same form of words can be misleading. Similarly, a definition which becomes inflexible can lead to the production of stereotypes and exclude changes in the actual practice of a phenomenon. Finkelhor (1986) notes that there is no universally agreed definition of child sexual abuse and suggests that a divide exists between those who exclude non-contact acts such as flashing and those who say that anything that makes a child feel uncomfortable may constitute abuse.

So, what is needed in a definition? First, an idea of what constitutes child sexual abuse. If a narrow definition is used, such as that of incest as defined by criminal law (see e.g. Street 1980), it could result in a sample with a greater commonality of experience than a more flexible definition might produce. Such a sample would, however, leave unexplored much behaviour that is equally damaging (Driver and Droisen 1989; Faller 1990; Kelly 1988). And the low reported incidence of incest (Viinikka 1989) may allow it to be seen as a deviant act practised merely by those who are sick or evil. If sexual abuse is defined as a wider problem, or as part of a continuum of behaviour, as feminists have suggested, it can be seen to merge with the range of 'normal' experience of members of a given society (Driver and Droisen 1989). Such a definition would reveal abuses of power that can be perpetrated alongside apparent morality and respectability (Driver and Droisen 1989; Glaser and Frosh 1988; Kelly 1988; MacLeod and Saraga 1988; Reid 1989). This produces a need for a different perception of possible perpetrators. The broader view will be employed in this text.

A second area involves asking who is involved in child sexual abuse. Goddard and Hiller (1993) indicate that, generally, perpetrators are male and victims female. They state that 'victims are more frequently abused by family members or by people known to them' (p.20). They cite Russell (1986) and Baker and Duncan (1985) to justify this. Kelly, Regan and Burton (1991) found that the perpetrator in the majority of cases was a known male adult or peer. Hence, whilst sexual abuse by females is acknowledged, it is seen to be a less common problem; though Mendel (1995) suggests that abuse by females may less often be defined as such.

Third, the sort of behaviours which are considered to be abusive and their context are factors within a definition. The fact that perpetrators are more likely to be male does not make it any easier for such a definition to be applied to any specific male. Abuse is a secret activity and abusers rely on a number of devices to maintain such secrecy. Hooper (1993) argues that being able to name behaviour as abusive can empower a woman to take action. Often, abusive behaviour is shrouded behind illness, drunkenness or threat (Hooper 1992; Kelly 1988). If such behaviours are part of the norms of a family, it may be difficult for those involved to perceive what else is there. Here, the politics of definition within a family may be such that there are not consensual norms. An inappropriate amount of power held by one family member may affect the norms that operate. Other family members may comply to demands simply through the threat of retribution. Kirkwood (1993) has talked of women's need to redefine themselves after they have left abusive relationships that have caused them to devalue themselves and their own abilities. Such factors may be part of the dynamics which operate against defining situations for what they are. Sometimes a mother may be called upon to redefine incidents, of which she has been aware, after a child has complained about them (Hooper 1992). Comparably, a young child has an awareness only of the norms of its own family and may not recognise behaviour as abusive until it has a wider base of experience upon which to judge earlier incidents. As Ann C. Miller (1990) suggests, the transition between acceptable and abusive behaviour may be gradual and form part of a continuum. This may enable those involved to minimise its significance. Incidents described to me, both during and after the research, would indicate that this can be a difficulty for teachers and other workers involved in dealing with particular cases. Researchers stress that little research exists about 'normal' families (Conte 1990; Olson *et al.* 1989), so the scope for grey areas is immense. Smith and Grocke's (1995) study of sexual behaviour in British homes indicated that in 'normal' families behaviours occurred which could be misconstrued. They argue that such factors as the context, the participants and the interpretations of the behaviour may be more important than the behaviour itself. The differentiation between 'normal' and 'deviant' families may not be a useful one here anyway. Walker (1992) sees its existence as a defence mechanism on the part of society. This idea of society protecting itself from information about abuse is pursued by Hollows (1992).

If sexual abuse is perceived as part of a continuum of behaviour ranging from seductive (Herman and Hirschman 1981) or non-contact behaviours to violent incest or anal rape, it can also be seen as linking to other forms of abuse. Kirkwood (1993) has pointed to the presence of emotional abuse within other forms of abuse, whilst Goddard and Hiller (1993) pinpoint the high incidence of domestic violence to be found in conjunction with sexual abuse. Links to the misuse of power can thus be seen to be involved. This is an element of many of the definitions espoused by feminists who see sex abuse crimes as a way of objectifying and humiliating women and children (e.g. Hooper 1992; Kelly 1988; Woodcraft 1988).

The notion of consent and the ability to give consent is a fourth element within any definition. Most practitioners agree that a child is unable to give informed consent to activities of a sexually abusive nature. Hence, whilst the child may not object to the behaviour, she or he is unable to understand the full implications of what is being asked. An adult, or significantly older child, who takes advantage of a child's innocence or ignorance is betraying that child's trust (Driver and Droisen 1989; Finkelhor 1984; Glaser and Frosh 1988). Again, for the child who is, or has been, involved in an abusive situation, there is the problem of naming what has happened as abusive so as to be able to give meaning to such behaviour and to acknowledge the abuser's responsibility for it. Shepherd (1990), referring to Rattigan's therapeutic work with survivors of trauma, indicates that being able to begin to tell the story of what has happened is a stage in healing, and that often this stage is preceded by confusion and a lack of ability to categorise happenings. It is unlikely that informed consent would lead to such confusion.

Perhaps an important point for those dealing with this area is that they need to be able to relate to a definition. For survivors this will ensure that they have begun the process of classifying their experience, although they may be far from understanding it or coming to terms with it. For mothers, teachers, social workers or health professionals a sufficiently broad definition will allow them to filter some of the complexities and grey areas and appreciate what might be implicated. In my research, I allowed respondents to supply their own definitions of sexual abuse in line with what Kirkwood (1991) has suggested. This allowed respondents to perceive it as meaning whatever it did in the light of their own interpretations of a particular situation. This did not produce an homogeneous sample; rather, it allowed individual differences to be explored. Nevertheless, it is important for those dealing with abuse that definitions should be regularly revisited in the light of changing information and research findings.

The term 'disclosure' has been the subject of discussion in the literature. One of the interpretations of this term is used in connection with the process of helping a child to give information about the circumstances of personal abuse, as in O'Hagan's (1989) discussion of strategies for assisting disclosure. Elsewhere, disclosure has been defined as a process which continues over a period of time (Hooper 1992). It is this definition of disclosure which is used in the current book, since mothers or teachers and other professionals may experience indications, without knowing the cause, that a child has worries or problems. Over time, they may learn more detail. This may, in its turn, have further implications for them, as at different stages in discovering a child's story, different responses, emotions and skills may be required.

The issues to be addressed

This book commences with a chapter on how the mother–child relationship is perceived; the second deals with how perceptions may change when abuse colours the picture. The next chapter deals with issues relating to support and the aftermath of child sexual abuse. Then there are three chapters that provide a detailed exploration of each of the three groups – survivors, mothers and teachers – who took part in my research. There is some small element of comparison within these three chapters, although this tends to be kept to a minimum. The final two chapters deal more specifically with the interfaces between the three groups, which are explored through the use of a model based on issues which arose from the study itself and from the relevant literature. These chapters include practical discussion points, make recommendations and draw conclusions.

CHAPTER I

Reflections on the Mother–Child Relationship

What is a mother's role?

The question 'What is a mother?' is not one that most of us give much thought to, although we all have assumptions about it. The maternal role has been both idealised and damned. What is needed to be a 'good' mother is subject both to fashion and to historical period (Oakley 1986). A mother's role is open to criticism by politicians, the professions, her children and others with whom she comes into contact. Yet, she has very little preparation for playing this part (Welldon 1992).

Motherhood is not only about having a child; it is a source of identity (Richardson 1993) – a rite of passage to becoming a fully adult female. Boulton (1983), in her study of mothers with pre-school children, notes three main factors in the meaning women accord to motherhood. These are: feelings of being needed; hopes for the future of their children – usually seen as being an improvement on the woman's own childhood; and pride in their children – which needs to be reinforced by the views of other people. Hooper (1992) notes differing perceptions of children. Some see children as the reason for marriage, others as the consequence of marriage or as the payment for being married. Such perceptions affect the practice of mothering and the meaning it holds. Askham (1984) writes that women mention child care as an activity of marriage but classify it as one which is not always liked.

Research, and commentary, on mothers comes from varying perspectives and sometimes the individual performing the role is excluded from the picture. The ideal mother, according to Bowlby (1965), is selfless, constantly on call, and totally satisfied by caring for her child. This, Sommerfeld (1989) notes, has led to maternal shortcomings being credited with producing an instant, linear explanation for defects in the child. Smith (1991) remarks that mothers who turn to official sources for help can often perceive themselves as failures for needing to take such action. Those who have looked at individual mothers and their practice of motherhood are aware of wide variations. In contrast to Bowlby's notion of satisfaction from child care, Sanford and Donovan (1984) argue that many women find motherhood less pleasurable than Western culture leads them to believe it should be. They argue against classifying mothers as 'good' or 'bad' without any middle view. Richardson (1993) suggests that an idealistic view of mothers prevents women from being able to express frustrations with this role as they are made to feel guilty about dissatisfaction. The idea of 24-hour availability is challenged by others. Angela Phillips (1993) points to gender differences in how much time a mother needs to spend with her child. Dally (1982), Kitzinger (1978) and Oakley (1985) recognise that, generally, mothers need to spend more time with very young children; but they stress that the relationship is dynamic and calls upon different skills at different ages and stages. Round-the-clock devotion to children assumes not only that a woman never gets tired or moody, but also that she is willing to sacrifice her own ambitions and become economically dependent. This involves a reduction of her own power and status outside the family. Oakley (1985) sees motherhood as involving a sacrifice of elements of identity and independence, noting that often a woman's status becomes a reflection of the breadwinner in the family. However, whilst studies dealing with the actual lives of mothers demonstrate the difficulties of ideals in practice, the ideal is nevertheless embedded in Western culture, providing both an unattainable standard and a source of guilt and blame. Dally (1982) argues that individual needs of both mother and child can be ignored if the objective of keeping them together is seen as essential.

Motherhood is often lonely and isolating (Adamakos *et al.* 1986; Dally 1982; Hooper 1992; Kitzinger 1978; Richardson 1993) and may damage women's social lives (Richardson 1993). Adamakos *et al.* (1986) point to mothers' own need for support if they are to have a stimulating relationship with their children. Piachaud (1984) found that even when women work they are still regarded as responsible for household tasks and for their children. Sometimes mothers choose to work, sometimes they work in order to meet household expenses. The effect of such factors within motherhood affects the way it is experienced. Welldon (1992) notes that mothers are expected to handle all aspects of their relationship with their children competently, and expresses surprise that society finds it so difficult to understand if this relationship goes wrong or a mother is unable to cope.

Since motherhood is invested with so much responsibility and attracts so little by way of preparation, it is surprising that mothers achieve what they do. Caplan (1990) demands that, far from blaming mothers when problems occur, professionals should applaud what they actually do.

So, why are mothers blamed? Traditionally, mothers are responsible for the interpersonal, affective areas of a family's relationship. The ideal mother is expected to be sensitive, nurturing, caring, able to express emotion and available, both emotionally and physically, to her children. When these areas go wrong, she is assumed to have made mistakes (e.g. Schonberg 1990). Feminists, such as Sommerfeld (1989) and Caplan (1990), have helped to make mother blaming visible by linking it to the expectations society has of mothers, and to the power structures it sanctions, rather than to the behaviour of individual women. Sometimes individual women do abuse their children, but until very recently (Hooper 1992) no differentiation was made between the parent who abused and the one who did not – such terms as 'the incest family' (Furniss 1984) reflected and perpetuated this joint culpability. Gordon (1989) looks at the shifting constructions of motherhood and mother blame. Currently, mothering is constructed in such a way that it does involve responsibilities; but there is also a need to make visible the fact that mothers are not solely responsible for everything that goes wrong, as Caplan (1990) has indicated. Campbell (1993) and Melanie Phillips (1993) note recent attempts by politicians to link rising crime to increasing numbers of single-parent (generally read to mean single-mother) families, which illustrates a trend towards blaming.

It is perhaps necessary to revisit the question of what a mother's responsibilities are. Askham (1984) queried the responsibilities involved in marriage – most concerned duties towards spouse and children. Women discussed how money was managed, how food and clothes were provided, and how child care was supplied. Whilst families evolve their own divisions of tasks, it is the general pattern in our society that mothers are responsible for the physical and emotional needs of their children. The responsibilities placed on the shoulders of women are heavy. As Parton (1990) comments, the assumption behind social policy provisions is that women will carry out those tasks which relate to the maintenance of a family's health. The current political emphasis of placing responsibility on the family frequently increases the load on the woman. This role is not subject to financial reward, effectively devaluing its importance in comparison to the status afforded by work – although, unlike with many low-status jobs, the consequences of failure can be profound. The Children Act 1989 uses the concept of 'reasonable parents'. Herbert (1993) defines this as including: provision for survival – food, shelter and physical care; psychosocial functioning – the ability to give love and a sense of security, paying attention to the child, providing new experiences, giving praise, educating, and imbuing the child with a sense of belonging. Barber (1996) notes the impact of a good relationship with parents on the development of self-esteem.

In terms of practice, it would seem that mothers are likely to bear the brunt of the parenting role (Piachaud 1984). The degree of responsibility a mother has may not be matched by her power within a family, perhaps a particularly salient connection when abuse is an issue. Currently, then, mothers have to contend with the requirements of an idealised role that promises satisfactions they do not always experience; have little training; have high responsibilities in connection with their children and their families; and are an interface with local and professional communities. They may be subject to blame from any, or all, of these groups when problems occur.

What is the role of a child?

How children are regarded is also subject to historical and current beliefs. Some literary writers, such as Wordsworth, have idealised childhood innocence; others, such as William Golding, have seen children as savages in need of civilising. Currently, children are regarded as needing protection and tender loving care – it is generally thought that what happens to children in their earliest years may have a tremendous impact on their later personalities (Dally 1982; Richardson 1993). However, Richardson does note that different theories of how to raise children are still current in practice.

So how might vestiges of past child-rearing practices still be apparent today? Reynolds (1999) observes that in the eighteenth century children from aristocratic families were regarded as being very like their parents, whereas lower-class children were seen in a more symbolic light – perhaps as victims of circumstance, perhaps as evil, perhaps as a source of purity or inspiration. Elements of this view may still exist in some arguments about the impacts of social disadvantage and the mistaken perception of abuse as a simple linear progression from this. In the 1930s, many regarded children as being born with a complement of vices that needed to be eradicated by training. Children were punished in ways which would today seem to many to be abusive. In line with the view of the child as intrinsically evil, children involved in sexual abuse were often regarded as young seducers rather than victims. Whilst this view persisted in some quarters (as indeed it does still – for example, a QC recently referred to an eight-year-old victim of child sexual abuse as 'no angel herself' (Johnstone 1993)), by the 1950s and 1960s, when childcare gurus Bowlby and Spock were both writing, it was beginning to give way to more liberal thinking.

Spock believed that children were able to regulate their own needs, arguing that they should never be punished, as this may repress or damage them. This view, coupled with the libertarian thinking of Kinsey, the American researcher into human sexuality, provided the basis of an argument, used by paedophiles, that children enjoyed sexual acts and should be allowed to indulge in them with adults should they so desire (Ennew 1986; MacLeod and Saraga 1988). More recently, research has indicated that children need to be aware of boundaries and that the imposition of restrictions on their behaviour gives them a sense of security (e.g. Dally 1982). Christopoulos and Dell (1989), in their study of social competence in seven-year-old children, suggest that children need their mother to be available when they need her, but not always there watching what they are doing. They found that children socialise best if a mother is warm and controlling, but state that too close companionship may have detrimental results. They found that boys who spent a lot of time with their mothers were perceived as more disruptive than their peers. Dally (1982) notes that parents appreciate a caring attitude on the part of their child, and that this seems to be part of normal motherhood. Hence some of what is dubbed 'parentification' – when a child assumes aspects of a parenting role towards an adult – and condemned in 'abusive' situations is expected or welcome behaviour in 'normal' ones.

It is clear that children's needs vary with age and gender. Cullingford (1997) argues that, even in children aged six to nine, a desire for independence coexists with a need for support. Sabatelli and Anderson (1991) note that adolescents need to develop autonomy whilst retaining a sense of 'emotional connectedness' (p.363). They stress the importance of relationships with both family and peers for healthy adolescent development.

Child-rearing practice is varied and complex. Ribbens (1994) points particularly to the inculcation of a sense of individuality in our children. Ribbens notes that families, while they want individuality for their children, can be seen simultaneously to be restricting the areas in which that can be given expression. If our children are seen as individuals, it follows that different interpretations will be given to the behaviour of different children. A child's particular meaning may influence how a family, or a particular parent, deals with him or her.

Reder, Duncan and Gray (1993) pursue the idea of a child performing a role in a script, noting that children are expected to further the aspirations of their parents. Sometimes, they suggest, the child finds his or her own characteristics being submerged in the pursuit of this role. In our construction of individuality for our children, we may note specific characteristics and reinforce them, as Ribbens (1994) intimates. Reder *et al.* (1993) recognise that families attribute meaning to their children but argue that sometimes this can be a distorted meaning. Children who are conceived to patch up a marriage may not succeed in this preordained role and may be scapegoated as an unconscious result. Similarly, children born after a tragedy may be linked with this, and hence treated differently from other family members. It may be that something pertaining to this meaning of an individual child in a family singles him or her out for abuse. Although frequently, as Reder *et al.* (1993) argue, abuse is meted out in greater or lesser degree to all members of a family. However, their study does note that in sexual abuse specifically this may differ and that only one child may be the focus of this sort of abuse.

What are the differences in male and female socialisation?

The ideals of masculinity and femininity upheld by our society are central to some of the gender differences which exist. Angela Phillips (1993) argues that boys often rebel in particularly hurtful ways precisely to escape from the influence of those very characteristics which the 'ideal' mother possesses. A boy may be loud, impatient, rude and cruel just to provoke his mother to react in a less 'caring' way.

Children are born with sexual characteristics and acquire information about gender differences from the socialising agencies they encounter. Golombok and Fivush (1994) report that males subscribe more to stereotypes than females, but perhaps that is because certain stereotypes are more rigidly enforced for males than for females – for example, dress codes. Even when children are brought up by parents who do not actively differentiate between gender roles, they soon learn what is expected of males or females when they mix with other children. Golombok and Fivush cite three American studies which indicate that young children apply sex stereotypes even more strongly than adults do.

Whilst gender roles are subject to change, several writers have noted a range of characteristics associated with masculinity or femininity. Oakley (1985) attributes aggression, independence, courage, extroversion and confidence to males; and sensitivity, perception, dependence on others, introversion, domesticity and emotionality to females. Smith (1989) notes that women are expected to exist, rather than to achieve. Horsfall (1991) observes that the most important thing about such gender lists is that they are dichotomies: men are what women are not, and vice versa.

Levy and Carter (1989) have developed the concept of gender schematisation, the strategy by which children assimilate views of gender and thereby form their individual differences. Some children see gender as being much more important than others. It may be that those who do not match the conventional stereotype for their sex have more problems with identity. Angela Phillips (1993) notes the importance of belonging to a group to confirm one's identity. She suggests that, for many, such a need may exaggerate the differences between the in-group and those who do not belong. Phillips submits that this is one of the reasons why gender differences are so exaggerated in Western society.

Differences begin in childhood; it is commonly suggested (e.g. Golombok and Fivush 1994; A. Phillips 1993) that girls have more regular access to gender models than boys do. Traditionally, child care is undertaken by women, and primary school education is female dominated. Children often see less of their fathers than their mothers. If fathers are absent, Angela Phillips suggests, boys may grow up with an idealised view of men, possibly based on brief contact with fathers or media images. According to Horsfall (1991), this lack of contact with their fathers may lead to a stereotyped view with boys identifying with the sort of personal and position roles men are portrayed as filling in the media, as this is how many boys receive their images of masculinity. In some families, gender roles are more strictly enforced than in others. Oakley (1985) notes that mothers have different expectations of male and female babies and that they may impose more restrictions upon their daughters than their sons. Daughters are more likely to be expected to take their part in household chores and to share child care (Arcana 1981). Arcana also suggests that mothers are more likely both to condone aggression in their sons and to excuse them from household tasks.

Hinde and Stevenson-Hinde (1987) noted that in pre-school children gender differences were found both in 'particular types of interactions' and 'in the two-way influences between individual characteristics and relationships' (p.221). There is evidence here that not only do gender differences occur in young children but they are reinforced by interactions with others. This may mean that such factors as maternal mood have different effects on sons and daughters. This, they argue, may be a result of gender stereotypes held by the mothers themselves.

Olver, Aries and Batgos (1989) suggest that girls may never achieve the same degree of self–other differentiation as boys; they see continuing dependence on mothers by their adult daughters as one indicator of this. Daughters may feel betrayed by the discovery that the apparent power their mothers have in the family is overshadowed by the real power men have in the outside world. Hite, 'the popular American researcher on sexual mores' has noted that 75 per cent of boys express pain and ambivalence at being taunted to become a man (Grice 1994). Boys experience conflict at the prospect of leaving the comparatively known world of women for the less familiar world of men. Kenway and Fitzclarence (1997) perceive that there is a cost involved when boys become part of a male peer group: they may be torn between the need to be seen to be masculine and confident, and an inner feeling of loneliness and uncertainty. They may also become unsure of what emotions it is acceptable to show as a young male.

Indeed, several writers comment on a boy's need to sacrifice freedom of emotional expression to become a man (e.g. Finkelhor 1984; A. Phillips 1993). Mac an Ghaill (1994) argues that male-dominated society pays little attention to boys' problems and suggests that boys are faced with different masculinities which coexist in society. They have to be confident in public, though they may have private insecurities, and they are called upon by their peer groups to separate their emotions from their sexuality. This vulnerability, he suggests, often manifests itself in bullying those, often women, who seem weak.

What is important about the mother–child relationship?

The mother–child relationship will be examined here in connection with differing theoretical perspectives. As has been suggested already, this relationship demands different skills at different ages and with different children. The needs of the young child differ from those of the adolescent.

Gender differences within this relationship have been noted by a number of studies, as Fivush (1989) points out. In particular regard to the current topic, Fivush found that how boys and girls talked with their mothers about emotions, and about memories of the past involving emotions, was different in children as young as three years old.

Age and developmental differences are also important. Honess and Lintern (1990) note the adolescent's quest for individuation and see conflict as stemming from the need to belong but be separate. In interviews with adolescent sons and daughters and their mothers, they found that all parties acknowledged that mothers were supportive but that children would not consult their mothers on certain of the specific areas which the mothers had believed they would. At the age of 16, boys tended to be more independent than girls. A second study carried out by the same researchers, with post-adolescent girls, indicates that by about 20, girls are more able to acknowledge areas of interdependence with their mothers. They see them as people, rather than simply as mothers. A comparable second study was not done with males.

Monck (1991) found that mothers were the most frequently named confidante for teenage girls, but from the age of about 15, female friends were more likely to be told about intimate details. Borduin and Henggeler (1987), in researching post-divorce mother–son relationships, noted that these tended to be less warm than when a father was present. This, they suggest, may be because of greater stress on the mother in having sole responsibility for the running of the family. A second reason they posit is the absence of a second adult to act as a buffer when there is conflict between mother and son. Greene and Leslie (1989) reiterate this concern in relation to any single-parent family.

Theoretical perspectives

If a number of theoretical perspectives on the mother–child relationship are explored, whilst none would question the centrality of the mother–child relationship to mental, physical and emotional development, there emerge differing interpretations of the mechanisms involved. Psychoanalysis, the systems view, attachment theory, transactional analysis and the feminist perspective are considered.

Psychoanalysis

Freud regarded the mother–child relationship as central to human development, and likely to be implicated in problems in later life. Freud saw nurture as important to the study of personality (Brown 1969) and did not assume solely genetic determination. Childhood events, often repressed before adulthood, were held to affect an individual's personality and responsibility for self. Mothers were seen as preparing children for the realities of society by helping in the formation of the ego, thus reducing the amoral pleasure-seeking tendencies of the id. This process operated both at conscious and unconscious levels and involved conflict. Klein, a post-Freudian who was particularly interested in early childhood, argued that the breast as a source of food for the infant provides boundless pleasure, its removal intense anger (Mitchell 1974). Hence, mothers are capable of arousing deep, diametrically opposed feelings in children. The whole process of infantile sexuality is one of conflict: primal instincts versus societal demands. Freud regarded this conflict as universal. Whilst society demands people love and esteem mothers, experience indicates that they can never satisfy us (Mitchell 1974). The relationship is a struggle as children move between dependency and independence. Freud believed that girls marry men like their fathers, but behave towards their husbands as they did towards their mothers. Therefore, in subsequent 'love' relationships they experience the same hostilities. This school of thought suggests that defence mechanisms form the means of coping with reality, protecting the ego from impossible desires. Mitchell (1974) centres this within patriarchy. Freud viewed women as intrinsically jealous of, and inferior to, men – incomplete without them. The patriarchy of society is re-enacted in families where the real motivations for behaviours lurk beneath the veneer of respectability.

Dally (1982), in exploring this view of the mother–child relationship, cites De Mause (author of a text on the history of childhood that was published in 1974), who posits three major adult reactions towards children:

- *Projection* – the adult's own fears become the child's. De Mause locates this historically in events such as parents taking children to public executions; dealing with the child's reaction becomes a means of exorcising adult fear. Dally argues that projection continues in both negative and positive ways. For example, pride and ambition for their children motivates adults' investment in them and subsequent enrichment from them.

- *Reversal reaction* – children are seen as substitutes for figures who were important to parents; children care, or fulfil needs, for parents. Dally acknowledges this reciprocal love as part of parenting, noting such reciprocity is difficult with autistic children. Reversal reactions may be overt or damaging where parents have problematical adult relationships.

- *Conflicting reaction* – the child is seen as simultaneously bad and loving. A child may be punished in the name of love, for its own good.

Family systems

In contrast to the psychoanalytic view, family systems theories locate the mother–child relationship within the context of a family. They involve looking at patterns, resistances and boundaries to ascertain how families function, process information, behave and manage interactions. This model of analysing functioning was adopted by therapists in the 1970s. It is a holistic approach and centres on the interrelationship of cause and effect. Masson and O'Byrne (1990) argue that, despite different approaches to family therapy, the central notions of a search for homoeostasis and resistance to change remain common to family systems thinking.

The impact of postmodern and feminist thinking on family systems is significant, as will be argued. For example, Perelberg and Miller (1990) argue that if family systems thinking is grounded in notions of circularity and self-regulation of the group over time – perhaps involving several generations – issues of gender or historical perspective become invisible. The argument is that power issues are often considered within the context of how power operates within the family, rather than by exploring any one individual's abuse of power. Hence, individual imbalances within the family system are not redressed.

Complications may ensue if, when family difficulties occur, the therapeutic model embraced is based on theoretical notions of hierarchical relations within a family, or focuses on conformity to a patriarchal model. Goldner (1985) argues that an awareness of motherhood and fatherhood as idealised states, not naturally occurring phenomena, needs to be central to family systems thinking and discourse. The family is a social construction; those working with families need to develop an awareness of how their own notions of family have evolved and to move beyond a value-limited view. Normality should be explored within the context of how families actually function. White (1986) suggests that therapists should develop explicit statements of their own assumptions in order to critique themselves. Bauman (1993), discussing postmodern ethics, notes the need to respect ambiguity and to accept that actions can be for no purpose or without calculation.

The systems view of the mother–child relationship puts it in a family context, postulating that family dynamics are affected by interactions with those both within and outside the family. How a family copes with its experiences is determined by the interaction of all involved.

Attachment theory

Attachment theory originated with Bowlby (1951) and was extended by Ainsworth (1962) and others. Bowlby (1987) summarises seven main features of attachment theory:

1. Attachment is directed towards one or few specific individuals, usually with an order of preference.

2. It endures for much of the life cycle. Early attachments commonly persist.

3. It involves emotions. Bond formation is falling in love, its maintenance loving someone. Fear of breaking a bond brings anxiety, its loss sorrow and mourning. Unchallenged bond maintenance provides security.

4. It generally develops during the first nine months of life. The more interaction between infant and adult the more likely is attachment. The person most involved will become the principal attachment figure. Attachment behaviour is readily activated until three years of age, less easily thereafter.

5. It involves learning to recognise familiar from strange. The familiar does not need positive reward; attachment can develop alongside constant punishment.

6. It is triggered by simple stimuli in the early stages, becoming increasingly complex; is dependent on internal and external causes. It may be activated by hunger, fatigue or anything strange and is reduced by interaction with the attachment figure. If this figure is nearby, the child will be confident to explore his environment.

7. It occurs in the young of almost all mammals and can persist through adulthood, suggesting its importance in survival.

Bowlby suggests the ability to form subsequent affectional bonds is dependent on an individual's earliest experiences of attachment. Ainsworth, Bell and Stayton (1971) posit three types of attachment behaviour:

1. *Secure attachment* – trusting, confident children believe parents will help in adversity and thus feel safe and empowered to act.

2. *Anxious resistant attachment* – children are unsure of parental availability or help, are anxious and unwilling to explore the world.

3. *Anxious avoidant attachment* – children have no expectation of help, expect rebuffs, and see no benefit in dependency.

A fourth type of attachment behaviour, arguably the most damaging (Bowlby 1988), is disorganised attachment (Main and Weston 1981). This contains elements of resistant and avoidant styles and fails to provide individuals with consistent coping strategies. It is often linked with physical abuse or gross neglect. Bowlby acknowledged both that people need dependable figures throughout their life cycle to provide personal security and value, and that they need an internal attachment model to discern when to trust others.

Van den Boom (1994), summarising research, links insecure attachment to reduced levels of functioning in interpersonal relationships, or when facing challenges. Poorly attached children are more likely to exhibit behavioural problems. She suggests that mothers' sensitivity to infants can be increased, strengthening secure attachment, although this is untested longitudinally. Again, in a more recent review of research, Honig (1998) argues for the importance of attachment, noting its impact on socio-emotional functioning.

Pearce and Pezzot-Pearce (1994) note that whilst many theorists accept that poor internal models of self can be modified, most agree that in adversity, coping strategies embodied within the internal model re-emerge. These strategies, learnt in early infancy, are incorporated as a response to original attachment with the primary caretaker. Benoit and Parker's (1994) longitudinal study of three-generation families found that a simple parent-to-child model accounts for such transmission of attachment.

Transactional analysis

Transactional analysis (TA) centres round ego states, life positions, life scripts and indulgence in games. It holds that if an individual understands relations, with self and others, then change to existing beliefs or functioning is possible. TA is both a means of analysing communication and explaining individual personality. This duality makes it useful in exploring relationships within families or broader organisations. The system is based upon the parent, adult and child ego states of individuals and their use in communication. Sometimes possible ego states are excluded, limiting functioning; for example, if an individual persistently takes a child role rather than using the more assertive adult role.

During childhood, messages are given which affect how the world is perceived. Hence, abused or neglected children may believe that they are of no value. This may affect interaction with others, ability to trust, and willingness to face new situations. Such perspectives may be incorporated into the 'life script' formed in early childhood. Transactional analysts (e.g. Berne 1964; Harris 1978) have described the concept of a life script, which they suggest is in place in children by about the age of three. This contains such notions as whether the child will succeed or fail and whether he is good or bad, and shapes his expectations of how he will be treated in future. Families which praise and encourage children, and which make them feel good and useful, are helping to provide them with scripts in which they value themselves and others. Other families may set up very different scripts.

This notion has resonances with attachment theory (Bowlby 1965), where bonding is seen as the device which lays down patterns of trust and relationships for later life. Transactional analysis suggests that life scripts may be compounded by the sort of 'games' (Berne 1983) people play, rather than confront central issues. Whereas a confident well-adjusted person has all of the ego states available, can use them appropriately, and is capable of intimacy, those with a less positive self-image may be unable to use certain states, or may spend more time playing games – an ultimately destructive pursuit. Here, those who have contact with the young child are seen as responsible for the internal model of self, the life script.

Whereas psychoanalysis embraces the role of the unconscious throughout life, TA acknowledges the possibility of behavioural modification at any stage. Such modification comes from gaining theoretical insight – hence being able to view one's individual use of ego states and game playing in both internal and external transactions. In this theoretical framework, coping strategies may be perceived to be based on playing games, or on the use of certain ego states in preference to others.

Feminism

Goldner (1985) suggests feminists came late to the study of mothers as they began by exploring their role as daughters – women wanting to leave their mothers to establish their own lives (e.g. de Beauvoir 1958). The family is now established as part of feminist concern, Goldner proposes, as a result of early feminists becoming mothers themselves and bringing their brand of enquiry to their own situations, and to mothers in general.

Feminism explores the societal construction of motherhood and how models and systems impact on this. Oakley (1986) notes that the development of professional knowledge about child rearing and childhood diminishes the knowledge of mothers, both literally and figuratively. She argues that the construction of a good mother is linked to historical and idealised maternal roles:

> Probably the most critical aspect of motherhood's fate in the twentieth century [is] that women's own knowledge of it has become, in the professionalised image, inauthentic. Stripped of its internal authenticity, motherhood becomes an exercise in professional consultation, an axis of self-doubt, and a black hole into which liberated women disappear

only to be besieged by visions of what they gave up (or never had) in order to fulfil this one great intimate destiny. (p.134)

This is one way in which mothers are denied power within the mother–child relationship. Mothering is subject to contradiction by superior, professional knowledge. This affects a mother's power in terms of status, decision making and access to resources. She is regarded as responsible for her children, but professional interpretations of that responsibility increase her opportunities for blame, or errors (e.g. Caplan 1990), and constrain her ability to act. Differences in gender socialisation account for further diminutions of a mother's power within the family. These may be structural: differing expectations affect the roles played; they may be developmental: males acquire additional power within the family as they grow, often rejecting feminine caring values to become more masculine (Grice 1994).

Oakley (1986) acknowledges dangers in seeing motherhood negatively. She cites the 'falling in love' between mother and baby, and the satisfactions that many women experience from mothering. Feminists do not dispute that satisfactions occur, but see them as easily manipulated into the double bind which ties women to a caring role. By exploring individual lives and people's own perception of situations, feminists discover issues which prevailing systems have rendered invisible, both at micro and macro levels. Coping strategies within this model are complex, may be individual or group, and are dependent on limitations of choice, inequalities of power, and restricted opportunity. Explorations of how people cope is central – not identifying methods of coping and fitting them to the situations being analysed.

These theoretical perspectives will be revisited in the next chapter in connection with the impacts of abuse.

CHAPTER 2

Abuse and Its Aftermath

Mothers and sexual abuse

An issue identified in the previous chapter was the tendency to blame mothers for problems within the family. The mothers of those who are sexually abused as children have been singled out by many writers as one of the causes of abuse in that, for whatever reason, they have been insufficiently protective of their children (Bentovim *et al.* 1988; Reis and Heppner 1993). A mother in Dempster's (1993) study demonstrates women's own awareness of this tendency. After finding out about her child's abuse by her current boyfriend, she said: 'I may not have been the best mother in the world but over the past 15 years I have struggled to do what's best for the kids. That won't count now' (p.65).

Mother blaming is sometimes linked to the mother's non-availability when the abuse occurred – resonating with Bowlby's view that mothers should provide 24-hour devotion. Most researchers now see the withdrawal (either physical or psychological) of a mother as only one of the possible factors involved (Glaser and Frosh 1988). But whether this should be seen as her fault is still a subject which arouses some debate, as is shown by discussion of Finkelhor's (1984) four preconditions model of child sexual abuse. This argues that, first, there must be some motivation for the would-be offender; second, internal inhibitions to this motivation must be diminished; third, external constraints must be eliminated; and fourth, the child's own resistance needs to be overcome. Whilst the first two preconditions are the sole responsibility of the offender, the third and fourth bring in other variables, which could involve the mother. This will not happen if a mother is permanently with her child (Bowlby's ideal), unless she also consents to the abuse of the child – a contravention of her caring, nurturing role. Reynolds (1999) notes how women who abuse or kill children are regarded as 'exceptionally and unforgivably depraved' (p.100).

In reality, 24-hour surveillance is improbable – mothers need to sleep. MacLeod and Saraga (1991) disagree that the third and fourth preconditions explain why abuse occurs but suggest that they describe 'how'. The comment by Bentovim *et al.* (1988) that no child is safe without the presence of its mother suggests that no substitute of either sex will do and maintains scope for blaming mothers. This is actually a very damning statement, as it seems to exclude moral choice by those who care for children. Hooper (1992) notes that even those family therapists who attribute a causal role to mothers now split this from the responsibility for the actual abuse which is centred on the perpetrator.

The reasons for mother blame in connection with child sexual abuse are various, though such blame is being challenged. Birns and Meyer (1993) argue that the existing theories may be what is dysfunctional. Featherstone and Fawcett (1994/95), applying a postmodern framework, argue for the need to explore the meanings associated with circumstances in order to appreciate complexities, rather than depending on orthodox or dogmatic understandings. Mothers of sexually abused children have been charged with a variety of defects:

- *Collusion.* Kempe and Kempe (1978) asserted that they had never seen an innocent mother in cases of long-standing incest.

- *Failing in their marital duties.* The assumption here, as exemplified by Laing, is that mothers tire of the sexual chore and hand their daughters over to their husbands.[1] The hidden message is that men are unable to control their sexual urges and need an outlet; if the conventional one is unavailable, they will use another – again, a negation of their moral choice. Failure in marital duties is also the charge when mothers are too tired or ill to carry them out. This, as Reis and Heppner (1993) note, may lead to the parentification of a daughter who thereby also assumes other aspects of her mother's role. However, other researchers do point to women whose sexual relationships with their husbands were good whilst these men were either concurrently abusing a daughter (e.g. Johnson 1992; Reid 1989) or having affairs elsewhere (Horton *et al.* 1990), or both.

1   Tougas, Shandel and Feldmar (1989).

- *Emotional inadequacy.* Salt *et al.*, cited in Gomes-Schwartz, Horowitz and Cardarelli (1990), comment on the physical or emotional unavailability of mothers; they note especially the particular passivity and dependency with which such mothers have been credited. This is not a direct cause of sexual abuse, although it may increase a child's vulnerability as the child may seek affection elsewhere.

  As Ward (1984) comments: '...even if a Daughter does experience her Mother as rejecting, neither she nor the Mother are asking for the Father to rape her' (p.174). Distancing of a child from its mother may (Christiansen and Blake 1990) be a device used by perpetrators to separate the child from sources of help.

- *Poor self-image.* Lack of faith in their own ability to solve problems is seen as characteristic of such mothers. But researchers have no means of exploring whether the abuse has caused this, or whether such characteristics preceded it. Whilst some mothers will have been inadequate before the abuse was discovered (Hall and Lloyd 1993), it is important to look at individuals rather than generalising about a group or a cause. After any stressful event, it may be difficult to assess the characteristics which predated it. Sirles and Franke (1989) query whether the sort of trust which is the basis of a family relationship can coexist with the suspicion that a partner might abuse one of the children. They suggest that mothers are not primed to be on the alert for abuse, so this should not be a reason to blame mothers.

- *Perpetuating abuse.* Those who themselves have been sexually abused will go on to become the mothers of sexually abused children. The British study by Kelly *et al.* (1991) suggests that given the prevalence of child sexual abuse it is unlikely that this will not be the case for many women. Alice Miller (1990) conjectures that an abused woman may not notice her child's abuse because she is repressing her own memories that are too painful for her to acknowledge. Feminists agree that the sexual abuse of a child may trigger a woman's memories of her own abuse, but not with any implication that this may constitute an element in causation (Courtois and Sprei 1988; Walker 1992). This research has not been noted by Reis and Heppner (1993), who comment that a much higher percentage of the mothers of sexually abused daughters in their sample had themselves been abused than had the mothers of the control group.

It may be that women who have not had to face the abuse of their own child have not had to redefine parts of their own experience as abusive, or they may define sexual abuse differently and thus discount incidents in their own experience. Studies which attempt to isolate specific factors in causation may be taking what is essentially a linear view of a multi-faceted problem.

Johnson (1992), in her study of mothers of sexually abused girls, notes that threads of all the myths about mothers of sexually abused children were there in those she interviewed. However, each of these individuals was, or had been, involved in a unique situation which contained differing explanations for such behaviours. Feminists would suggest that it is safer for society to deal with a phenomenon such as child sexual abuse by attributing its incidence to groups which in some way differ from those of us who are 'normal'. Again, this provides evidence of the societal defence mechanism referred to by Walker (1992).

Within the specific context of sexual abuse, societal pressure will ensure that women feel that they have failed their children if they become the victims. Indeed, Breckenridge and Baldry (1997) perceive the institutionalised blaming of mothers as a detrimental factor in both policy making and social work interactions. Despite this blame, mothers are often expected to make far-reaching decisions if their child is abused. In some American states, the law requires mothers to protect their children by informing the police of suspected abuse (Besharov 1990). Ironically, Hooper (1992) notes that women who report child abuse during divorce or custody proceedings may be regarded as vindictive and their stories less credible. Humphreys (1997) reiterates this concern, suggesting there is little empirical basis for such assumptions. Hence, mothers may be damned for action as well as for inaction. It is more likely, if Kirkwood's (1991) argument is pursued, that the distance from the abuser has given remaining family members the security needed to be able to disclose abuse.

Decisions, about how to deal with the abuse, will have to be taken when a mother is particularly vulnerable, especially if her child's abuser is a current partner. As well as dealing with her own problems, she will be expected to support and protect her child and deal with whatever problems the abuse may have caused the child. Coping with her responsibility towards her child may face her with stark choices. Perhaps the responsibility mothers are expected to assume is too great.

The sexually abused child

The sexual abuse of a child is always disturbing, but may evoke different reactions depending on the age or gender of the child involved (e.g. Feiring, Taska and Lewis 1999; Maynard and Wiederman 1997). In terms of age, if a baby or very young child is abused it provokes outrage. Unquestionably, the victim was not responsible for what happened. Back (1998) suggests that age of victim may impact on the allocation of blame, either placing responsibility with the victim or on non-offending parents. As children become older, it is assumed that they will take more responsibility for their own behaviour and will have greater awareness of the consequences of their actions. It is here that definitions may become problematical.

A sexually abused child may have learnt that the only way in which to gain affection is through sex; hence, that child may exhibit sexually provocative behaviour without understanding the implications of such behaviour. Such children may be regarded as 'bad' because their behaviour is not acceptable (Bray 1991; Wattam, Hughes and Blagg 1989). Blagg (Wattam et al. 1989) warns of the danger of seeing a victimised child as bad, since it is likely that the worse the victimisation is, the worse, in adult terms, the behaviour may appear. Such an area is particularly difficult if a parent or professional does not realise what is causing the behaviour and attributes a different meaning to it. That adult may, likewise, be in a difficult situation which is exacerbated by the child's behaviour. For instance, a mother who has just left her partner may find difficult behaviour by her child to be especially hard to tolerate.

The question of informed consent is at issue here, as is the inequality of power between victim and perpetrator. Whereas most adults understand the implications of their actions, children understand only a limited part. A charge which has been levelled at children is that they lie about abuse. Whilst in a few cases this is true, in the vast majority it is not. Many factsheets for mothers or teachers stress that children's allegations should be believed (e.g. Elliott (n.d.); Humberside County Council 1992; Lambeth Women and Children's Health Project 1993).

Unfortunately, there is an unwillingness in society to believe the stories of those who are less powerful (Stanko 1985). This, coupled with what has been dubbed 'false memory syndrome', has provided sceptics with a weapon against believing what victims claim. Grant (1994) challenges this syndrome, claiming that in her examination of false memory cases it was generally a characteristic that the girls involved had been brought up by fathers who blurred the boundaries between the generations and in some way disturbed their daughters sexually. Herman and Hirschman's (1981) research on 'seductive' fathers – men who behaved flirtatiously towards their daughters – indicates that such behaviour by men can produce symptoms in their daughters which are milder than, but similar to, those suffered by incest victims. This may call into question some of what Smith and Grocke (1995) have been prepared to define as 'normal'.

In relation to gender, most studies indicate that there is a likelihood that perpetrators will be male and victims female (Finkelhor 1986; Kelly *et al.* 1991). Finkelhor (1986) has, however, warned that since boys find it more difficult to talk about their abuse it is probable that numbers may be higher than they appear to be. He adds that 'boys may be reluctant to admit victimization because it clashes with the expectations of masculinity. The homosexual character of most abuse of boys may also inhibit disclosure.' (p.62.) Further, he worries that stereotypes about victims may prevent parents and professionals from being as likely to identify abused boys. Finkelhor (1986) has suggested that boys are both less likely to talk about their experiences and potentially more likely to use devices such as acting out or identification with the aggressor. Draucker (1992) has put forward the idea that sexually abused boys may overcompensate by becoming extra aggressive or macho, or may use controlling or compulsive behaviours. Watkins and Bentovim (1992) have suggested that the effects of abuse on boys are serious and have called for further research into the area. According to Gill and Tutty (1997), male survivors may experience problems with sexual identity. Beitchman *et al.* (1992) say that insufficient research has been done on long-term effects on boys. Waterhouse (1993) echoes these concerns and thinks boys may be less willing to talk to female researchers.

Since girls are encouraged to talk more openly about their feelings, both to parents and peers, it may be that gender factors are involved in the healing process itself. This may also have implications for whether mothers are the most appropriate people to help their sons overcome abuse. If mothers have a fear or dislike of aspects of male behaviour, this may affect the messages their children receive. Perhaps boys need a stable and caring male figure in order to unravel the issues relating to masculinity.

Any or all of these areas may relate to every mother–child relationship. Esparza (1993) found no significant differences in the level of support which mothers of sexually abused and non-abused daughters provided. However, she pinpoints what may be a crucial difference. 'A possible explanation…is that the additional stress of sexual abuse in the abused group was such that the level of maternal support necessary for the girl to maintain her coping equilibrium became more of a critical factor' (p.100).

O'Hagan (1989) identifies the importance of support at the time of disclosure, indicating that at this time the mother has the greater difficulty in dealing with the information, but that the child has need of her overt support despite this.

As has been argued, the mother–child relationship is dynamic. Whilst a number of researchers have pointed to the ways in which this relationship can ameliorate the problems of abuse or 'uncouple' it from its lasting effects (Wyatt and Mickey 1987), it is important to explore both of those involved in the relationship and how they interact. This relationship does not commence at the end of the abuse or with its discovery or disclosure. As Hooper (1992) has pointed out, discovery is often a process, not simply a point in time. During this process, mother and child may construct divergent meanings for the behaviour of the other. Children may think that their mothers know about the abuse when in fact they do not, and may blame them for not putting a stop to it (Jacobs 1990). Goldstein (1992) notes that the effects of abuse on the child and the loss of the view of a world which is safe and just may in itself make the relationship with the mother 'particularly vulnerable and fragile' (p.63). The child may not be able to view home as a safe place.

In other instances, children may try to protect their mothers because they know they are having difficulties themselves (Todd and Ellis 1992). Or they may prevent mothers from gaining information because they fear either that mothers will send them or the abuser away or that the family may break up. Abusers often use threats of what might happen to prevent a child from disclosing to anyone (Horton *et al.* 1990). Reilly and DiAngelo (1990), writing of organisational contexts, have argued that, if communication is to be effective, hidden and overt messages should match and that for this to happen an atmosphere of trust and security is needed. Such an atmosphere may be difficult to generate in the immediate aftermath of disclosure. Mothers who have separated from a partner who was the abuser may find it easier to relate to a daughter than a son, as they may perceive male children as representative of the rejected spouse (Wallerstein and Kelly 1980). Hooper (1993) warns that researchers talking to children should not put too great a credence on the child's belief that a mother knew. Before a mother and child can begin to clarify what was known, or not known, both have to be able to talk. The repair of the damage done to their relationship may take a long time.

Theoretical perspectives on coping with sexual abuse

The theories examined in the previous chapter apply to coping with child sexual abuse. Arguably, some theories, such as the Freudian notion of the Oedipus complex, may also have helped to construct some of the problems. Exploring differing perspectives highlights the notion that coping with abuse may affect individuals and groups differently.

Psychoanalysis

Glaser and Frosh (1988) argue that Freud discovered child sexual abuse in many of his clients but denied its existence, thus disadvantaging several generations. They accuse psychoanalysis of 'supporting a climate' (p.28) in which victims' stories are disbelieved. The notion of infantile sexuality can cause confusions. If the Oedipal stage is seen as involving children's fantasies about parents, it is easier to refute real acts, or blame victims for collusion. Defence mechanisms, argued to be integral to family processes, can, paradoxically, work against healthy functioning.

Problematically, psychoanalysis locates desires and motives in the unconscious, thus diminishing awareness of, and responsibility for, actions, whilst increasing scope for blame. A man who abuses his daughter may be seen as re-enacting repressed Oedipal fantasies, so diminishing his overt responsibility. A woman, unaware of her child's abuse, may be seen as unconsciously colluding in it by allowing certain conditions to prevail; that she might be guiltless is not considered. Psychoanalysis validates the fantasy of a parent–child sexual relationship as part of normal childhood. This provides some with a potential rationale for translating fantasy into reality.

Glaser and Frosh (1988) maintain that viewing children as oriented towards pleasure seeking demolishes the romanticised notion of them as innocents needing protection from knowledge of sexuality; this, they argue, has protective potential. The converse interpretation of such pleasure seeking (Parton 1990) is embodied in the libertarian view of children as sexual beings with the right to indulge in activities associated with adult sexuality.

Psychoanalysis centres the mother–child relationship, with its attendant adjustment hostilities, within a patriarchal unit. Thus, problems for mother or child may complicate adaptation. If mothers are the source of pleasure and pain, an impaired relationship may not resolve enough of a child's conflicts to allow the realisation that ideal mothers do not exist. The desire for perfection thus continues into other relationships, or in imagination. Perpetrators often employ different methods or processes of grooming to make a child more susceptible to abuse. Christiansen and Blake (1990) argue that this may isolate children from mothers, and this isolation, it is argued, serves to increase children's need for infinite care, and may fixate some in a childish belief that perfect mothers exist. The belief that perfect mothers exist elsewhere may be an immature response to the real or perceived failure of one's own mother. If, as Honess and Lintern (1990) contend, before the age of 20 girls are unlikely to regard their mothers as people in their own right and so fail to accept their imperfections, an early break in that relationship may prevent such differentiation, or acceptance, from occurring. Consequently, survivors may demand unattainable devotion from subsequent love figures, constantly exacerbating a sense of loss, rather than resolving their quest for perfection.

More positively, psychoanalysis has implications when listening to survivors' stories of their perceptions and expectations of mothers. It also addresses how defence mechanisms are used in coping with abuse or its aftermath. Parry (1991) suggests that Freud validated people by allowing them to tell their stories to an attentive listener. Freud's was a particular agenda, but by telling their stories people can gain their own voice and explore their interpretations of events. This device is central to a study exploring the effects of abuse.

Family systems

Since the family systems view deals overtly with relationships between family members, how normality is seen by therapists working with such families can affect outcomes. Feminists argue that unless issues related to power inequalities within the family are addressed, damaging systems may be perpetuated even by those purporting to help.

Much of the 1980s 'orthodox' view in dealing with child sexual abuse was based upon systems. The idea that dysfunctional families provided conditions which encouraged abuse was commonplace and largely unchallenged (MacLeod and Saraga 1988). The whole family was responsible: there was no differentiation between offending and non-offending mothers, and little recognition of the individual responsibility of perpetrators.

Furniss (1991) describes conflict-avoiding and conflict-regulating families as representing polarities of a continuum. In the former, the family avoids the issues, and abuse 'serves as a means of denying any emotional and sexual imbalance and tension between the marital partners' (p.54). In the latter, there is open family conflict, and abuse 'helps to decrease marital conflict which could lead to family break-up' (p.56). Whilst Furniss acknowledges individual reasons for abuse, he argues that family conditions contribute to its maintenance and explain how families handle disclosure. He believes the change in family relationships causes problems rather than abuse itself. The disturbance of family homoeostasis prompts certain actions. He theorises that a mother's initiation of prompt legal action is to alleviate her own 'acute sense of guilt and shock' (p.57), particularly within conflict-avoiding families, because of the effect on family status of what has emerged.

The notion of circular causality implicit in family systems theory, and its associated mother blaming, is criticised by feminists. If misuse of power is a characteristic of child abuse, family dynamics may stem from how power issues are handled. Jacobs (1994) argues the case for viewing incest, and its effects on the mother–daughter relationship, against the backdrop of patriarchy. Goldner (1985) comments that family systems theorists have for years believed that family function 'is best understood as a clinical problem...'. She reframes it as:

> ...the product of a historical process two hundred years in the making and that power relationships between men and women in families function in terms of paradoxical, incongruous hierarchies that reflect the complex interpenetration between the structure of family relations and the world of work. (p.31)

As a reaction to family systems orthodoxy, in the late 1980s feminist researchers began to explore what mothers actually did (e.g. Hooper 1992; Johnson 1992; Orr 1995) and to suggest that they simply may not have known what was happening to their child (Carter 1993). Despite orthodoxy viewing mothers as culpable, Print and Dey (1992) argue that professionals nonetheless expected them to protect their children from offenders.

The assumptions that mothers, rather than fathers, should provide emotional stability within the family (e.g. Schonberg 1990), should prevent their mates from the sexual excesses they would otherwise perpetrate (Bentovim et al. 1988) and should be constantly emotionally and physically available to their children (Bowlby 1965) have been questioned already. Orr (1995) stresses the complexity and unstructured nature of real experience. Wolin and Wolin (1995) pinpoint the inadequacy of models that explore only how families damage their offspring, which thus neglect individual differences.

Those studying family behaviour and sexual abuse have noted significant links to domestic violence (Deblinger et al. 1993; Goddard and Hiller 1993), and a measurable tendency for perpetrators to misuse alcohol (Glaser and

Frosh 1988). Hence, women and children may be coping with the effects of other behavioural, financial or personal problems in addition to abuse. This would have an effect upon how the family organised itself. Children might not confide in mothers in order to protect them, perceiving that they have other problems (Todd and Ellis 1992), again potentially affecting family dynamics. Most child survivors in Lovett's (1995) study described relationships with their mothers as warm and supportive, yet under one-third disclosed to them.

It has been argued that the secrecy and grooming of victims accompanying abuse (Christiansen and Blake 1990) may distance children from mothers. Stow (1994) further suggests that fathers may groom whole families well before abusive behaviour begins, engendering changes in family operation. Real life is often messy and unpredictable (Orr 1995); mothers are not automatons, do not have insights they 'ought' to have had, do make mistakes or poor judgements, and are sometimes lonely or depressed (e.g. Adamakos et al. 1986; Dally 1982).

Systems thinking allows relationships to be explored. It potentially provides a means for empowerment, and for participants to observe their roles within their construction of family and to assess or reframe patterns. Hoffman (1988) notes the inappropriateness of the 'old repairman' notion of family therapy which implies that the therapist 'mends' the sufferer (p.112), though Minuchin (1991) warns against devaluing what the therapist can contribute by dismissing old methods. Parry (1991), commenting on postmodernism and family therapy, sees notions of hierarchy, specialist knowledge and underlying structures as redundant. He recommends the use of a 'narrative paradigm' which allows people to own their experiences, instead of trying to fit their life stories to a particular norm of society – 'the tyranny of pathologizing' (p.41). As Mason (1993) argues, this narrative paradigm technique, rather than being prescriptive, allows family members to assess their own experiences – placing new perspectives against the old, exploring how individuals might rewrite, reorganise, reselect or deselect, and so changing outcomes. These are devices which transactional analysis would endorse. Flaskas and Humphreys (1993) see this as allowing for a difference in the way power issues are regarded by traditional family therapy – any participant's use of power can be explored. Here, Foucault's (1981) analysis of interactional power replaces a linear, hierarchical view of power (e.g. Featherstone and Fawcett 1994/95). The narrative paradigm appears beneficial for families involved in an abusive situation, though individuals may require specific attention before feeling ready to explore stories as a family (Sgroi 1982).

By exploring individual assumptions, or attributions of meaning, people can realise how they have played in someone else's script and can gain, or give themselves, permission to have rights of their own. Exploring one's own interpretations of events alongside the meanings others have ascribed to them is of potential benefit. The opportunity to relinquish labels may be essential to healing and cannot, necessarily, happen in isolation. Postmodernist family therapy accepts that, although we play in our own stories, we are also characters in the stories of others, both at family and societal level. That stories cannot be lived out without regard to others is both a constraint and, arguably, a liberation. It is regulating to become aware of one's own impact, but potentially liberating to view others' stories as similar to one's own. Feminist group work would endorse this (e.g. Priest, Mockridge and Clear 1993). Linkages between stories can empower by allowing the isolating devices of more powerful people to be revealed, as in the feminists' reworking of patriarchy. As Ann C. Miller (1990) comments:

> ...work which focuses on the differences and similarities between mother and daughter in being part of a system which includes real differences in power between men and women is likely to seek out the strengths in both mothers and daughters and to help women construct realities in which they can challenge abuses of power. Otherwise therapy runs the risk of reproducing the structures of power that keep women in the position of mutual betrayal. (p.147)

Attachment theory

Alexander (1992, 1993) describes how differing patterns of attachment behaviour, based on the child's learning to care whilst being cared for, affect how people care for their own children. She links different modes of insecure attachment to the 'wide array of family dynamics associated with the onset of sexual abuse' (1992, p.187). She believes the attachment patterns of both males and females affect consequent family dynamics, and that attachment may act as mediator, or precursor, for the potential long-term effects. Alexander (1993) notes the need to differentiate between symptoms caused by the specific abuse or by family dynamics. Certain symptoms are associated with trauma; others are connected to basic personality structure and patterns of attachment.

Attachment theory acknowledges that children may be abused where mother and child are securely attached, but posits that insecure attachment may contribute to children being both at greater risk and less able to cope with the effects of abuse if it occurs. It suggests that such children will not only be coping with the trauma of abuse, but also operating with internal models of self less well suited to overcoming problems.

The attachment model offers hope for many survivors, recognising that problems may not stem solely from abuse, but also from other factors within individual development. It acknowledges possibilities for learning, for change, and for interventions to be made which might strengthen the security of an infant's attachment. It emphasises the importance of secure attachment – this may exacerbate the sense of failure of non-abusing mothers who have not provided that security, but reassures others that secure attachment can mediate in overcoming trauma.

Alexander (1992) observes that since certain family characteristics – the presence of a stepfather, maternal absence, marital conflict and violence – are statistically likely within sexually abusive situations, it is worth examining patterns of attachment within this context. In similar vein, Gillham and Thomson (1996) note that whilst correlates of abuse are not causes, there is benefit in implementing measures to promote child safety and avoid the twin risks of failure to identify abusers and targeting those who do not actually abuse. If van den Boom's (1994) suggestion that attachment can be strengthened is pursued, everybody may benefit from training to sensitise them to their children's needs as a preventive measure. This would not diminish the individual responsibility of perpetrators but might, in the event of abuse, enable others to respond differently or cope better.

Alexander (1992) questions whether a father who is securely attached to a child could abuse that child. She notes that family variables such as conflict, cohesion or maternal warmth had more influence on the eventual outcomes of abuse than did abuse-specific characteristics – a second strand to the rationale that secure attachment mediates abuse trauma. More recently, Alexander et al. (1998) suggest that insecure attachment predicates exacerbated long-term outcomes. Alexander warns that the value of attachment theory in this connection is based on attachment being sustained over generations. The theoretical implications for coping skills or changes in attachment style would be affected if longitudinal studies demonstrated otherwise. Reports by adult survivors are subject to their constructions of abuse events, their sequelae and family relations; they may not be a valid basis for assumptions about attachment. As has been noted, Hooper (1992) has warned that survivors sometimes construct their own stories assuming mothers knew about abuse when they did not.

Wolin and Wolin's (1995) study of substance-abusing families suggests a challenge model which examines the experiences children have within families. Such a model does not underestimate the problems of coping with abuse but offers some positive outcomes, suggesting that children learn positive skills from their experiences. If families teach how to filter experiences, we may concentrate on how family deficiencies provide stumbling blocks, or investigate how people cope. The Wolins' seven resiliences – insight, independence, relationships, initiative, creativity, humour and morality – often develop despite family inadequacies. They stress the need to build self-esteem upon such acquired resources, despite the problems, and to explore potential rather than damage. Osborn (1990) points to the value of the resiliences abused children can demonstrate, listing twelve characteristics. Benishek and Morrow (1995) note differences between coping and resilience, suggesting resilience allows individuals to move beyond hardships.

Elsewhere, resilience forms part of Gilgun's (1991) view that supportive relationships with mothers, or other trusted adults, can ameliorate the effects of abuse, allowing healing and resilience to develop. The ability of such relationships to 'uncouple' abuse from potentially lasting effects is supported elsewhere (Esparza 1993; Wyatt and Mickey 1987). Weissmann-Wind and Silvern (1994) note that to develop self-esteem and avoid depression, children need parents who demonstrate empathy, provide a mirror for behaviour, are emotionally available and practise Rogers's (1967) concept of 'unconditional positive regard'. Attachment theory supports this view. Indeed, George (1996) proposes that relationships characterised by secure attachment are the most flexible and can adapt to deal with problems or trauma most readily. Feinauer, Callahan and Hilton (1996) suggest that subsequent positive intimate relationships can offer benefits to adult survivors.

Alexander (1992) argues that attachment theory forms a useful perspective from which to view the effects of sexual abuse, and may reduce the risk of its occurrence. But she warns that its tenets should not be regarded as absolute until a wider range of research has confirmed its predictions.

Transactional analysis

Harris and Harris (1985), taking a transactional analysis (TA) perspective, describe how an abused child depends on the abuser 'because the child has nowhere else to go, he forces his perceptions into the moulds of his need, and distortion in thinking, or incorrect assumptions, are not only possible but probable' (p.29).

Like attachment theory, TA explores how life positions and life scripts form the basis of internal models of self. In this context, of the internalisation of parent, adult and child voices into the personality, it is useful to note Herman's (1992) perception of the effects of trauma. Herman's model of complex post-traumatic stress notes alterations to aspects of self and situations, including: regulation of emotions; remembering or banishing experiences from memory; perception of self and of the perpetrator; how relationships are conducted or avoided; and how meaning is attributed to situations or beliefs. Herman differentiates the effects of trauma between children and adults. Adults have a personality structure in place that may be eroded by repeated trauma; whereas children's personality *formation* is damaged or deformed by trauma. Finkelhor and Browne (1988) acknowledge the value of seeing sexual abuse as a traumatic event, but their model examines cognitive as well as affective areas; hence, distorted beliefs may be involved as well as phenomena like flashbacks.

The adapted child and critical parent voices[2] may be particularly significant in the way abuse trauma is handled by the personality, carrying implications for future interpersonal relationships. Survivors may play victim games, or may conceptualise the abuse as the source of future problems. Here an individual may use the fact of the abuse as a reason for not being able to do certain things, rather than allowing for change and healing.

TA provides a framework for mothers and children to explore styles of interaction and individual functioning, to change how they perceive themselves in relation to others and offers the possibility of healing. Strawbridge (1992) sees it as dynamic and 'liberating' (p.176). As with narrative therapy, people can develop their own voices, explore roles they play in their life script and examine games they use. Like attachment theory, TA may offer protective potential. Families or individuals could be taught to recognise the ego states they are using and thus to take charge and change behaviours.

Feminism

Feminists initially examined how existing models of abuse made assumptions about certain groups. Once damned for believing that women were always victims, feminists acknowledge this is not so, and have been successful in prompting theorists to review their assumptions. Hooper and Humphreys (1998) identify that feminism itself is changing and that

---

2   The 'adapted child' state is where behaviour often centres around compliance or withdrawal: the 'critical parent' state is characterised by prohibitive behaviour and censure. These states are not confined to children and parents but may be exhibited by anyone. For those who have been abused they may become a form of defence to protect the individual from more spontaneous or intimate behaviours.

understanding both the complexities of the mother–child relationship and the contribution of family therapy is an important factor providing for survivors and their families.

If misused power is characteristic of child abuse, family dynamics may stem from how power issues are handled. Jacobs (1994) argues the need to view incest, and its effects on the mother–daughter relationship, against the backdrop of patriarchy.

If mothers are responsible for their children, what does this entail? Is too much responsibility put on mothers? (Hooper 1992.) What, in reality, can a mother be expected to know? Why should a mother suspect her spouse, or male friend, of sexually abusing her child? (Nelson 1987.) How can this be called collusion? (Walby *et al.* 1989.) Why are mothers expected to be with their children all the time? (Bowlby 1965.) As has been argued, feminists take the view that everyday life is messy (Orr 1995). Linked to such messiness is the question of disclosure. Many children disclose abuse to their mothers, and many mothers report this abuse. Hughes's (1993) Hereford study noted that 59 of 148 referrals of child sexual abuse were made by close relations, mainly mothers.

As discussed, Hooper (1992) has described discovery as a process rather than an event. This process has at least two players – the perpetrator and the child – who know what is happening and hide this information for various reasons. (The child may think the mother knows, when she may not.) The third player, the mother, may or may not know, may suspect and have personal reasons for pursuing, or not pursuing, her suspicions. The ramifications are as individual as the occurrence.

The argument of whether the abuse causes the dynamics, or vice versa, is central to the mother–child relationship and can only be answered by longitudinal studies. Kelly, in the foreword to Orr (1995), notes the need to challenge perceptions of what abuse is and who abusers are.

Feminist questioning re-explores existing assumptions and theories by re-visiting the phenomena concerned. The accounts of those who have been abused have been constructed for a purpose. Memories of the time before abuse may have been damaged by the subsequent lack of trust and betrayal. Incidents may be differently interpreted in hindsight. The story is important, indeed central, but so are the questions of why it is told and what is omitted. Whilst abuse is taking place, both mother and child may formulate explanations for changes in behaviour. The effects of abuse on mothers and children, and their relationship, do not disappear with disclosure (Giarretto 1982). Often the impact can appear greater, as action is demanded that may involve stress and privation. The mother's responsibility intensifies as she is expected to believe, act, repair, support and be strong despite her losses within the situation.

Often losses are psychological and material. Both mother and child may exhibit symptoms of trauma (Dempster 1993), may react differently (Herman 1992) and may be at different stages of adjustment concurrently, as exemplified by Remer and Elliott's (1988) research on victimisation. Neate (1992) notes the effects on partners of supporting victims coming to terms with abuse. Any combination of these factors can intensify difficulties. Priest et al. (1993) note the prognosis for children is better if mothers are supported, and they endorse mothers joining survivors' groups. Barrett (1993) stresses the need to link insights between theoretical perspectives in order to retain flexibility and be open to change, rather than feel that one view is the correct one. Hence, there is a need to examine the strategies employed by individuals involved in coping with abuse, and to recognise and explore them using interpretations determined both by those involved and by existing theoretical perspectives.

One of the crucial areas in the healing process is for the child's story to be believed. The extent to which a mother is supportive is a factor which will be scrutinised by any official body called upon to intervene in the aftermath of child sexual abuse. As mentioned, research is beginning to indicate that mothers do generally believe their children (Hooper 1993). What may also be of significance is whether children come to accept that their mothers did not know what was happening if they believed their mothers did know.

Hooper (1993), in reviewing recent research, has noted that the majority of mothers are prepared to respond positively towards their child once they know about the abuse. A high percentage of mothers are likely to believe at least part of what their children allege (Deblinger et al. 1993). Timmons-Mitchell and Gardner (1991) note that there are degrees of belief involved, which may include denial that the abuse has occurred. But they suggest that a child may also be damaged if a parent tries to minimise the child's feelings about the abuse or makes the child feel responsible for not disclosing the abuse earlier.

A factor which has been found in a number of studies is that mothers are less likely to be supportive where the abuser is their present partner (Faller 1988; Gomes-Schwartz et al. 1990; Sirles and Franke 1989) or when the abuser is the child's father (Gomes-Schwartz et al. 1990). However, Deblinger et al. (1993) did not find any significant differences in this area. It is arguably simplistic to look for specific factors that may predispose a mother to be less supportive, since each incidence of abuse is unique and those involved in it will react in ways which are more complex than a sum of knee-jerk responses to the variety of factors involved. As Johnson (1992) has suggested, each story is different and involves its own patterns and reasons.

The effects of sexual abuse on mothers and children will be explored in the following chapter but it is important, here, to examine why the mother–child relationship has been seen to be important in terms of survival and healing. Professionals may view the mother–child relationship as important, in that it provides a means of ensuring protection from the offender in the future (Print and Dey 1992). Gilgun (1991) has pointed to a mother's role in helping a child to develop resilience and has indicated that, whilst this role can also be played by a trusted adult in whom the child can confide, there needs to be a relationship of this sort if healing is to take place. Wyatt and Mickey (1987), in a study of 248 adult women, found that the support of parents and others can ameliorate the damage caused by sexual abuse and can 'uncouple' it from lasting effects. Esparza (1993) notes that nurturing and supportive parenting is likely to mediate positively, whereas punitive measures or distance will have a negative influence on the child's perception of the abuse. Giarretto (1982) suggests that 'alienation from one's parents is intolerable at any age and is particularly painful when the mother–daughter bond is broken' (p.269).

Weissmann-Wind and Silvern (1994) have shown that all children require parents who demonstrate empathy, provide role models and are emotionally available, enabling children to develop self-esteem and avoid depression. Gomes-Schwartz et al. (1990) found that a mother's initial reactions to the abuse, such as anger or punishment, had an effect on both the child's self-esteem and the amount of distress the child suffered. Beitchman et al. (1992) note that the child's perception of the mother's response may be one of the most important factors in the prevention of long-term depression as an after-effect of child sexual abuse. In relation to negative divorce events, which may in a number of cases also be implicated in the aftermath of abuse, Mazur and Wolchik (1992) found that maternal support could lead to a reduction in negative perceptions and improved outcomes. Hence, mothers, even if they are not involved in the abuse, can increase or lessen its effects on the child. Their ability to provide support may depend on the effects they suffer in consequence of the abuse.

CHAPTER 3

Impacts, Responses and Coping

Coping with trauma

Coming to terms with crises takes time, and stages of adjustment in survival have been noted (Herman 1992). Post-traumatic stress disorder (PTSD) is now a recognised complaint with a cluster of associated symptoms. Originally designated as a specific complaint by researchers looking at the reactions of veterans of the Vietnam War, research has examined how people cope with traumas ranging from hijacking to surviving disasters (e.g. Collins 1992; Jackson 1991). Links to PTSD have similarly been made with child sexual abuse (e.g. Patten *et al.* 1989; Wolfe, Sas and Wekerle 1994) and in relation to the impact on mothers of victims of child sexual abuse (Famularo *et al.* 1994). Finkelhor (1988) notes that PTSD involves several components:

1. The presence of an identifiable cause of stress which would produce noticeable signs of distress in most people.

2. The reliving of the traumatic situation through such things as:

   a) recurring and unpredictable memories;

   b) nightmares; and

   c) uncontrollable emotional sensations.

3. A feeling of numbness or reduced involvement in life – perhaps shown by reduced activity, poor relationships and a limited range of emotional response.

As well as this, he notes that for a diagnosis of PTSD to be made, at least two of the following need to be present: '...hyperalertness, sleep problems, survival guilt, problems with memory or concentration, avoidance of activities with intensification of symptoms when exposed to stimuli related to the traumatic event' (p.63). Finkelhor observes that the recognition of child sexual abuse as part of PTSD has been important in allowing sexual abuse to be seen as sharing the dynamics of trauma and not producing a unique cluster of symptoms.

As already referred to in the previous chapter, Herman (1992) differentiates the effects of trauma between children and adults. She posits that 'repeated trauma in adult life erodes the structure of the personality already formed, but repeated trauma in childhood forms and deforms the personality' (p.96). Her model of complex PSTD notes a series of alterations to aspects of self and situations (see p.46).

The process of coping with the knowledge and the emotions of survival can lead to healing, although some people never work through this process and may remain trapped in disbelief or unresolved anger. Quinton (1994) notes that those suffering from the effects of trauma should be allowed to recover at their own speed. Too often there is pressure on survivors to resume their lives as if nothing has happened. She indicates that survivors should be allowed to tell their stories, advising that pressure on them to feel better is often counterproductive.

Finkelhor and Browne (1988) propose a model of traumagenic dynamics to explain the effects of child sexual abuse. This model suggests that the experience of child sexual abuse may involve four factors: stigmatisation, powerlessness, betrayal and traumatic sexualisation. These factors are seen to affect the subject's perceptions of self and others:

1. *Stigmatisation* includes the feelings of shame, guilt or badness which the child experiences in relation to the abuse.

2. *Powerlessness* involves the child's response to the unwanted invasion of his or her body and may be intensified if attempts at disclosure are not believed.

3. *Betrayal* is the child's realisation that he or she has been cheated or manipulated by a trusted adult.

4. *Traumatic sexualisation* is how the child now views sexual behaviour – the child may see such behaviour as the only way to gain affection, or may completely avoid sexual intimacy.

Finkelhor (1988), whilst acknowledging the value of seeing sexual abuse as part of PTSD, argues in defence of this model that there are differences of emphasis. PTSD locates problems in the affective area only, whilst his model brings in the cognitive sphere, allowing distorted beliefs to be involved. Some victims do not suffer PTSD, but this does not mean that they have not been abused. Finkelhor and Browne's (1988) traumagenic dynamics model is applied by Dempster (1993) to mothers of survivors.

By exploring the meaning experiences have for individuals, researchers can produce insights which encompass differences. Personality and trauma factors are again evident in Spaccarelli's (1994) model of coping. This emphasises 'multiple factors that threaten or potentiate poor developmental outcomes' (p.343), noting that stress may be related to the actual abuse, to events surrounding it, and in connection with disclosure. Spaccarelli does not predict problems with coping; rather, he explores areas which could be implicated, arguing that theoretical assumptions are less useful than individual perceptions of stress. This bias towards individual strategies and response has value in examining every stage of the mother–child relationship.

Effects of child sexual abuse

Finkelhor's model, which allows that victims may or may not exhibit symptoms of PTSD, will form the basis of this overview of effects. The effects on children have been split into initial and long-term effects.

Initial effects

Initial effects are defined by Finkelhor (1986) as occurring during the two years after the abuse has ended. He concludes from his survey of studies carried out prior to 1986 that such effects may depend on the age and gender of the child. Effects include: emotional disturbance, most commonly fear and anxiety; anger and hostility, which may be directed at a wider group of people than were involved in the abuse; and inappropriate sexual behaviour. O'Hagan (1989) notes the incidence of sleeping and eating problems in sexually abused children, citing evidence from a number of studies to substantiate this. Wells et al. (1995) mention 'sleep problems and emotional and behavioural changes' (p.160) as the most commonly reported effects in prepubescent females.

Goldstein (1992) cites how theorists have linked child sexual abuse to the 'just world theory', whence primary assumptions about the world as meaningful are challenged, as are a child's feelings of security and personal value. Timmons-Mitchell and Gardner (1991) note that abuse may cause children to mistrust their own judgement, perceptions and actions. Similarly, differences in the behaviours exhibited by children of differing ages in response to sexual abuse have been noted. Gomes-Schwartz et al. (1990) have tabulated the work of different researchers and demonstrated that effects are influenced by such factors as developmental age and previous history. In relation to the former, Tuft's study, quoted by Finkelhor (1986), found that highly sexualised behaviour is more common in the 7–13 age group. For the latter, Gomes-Schwartz *et al.* suggest that cases of long-standing abuse tend to exacerbate the problems and the nature of the sexual abuse. For instance, Wyatt and Powell (1988) suggest that the relationship of the perpetrator to the child and the degree of violence involved may be more significant factors than the nature of the sexual act itself.

There are implications, therefore, that where siblings have all been abused each may exhibit different behaviours in response to the abuse. How information on the initial effects of child sexual abuse is actually collected is important here. Sauzier *et al.* (in Gomes-Schwartz *et al.* 1990) have described three approaches: talking to 'normal' adults about their experience; interviewing those seeking clinical services later in life; and talking to children immediately after disclosure. Each of these strategies will produce a different picture of effects, but none includes those who have not disclosed, or those who have not been believed.

Long-term effects

By discussing the long-term effects of child sexual abuse, researchers have demonstrated how certain effects may continue into adulthood. Sometimes, disclosure first occurs in adulthood; and there are numerous instances of adults experiencing mental health problems and later discovering that their own sexual abuse had been the cause (e.g. Hall and Lloyd 1993). Sometimes, what were initial effects persist as long-term effects. Wyatt and Newcomb (1990) note the degree of violence and the relationship of victim to perpetrator as predictors of long-term negative effects and elements such as self-blame which persists or non-disclosure as additional factors.

Finkelhor (1986) refers to depression as the most commonly reported long-term symptom and cites a variety of studies which endorse this. Beitchman *et al.* (1992) note that six out of eight studies found a link to depression as a long-term result. Young (1992) suggests that the effects of trauma may not be so much related to time as to how comfortably one is able to live inside one's own body. The coping skills that some children have had to adopt to survive the abuse may need to be reassessed for healing to take place (Hall and Lloyd 1993). An example of this is Danica's (1989) description of her use of dissociation as a device for coping with abuse by her father. She was able to cope by regarding herself as 'the body' during the abuse, but the process of reintegrating her feelings was a long and painful one.

Whilst a variety of long-term effects ranging from low self-esteem and emotional reactions through various psychiatric symptoms to multiple personality disorder are possible, the most common effect is depression; and even that can be ameliorated if a supportive relationship is in place. Tsun (1999), in a study based in Hong Kong, notes the potential impacts of culture on coping, particularly where family loyalties may be regarded more highly than individual rights. In this particular instance, reporting abuse could be seen as disloyalty to the family, which is an extremely serious contravention of correct cultural behaviour.

My own study did not look at the incidence of different effects but at how mothers and children or teachers coped with them if they occurred. The different individual responses to the abuse and individual means of coping are the main focus here. How a mother responds to the news of the sexual abuse of her child may be used by the authorities to assess the extent to which she will be supportive. Anger is seen by professionals as a positive response (Todd and Ellis 1992). Carter (1993) describes the shock and inability to function experienced by some women, particularly those whose current partners are the abusers. It may be asking too much to expect all mothers to act quickly and positively on their child's behalf. If a woman is affected in this way, her anger may come later.

Dempster (1993) uses Finkelhor and Browne's (1988) traumagenic dynamics model to assess what happens to mothers. Mothers and children may not experience the effects of these factors in the same way. Research by Remer and Elliott (1988), which explored the concept of secondary victimisation in relation to the problems suffered by men whose wives had been raped, indicated that recovery did not follow the same path and that participants may be at different stages of recovery concurrently. This can be problematical when both parties are coping with different problems simultaneously and whilst, in the mother–child situation, one is specifically responsible for protecting and supporting the other.

Hooper (1992) draws attention to the scale of mothers' losses when their children are abused. She uses a model proposed by Marris (1986) to describe the process of working through grief. This model moves from the initial shock of discovery through acute distress to reintegration, which does not always occur. Hooper (1993) describes women's losses as 'multiple and ongoing' (p.12). She found that such losses include: the ability to trust the abuser; identity as a mother (and as a wife or partner, if the abuser was the partner); control over what happens to the child; expectations or hopes for the future; and memories of the past, as these can be sullied. Other sources of loss included the right to privacy and disruptions to the family.

Gerwert, Thurn and Fegert (1993) see disclosure as a multiple crisis for the mother as it causes her to reconsider her existing concepts of partnership, question her competence as a mother, doubt her own self-concept and degree of assertiveness, and undergo a form of bereavement or conflict in all her relationships; it may also cause material or economic crisis. Reis and Heppner (1993) noted how mothers of sexually abused girls, in their study, had lower self-esteem, less confidence in their own problem-solving ability and a higher degree of life stress. What is left unexplored by their study is how these women did seek to cope, and why some of them were more effective than others or had maintained better self-esteem.

Whilst some mothers may have had problems predating the discovery of their child's abuse, others have not. Muram, Rosenthal and Beck (1994) indicate that mothers of sexual abuse victims are significantly less impulsive and outgoing than mothers whose daughters have not been abused. Such studies cannot demonstrate what these mothers were like before the abuse occurred, although questions could be formulated to discover how mothers felt abuse had changed them.

It is possible, if the perpetrator is the current partner of the woman involved, that she is herself a victim. For example, five out of Johnson's (1992) six mothers had been beaten by their partners; nine of Hooper's (1992) eleven mothers whose partners had been the abusers had been physically, verbally and/or sexually abused by them. Goddard and Hiller (1993) see child sexual abuse as part of a continuum of domestic violence, and found that violence between the adults was a characteristic of just under half of sexual abuse cases and in just over half of physical abuse cases. Herman's (1992) complex post-traumatic stress disorder model may, likewise, be seen to have relevance to the mother's situation, particularly if she has been abused by a partner. Stanley (1997) has noted that social workers have for too long compartmentalised the problems in families and have only recently considered the linkages between domestic violence and child abuse. Especial consideration has only recently been given to other factors that might coexist alongside domestic violence.

Kirkwood's (1993) finding that emotional abuse underlies all other forms of abuse furthers the argument that the mothers themselves may be victims. Hence the impact of Finkelhor's model on them may be both as primary and secondary victims. In addition to the psychological impact of the discovery of the abuse of their child, mothers may have to make choices which, in turn, may cause further effects.

Reis and Heppner (1993) found that mothers of sexually abused children experienced a higher degree of family life stress. This is unsurprising. Mothers face decisions about whether to stay with their partner (if he is the abuser), whether to inform the authorities, and how to protect their children. They may face economic decisions like where and how to live, and decisions about whether to question other children in the family about their possible abuse. They may have to face family and friends who may be critical or disbelieving and may need to know where to turn for support. As the Lambeth Women and Children's Health Project (1993) booklet suggests, such decisions are forced upon women by the behaviour of the offender and are not their choice, even though they will live with the consequences of them. If rating scales of stress are used (Quick and Quick 1984), it could be argued that such a situation is a cause of multiple sources of stress. Reis and Heppner (1993) argue that mothers of sexually abused children are less able to cope with stress and that those in non-abusive families have better coping strategies in place. An exploration of the coping strategies that those in the study actually employed challenges this assumption.

Hooper (1992) found that many of the mothers she interviewed had difficulties in gaining access to the help and support which they needed to cope. This served to increase their sense of isolation. Massat and Lundy (1998) comment on the costs of reporting abuse that are experienced by non-offending parents, and note potential impacts on relationships, finance, the workplace and the area of residence. The needs of mother and child must be addressed in the aftermath of child sexual abuse. Often, both will need individual support before their relationship can become the healing one which is to be desired. Hence, Finkelhor and Browne's (1988) model may be further applied to the behaviours that mother and child exhibit towards each other before this healing process begins.

Coping strategies

Hooper (1993) suggests that, on the basis of only a small number of studies, there are indications that, despite their own distress at the discovery of abuse, most mothers are supportive and do take steps to prevent a recurrence. However, further research is needed in this area. Whilst the measures mothers take may not always be successful, it is important to look at what they do rather than judge them on how successful the measures are.

The mechanisms of coping are likely to involve mothers in contact with a wider network of people, be they official bodies, extended family or friends. There is a sense in which disclosure by the mother replicates the disclosure by the child. Her sense of being supported in her problem will be increased if those she tells believe her, do not blame her and are able to help her to prevent further abuse. Unfortunately, families may express disbelief or have divided loyalties, particularly if the abuser is a partner or other family member. Hooper (1993) points out that such responses may continue over a considerable period and may change as the situation changes, involving the mother in an ongoing process of negotiation and mediation. Whilst this may be the case with adult family members who live elsewhere, it can also be true of those in the immediate family, adding an extra dynamic to family interactions.

Carter (1993) found that some of the mothers in her study felt ostracised by their local community and that this would link with the stigmatisation of Finkelhor and Browne's (1988) model. Telling people is a risky activity – silence might be safer; yet to gain support and protection, others have to know. Herman (1992) points out that 'rigidly judgmental attitudes are widespread, and the people closest to the survivor are not immune' (p.67). If official bodies become involved, a mother may feel that matters have been taken out of her hands and that her own sense of powerlessness is increased. Again, she may be placed in a situation where she feels as if she is being judged (Reid 1989). It is unsurprising that women, despite their efforts to cope and be supportive, find themselves with little confidence in their own ability to take important decisions at this time.

As has been suggested, both mother and child may need access to counselling skills to facilitate healing. Wyatt and Mickey (1987), reviewing the factors which can ameliorate the effects of child sexual abuse, note the need for victims to be able to air their feelings. They also say that victims need to place the blame where it belongs, and not blame themselves for in some way encouraging the abuse. Such insights are equally applicable to mothers.

Whilst many different forms of counselling and therapy are available, Hooper (1992) found that mothers were frequently disappointed in the results when they turned to professionals for help. Sometimes, mothers are required to attend therapeutic sessions; such enforced therapy might only exacerbate a woman's sense that she is being blamed and increase her sense of powerlessness. Driver and Droisen (1989) and Perelberg and Miller (1990) have indicated that unless such therapy empowers a woman it does nothing to redress power imbalances within a family, some of which may predate the abuse. Reid (1989) has suggested that mother and child may need access to different workers, and Hooper (1992) has observed that supporting mothers is important not only from the view of their individual needs but also in terms of how much their support can benefit their child.

Hall and Lloyd (1993) stress the need to recognise the strengths of survivors and the value of the coping strategies they have employed. Even though these strategies may prevent healing and may need to be changed, it is important to acknowledge their value in the past. In helping mothers, such a sentiment would be an extension of Caplan's (1990) call for professionals to value what mothers actually do.

Counselling can provide a source of support for victims and can provide the opportunity for people to talk either one-to-one or as part of a group. Different methods have differing advantages and disadvantages, and some may be better suited than others to individual survivors, as Hall and Lloyd (1993) point out. Scott-Peck (1990) has suggested that the counselling relationship is comparable to that with a caring parent. It may be that some of the skills involved in counselling are appropriate for parenting and that these could be taught in school as an additional support to parenting.

How people construct meaning and how they learn to cope with their lives have implications for the current issue. According to Herbert (1993), Mowrer's two-factor theory of learning[1] may mean that any features present during the abuse can become triggers for comparable reactions and may lead to strict rules being employed by victims to control their own behaviour.

Lewin's theory of social learning (Schein 1988) may be of value both in how survival responses are learned and how they can be later changed. This theory suggests that people move, because of situations or learning events, into a state of disequilibrium that brings with it a need to restore a state of equilibrium. Equilibrium is restored either negatively by rejecting, distorting or suppressing what has happened, or more positively by exploring new modes of thinking or behaving and by their subsequent reinforcement. Lewin notes that this sort of change of learnt behaviours frequently involves pain. Survivors will need time and support to enable them to achieve this learning.

---

1   Mowrer's theory was that a sign – perhaps a sound, in this context, learned in an abusive situation – could lead to a solution – perhaps, here, dissociation. So the sound of a bedroom door opening might lead a survivor to block out ensuing events.

Effects on those dealing with abuse issues

The literature concerning the effects on workers dealing with sexually abused children and their families centres predominantly around the likely effects on social workers (Morrison 1992) and counsellors (Hall and Lloyd 1993). Morrison notes the effects that organisational climates can have on workers in the welfare professions and pays particular attention to how this might impact upon their own unresolved issues. She argues that they may use similar defence mechanisms in the work context as they did in response to their own problems. She particularly notes the stresses on those, including teachers, who have some responsibility for child protection embodied within their role.

Hall and Lloyd (1993) pursue into other areas the range of issues involved in helping survivors, noting that there may be different issues centred around a helper's gender, professional and personal responsibilities, their level of comfort with discussing sexual or emotive issues and the defence mechanisms they use to deal with the emotional content of a case or disclosure. Knight (1997) particularly points to the emotional issues faced by those who work with survivors.

As stated earlier (p.10), training for teachers seemed to pay very little heed to the potential effects of dealing with child sexual abuse on teachers, although teachers who had written about the subject (e.g. Maher 1988; New 1991) had commented on the personal impact they experienced when faced with this issue. A course (Webb 1997) being delivered to teachers at the end of my study noted that they may need support themselves and addressed general support issues during the final 15 minutes of a six-hour day. O'Hara (1988) remarks that a school policy must mesh with the school's atmosphere so that pupils are able to believe that teachers will support them, and comments that teachers need to appreciate the universality of incidence of sexual abuse and its prevalence in all social groups.

O'Hagan (1989) notes a tendency in the literature to contribute to understanding of the issue of child sexual abuse, of why it happens and of who it involves, but he adds that little of it is relevant to the needs of practitioners actually dealing with the problems of individuals or family groups.

Besharov (1990) notes that, over the past 20 years, in most American states, 'teachers, child care workers, social workers, law enforcement personnel...nurses, dentists, and mental health professionals...may be held liable for their negligent failure to identify and report maltreated children' (p.43). If this element of legal liability has been embodied in American practice for that length of time, it is perhaps unsurprising that the thrust of much of the literature available to professionals was concerned with signs and procedures. Indeed, whenever cases reach the headlines, as with Fred and Rosemary West, questions are asked about why schools or social workers failed to notice the problem earlier. A BBC news item, referring to the West case, reported that most health workers had not been trained to 'spot abuse'.[2] This perspective often underestimates the cunning of perpetrators, the uncertainties involved in dealing with abuse and the emotional impact on the workers involved.

O'Hagan (1989) notes that the sort of unchallenged ethics which formed the backbone of the welfare professions in the middle of the twentieth century did not prepare practitioners for some of the social situations which faced them in the 1980s and beyond. The complexities of situations concerning child abuse of whatever sort involve interactions between people and operate within a range of contexts of awareness. Some parents collude in abuse, some know nothing of it; others are located somewhere in between, where their knowledge is tempered by fear of taking action, or by an underestimation of the real nature of the problem. The professional who encounters this situation is not faced with simple choices or decisions but with a web of problems woven from what individuals have done within a group context. Braun (1988), in one of the few texts which deals with training for teachers to take account of such issues, notes that 'training needs to encourage teachers to trust their intuition about children. But it also needs to enable them to confront their feelings about abuse and abusers, and to recognise the ways these feelings might influence their actions.' (p.11.)

It might be argued that when teachers suspect that a child has been abused they begin to move into this same territory of problematical relationships and grey areas of understanding, and, as O'Hagan (1989) argues, potentially, though not necessarily, become involved with manipulative people. In other words, the procedures currently used in connection with reporting abuse may be a means of initiating action, but they do not facilitate dealing with individuals.

A role for education

Since teachers are the people who, after the family, have most contact with children, education may be seen to have an important role to play in addressing the problem of child sexual abuse (New 1993).

---

2   'West case that haunts NHS staff.' BBC Online, 15 December 1998.

One key area is the knowledge of child sexual abuse which individual teachers have available to them. The Hereford study, already referred to in connection with mothers (p.47), reported 148 referrals of child sexual abuse. 59 of these referrals were made by close relations, mainly mothers, and 67 by professionals, mainly teachers (Hughes 1993). One level of teachers' knowledge is thus concerned with recognising that this might be the problem a child has, which may involve knowing the procedures an educational authority requires them to follow (e.g. Humberside County Council 1992).

Teachers may be faced with handling disclosure but may also be faced with less definite hints, just as mothers sometimes are. An understanding of child sexual abuse as a problem that does not simply belong to 'problem groups' may increase their own perceptions of who might be a victim, as suggested by Finkelhor's (1986) comment about boys as victims. Esparza (1993) has suggested that supportive figures in a child's life need to be well informed about the consequences of sexual abuse for them to assist in recovery. Chamberlain (1993) goes further when she suggests that the texts which define sexual abuse may themselves restrict teachers' perception of what constitutes such abuse and hence their 'response to and management of any disclosure' (p.29).

There is still the possibility that professionals, including those in the caring professions, may hold stereotyped views of the type of child who is at risk and of the inadequacy (Reidy and Hochstadt 1993) or blameworthiness (Breckenridge and Baldry 1997) of the mother involved. This means that children from families that do not fit this stereotype may be at greater risk of the abuse going undiscovered. The Norwich Consultants On Sexual Violence (1988) and others (Abrahams, Casey and Daro 1992; New 1993; Wurtele and Schmitt 1992) suggest that their findings indicate a massive need for the training of teachers, particularly in terms of how to foster a safe environment for children's disclosures, rather than merely providing teachers with lists of symptoms that may suggest the presence of something sinister.

It would be valuable for teachers to be provided with information, perhaps during initial training, or on an in-service training (INSET) course, to allow them to challenge any preconceived notions they may hold and to gain a deeper understanding of the variety of issues involved, including the possible effects on themselves. Ideally, such knowledge should be regularly updated. New (1993) notes that the Department of Education and Science Circular 4/88 (Hancock 1988) suggests that there is a need for such INSET but 'stresses that no additional costs should be incurred by this training' (p.24).

Gender differences and their implications for education form another area on which teachers need knowledge. If, as feminists argue, child sexual abuse is part of a continuum of male power, ways of empowering children may be valuable in relation to long-term change. Golombok and Fivush (1994), referring to American studies, suggest that, especially in the early years at school, teachers reward boys and girls differently: boys are praised for knowledge, whereas girls are rewarded for obedience and compliance. In contrast, girls are reprimanded for not getting the right answer, whereas boys are reprimanded for bad behaviour. They suggest that boys learn that they can be clever without being good, while girls believe it is more important for them to comply than be clever by realising that they can get rewards for behaving well if they are not clever. This reinforces a passivity in females that does nothing to prepare them to take an active stance in situations where males are in positions of power. Dziuba-Leatherman and Finkelhor (1994), when exploring the effect of preventive education on boys' perceptions of risk of sexual abuse, state that 'exposure to these programs actually lessens boys' concerns about their risk of being abused, possibly by increasing their perceived control over such an event ... Because of this, there is the danger that boys may unknowingly put themselves in high-risk situations.' (p.566.) This implies that teachers need more awareness of how children may respond to preventive education. Knowledge of such research may underpin the need to provide children with information in single-sex groups, as O'Hara (1988) has suggested. It is possible that teachers do not want to know about sexual abuse and do not want the responsibility of having to deal with its survivors (Kenward 1988). To what extent teachers were prepared or willing to deal with this topic formed part of my research and provoked widely differing responses.

A second important education issue here is prevention. There is a move towards preventive education currently, but such education varies and is dependent upon the knowledge of those who provide it. Whilst sex education is supposed to be presented in a factual value-free way, it is probable that value judgements will creep in. It is easy to equate preventive education with merely teaching children to say 'no' (Mills 1988), but this fails to take account of the imbalance of power in the child abuse situation and may have the result of making the victim feel more responsible for what has happened. Children, Mills argues, do need information as well as assertiveness. There is a move in primary schools to encourage children to be more assertive and to challenge what they know to be wrong (Frost 1987). But this may be insufficient until imbalances of power are less sanctioned within the family. The school is only one of the socialising influences which children encounter.

Maher (1988) notes the potential dangers of preventive education. Knowledge of sexual abuse may sow seeds of doubt or mistrust in children who have been untroubled by such considerations – although those engaged in such programmes would refute this. Waterhouse, Carnie and Dobash (1993) argue that it is unethical to keep such knowledge from children as such dangers do exist. Hendessi (1992) recommends that sex education should include the topics of rape, domestic violence and sexual abuse at both primary and secondary school level. Francis (1992) reports that the whole issue needs opening up and making less secret, and argues that inaccurate perceptions of what child abuse is need to be corrected so that the public recognise both that it happens on a significant scale and that it needs to be prevented. Bogat and McGrath (1993) suggest that even pre-school children can recognise limits to adult authority and that such awareness can be increased through training.

Maher (1988) sees education's role as being one which fosters change in such areas as attitudes towards women, violence, parenthood and relationships. Such views are echoed by feminist writers (e.g. Kelly 1988; MacLeod and Saraga 1988). Gough (Murray and Gough 1991) says that the focus on strangers as the abusers is prevalent in much preventive work, and notes that whilst the concept of good or bad touch may be useful with young children, it is not necessarily the case that they will generalise this concept to known males, such as those within the family (Tutty 1992, 1994).

Preventive education programmes are still being evaluated in America (e.g. Carroll, Miltenberger and O'Neill 1992; Dziuba-Leatherman and Finkelhor 1994; Tutty 1994), Australia and New Zealand (e.g. Briggs and Hawkins-Russell 1994) and in Britain (e.g. Chamberlain 1993). Faulkner (1996) suggests that 'many prevention programs are pursued without research to determine their effectiveness' (p.3).

How such programmes define abuse and the issues involved is likely to continue to have implications for its treatment. Elrod and Rubin (1993) found that whilst parents want their children to know about certain aspects of sex education, there are other areas they would not feel comfortable to discuss. Archard (1993) notes that it is still the case that in Britain 'too much information is held to "frighten" children' (p.77). He counters that argument by saying that 'victims of sexual abuse often testify to the fact that they submitted to the assaults because they had been taught to respect and defer to adults' (p.78), and adds the warning that 'if children are to try to learn to say "no" to adults it cannot just be a localised and parentally approved negative that is encouraged' (p.78).

Hence, education might help in direct ways relating to sex and parenting and through the development of skills which may aid survivors to cope with abuse. Education may take place in the school context or be directed at groups of parents or survivors. In this second context, Parent Network[3] has found that such groups can lead to 'significant benefits to parents in terms of confidence, better communication with their children, improved under-standing of children's feelings and improved handling of children's behaviour' (Kahn 1994). Finkelhor (1986) also endorses the notion of educating parents as a preventive device, and mentions another form of preventive education as being that involved in educating those who have offended to enable them to see the victim's perspective with the aim of preventing further offence. Kaufman, Harbeck-Weber and Rudy (1994) involve the perspectives of both victims and offenders in determining what preventive education should be provided for others.

Kenward (1988) notes that teachers are the adults with whom a child comes into contact most after the family and are thus the next line of defence for a child. New (1993) argues that the school's role in this is significantly underplayed, as is the school's role in providing ongoing support after investigations have run their course. Teachers may be able to play the role of the trusted adult in providing support and nurturing resilience (Gilgun 1991); this may be of especial significance if the mother concerned is not particularly supportive or is enmeshed in her own set of problems brought about by disclosure.

In what is perhaps a less direct way, certain skill areas may help in enabling people to survive abuse. The storytelling, described by Rattigan as the way in which people use language to repair their own narratives in order for healing to take place, is such a skill. Shepherd (1990) sees such an increase in storytelling ability as a factor which increases the potential for re-evaluations and new perceptions of one's own situation. The area teems with questions. Does education do enough to provide people with the ability to tell their own stories? Are the stories we sanction the ones that are socially acceptable, rather than those that need to be told? Does school send some children the message that their stories are not to be told? David (1993)

---

3   A London-based support group set up by parents to give practical help to other
     parents experiencing stress about various child-rearing issues.

questions whether schools listen to children sufficiently or offer children enough time to make their own issues heard. Maher (1988) wonders whether children are helped to acquire sufficient language to describe their emotions fully.

Similarly, do schools really teach children to listen? The active listening skills that are part of the counselling relationship may be of benefit in the context of problem solving throughout life. Horsfall (1991) describes the need for communication skills and problem-solving skills, arguing that violent men often have poor vocabularies and are non-assertive. Being able to communicate effectively, to state one's point and not to be afraid of verbal conflict can all be valuable devices in overcoming stereotypical gender differences in the longer term.

Bloom *et al.* (1956) divide educational objectives into cognitive, affective and psychomotor domains. Whilst knowledge is of indisputable value in understanding child sexual abuse and in challenging stereotypes, perhaps the role of education in the affective domain may do more to challenge the value systems which maintain abuse. If what Mac an Ghaill (1994) has suggested about society's blindness to the needs of boys and their problems is valid, this too is an urgent need.

Interpersonal skills and the ability to express feelings are regarded as feminine characteristics (A. Phillips 1993). Education which permits men to acknowledge and value such areas in themselves may move people towards change (Horsfall 1991).

The role that teachers can play thus spans a number of areas, which range from the provision of skills that may prevent the continuation of abusive situations, to the ability to identify and assist individual survivors. At this more individual level, it may be that the teacher can support a child or parent in the aftermath of abuse as New (1993) suggests. Esparza (1993), discussing the implications for nurses helping those coping with abuse, makes points which are equally applicable to teachers. The teacher may provide the child with a source of support whilst the mother is facing her own trauma in connection with the abuse. Or the teacher may support the child's own coping by being someone with whom the child can talk through his or her own concerns. Similarly, Vulliamy and Webb (1992) have shown that head teachers often take on social worker roles towards parents within the school context. Hence, a mother may turn to the school for support with her own coping in the aftermath of her child's abuse. Several of these areas are acknowledged to be part of the school's role, others could be implemented if the right funding and resources were provided.

CHAPTER 4

The Survivors

This chapter deals with the stories of the survivors who formed part of the study. Their stories illustrate some of the complexities and confusions faced by those who have to cope with the reality of child sexual abuse. The survivors have had to deal with their own abuse without the benefit of whatever adult coping strategies the mother or teacher groups had acquired before their involvement with the situation. Certain of the themes to be found in this chapter will be visited in different chapters. For instance, the impact of the abuse and the coping strategies employed will be a focus for each of the groups studied.

Despite the fact that I did not mention gender in the letter inviting people to take part in the research, my sample was composed of women. Various researchers (eg Mendel 1995; Waterhouse 1993) would confirm that in a small sample obtained by a female researcher this is not surprising. In addition, Mendel (1995) cites twelve studies which have found that males are more reluctant to report sexual abuse than are females.

Seven women were interviewed, six of whom were white and one Anglo-Indian. Their ages ranged from 18 to 60. All responded to my letter in local newspapers seeking people who had been sexually abused by males that were either members of their families or well known to their families. In two cases the survivors had also been sexually abused by women. This seemed a high proportion of a small sample, especially a sample which had self-selected on the basis of having been abused by males. The stories of both women included details of contact abuse by their mothers. The acts described were such that it would have been difficult to rationalise them as other than abusive. Whilst several researchers argue that sexual abuse by women is extremely rare (eg Osborn 1990; Reid 1989; each citing several studies), Mendel (1995) argues that much female abuse goes unrecognised because it is more covert and subtle. Mendel states that female–female abuse is regarded as rare, but suggests that it, like abuse of males, may be underreported.

In fact, since the completion of the original research, Hetherton (1999) has suggested that female stereotypes may have caused professionals to minimise or discount what is beginning to emerge as a higher than anticipated incidence of female perpetration. Nelson and Oliver (1998) maintain that in this connection boys may tend to regard their contact with women as consensual but with males as abusive.

In addition to their sexual abuse, those in the sample had been subjected to varying degrees of physical and emotional abuse. How these areas are defined can have implications for how the experiences of those involved in the study are constructed. Gibbons *et al.* (1995) suggest that the whole area of what constitutes child maltreatment is socially constructed. Whether there is such a thing as 'reasonable' corporal punishment is frequently debated, and, as Besharov (1990) argues, 'reasonable' punishment may become emotionally abusive in itself. Farmer and Owen (1995) point to the difficulty of definition in such areas and also to the frequency of linkages between differing types of abuse. One survivor mentioned that her father always seemed to be smacking her for something. The smacking was not severe, but its emotional effect was marked: it was a constant threat which ensured her compliance. This would link with work on how perpetrators groom their victims (e.g. Horton *et al.* 1990). Kirkwood's (1993) conceptualisation of emotional abuse as a web, which entrapped the battered women she studied, is equally appropriate to the experience of these survivors.

The finding that more than one type of abuse was present in the lives of those interviewed, and that facets of the different types of abuse were intertwined, means that, as is common in such studies, it is difficult to isolate how sexual abuse specifically contributed to whatever problems the survivor encountered. Nevertheless, how the survivors perceived such effects can be explored, as can whether factors in their backgrounds may have ameliorated or exacerbated these effects.

All but one of the survivors had children of their own; all but one had been, or were currently, married; and all but one had had professional counselling or other psychiatric help. This intervention appeared to have resonances in the way they told their stories.

The youngest survivor was abused within the previous ten years, whilst the elder two had been abused over half a century before. The remaining four were abused during the 1960s and 1970s. Though all but one mentioned earlier attempts at disclosure, it was interesting that all of them had made fuller disclosures of their abuse within the last ten years and if they had had counselling it had been during that time. Kelly (in a preface to Orr (1995)) points to the way in which survivors are increasingly being enabled to tell their stories, though she acknowledges continuing problems associated with this.

In terms of my aim of examining the impact of dealing with survivors on those in education, it was interesting that only the youngest survivor had confided in a teacher at school. Additionally, this survivor had disclosed to her family earlier than others in the sample, and felt supported at home.

It may be argued that since child sexual abuse has become a more acknowledged problem during the last decade or so, this has permitted those who were abused many years ago to unburden themselves. Certainly professionals are more likely to perceive child sexual abuse as a possibility than in earlier decades. No survivor in the study cited one reason alone for seeking help. Those mentioned included personal problems (4), problems with relationships (3), nightmares or flashbacks (4), or reaching a point where they felt unable to function and being forced to seek help (3). This experience of 'help' had not been entirely beneficial for survivors, as will be discussed later.

If a link is made to the prevailing views on abuse at the times when these survivors were abused, it can be seen that disclosure may have involved hurdles which have since been reduced by current thinking about abuse. This is not to minimise the problems individuals now have when disclosing their abuse. Members of each of the three groups interviewed took issue with how the subject was handled by professionals and the law alike; but each group found some areas of support and understanding, though these were not always readily identifiable or easily accessible.

When the older survivors were children, many women entered marriage in a state of ignorance about adult sexuality, homosexuality was illegal, and precocious sexual behaviour could be rewarded by sectioning under the Mental Health Act (e.g. Grant 1994). The predicament of those who were abused was compounded by a taboo on knowledge and a climate of blaming the victim, who was often seen as a young seducer (e.g. Driver and Droisen 1989).

Whilst child-rearing practices were being somewhat liberalised by the 1950s and 1960s (e.g. Ennew 1986), when four of the survivors were children, the feminist movements which have facilitated discussion of such issues as child sexual abuse were unborn; it was not until the 1970s that these began to surface. Media discussion of abuse issues during the past decade has provided a climate in which survivors have been able to realise that others have shared some of their experiences, although this has to be seen in the context of the destructive, sensation-seeking face of journalism, which exposes some survivors to further abuses. Whilst these survivors may feel that the current systems do not best serve their needs, all were aware that sources of support do exist.

At a macro level the current climate of thought acknowledges that abuse happens; however, there still lurk remnants of earlier beliefs. Feminist researchers (e.g. Driver and Droisen 1989; Glaser and Frosh 1988; Hooper 1992; Kelly 1988) point to the vestiges of myths that remain in the public consciousness concerning who abuses, who is abused and why abuse happens. Whilst professionals and researchers may have moved to a new awareness of the nature and causes of abuse, the survivors in the study have experienced the effects of various myths at both intrapersonal and interpersonal levels. Driver and Droisen (1989) argue that myths may permeate both community stereotypes and academic or professional thinking. It was my experience that all three groups studied contained those who were still affected by earlier views.

All in the sample had been subjected to contact abuse, although the range involved was from inappropriate touching accompanied by demands for reciprocal touching to multiple incidents of intercourse and buggery by more than one perpetrator. Statistical studies that rank such variables as severity of abuse, proximity of offender and duration of abuse may point to likely outcomes (e.g. Wolfe *et al.* 1994), but the stories of these women point to the effects on individual lives of differing types of abuse and provide information which may remain hidden in statistical patterns. The survivor, or professional, whose knowledge derives solely from such sources, may, as Chamberlain (1993) suggests, be restricted by the definitions thus imposed and therefore less able to perceive or name what has happened.

Telling the story

I was interested in why these survivors chose to tell their stories and in how they chose to construct their stories for different purposes. I wondered whether, by incorporating change and learning within their stories, they were able to move towards healing, as Parry (1991) and Shepherd (1990) have suggested. My purpose, in common with others who have used the storytelling approach to the interview (e.g. Hooper 1992; Kirkwood 1993), was to allow respondents to tell their stories in their own words, to structure them in their own ways and to have control over what they chose to include.

One problem with the stories was that they were being told for the purpose of telling a researcher what it was like to be a survivor. Before the interviews began, how survivors constructed me and my purposes would have a bearing on their stories. I had described myself as involved in a research project aimed at producing insights which may help those facing a comparable situation. Six of the sample said they had responded because their stories might help others, the other hoped for help for herself. Whilst these were their stated purposes, were there any underlying purposes?

It may be that in their interpretation of my purpose they selected certain incidents and rejected others. Certainly two survivors apologised for reported swearing during the interview, whereas others swore readily without apology.

Were they sufficiently aware of the effects the interview might have on them? I had attempted to outline this and provided a list of sources of support should they need it after the event. Methodological and storytelling issues merged here. Lee (1993) notes how Brannen (1988) acknowledged her own need for support after interviewing on sensitive issues, and found that many of her respondents had themselves anticipated their needs by arranging for friends to be available to provide support after the interview. I had my own outlet, and six of my respondents had set up their own sources of support. These sources of support and the problems of finding appropriate support formed part of their stories, may have been a secondary reason for choosing to speak to me, and are an important issue for the study. One of the issues arising from the question of support was the decision about when and how to tell the story. In a sense, by being prepared to listen to the story, I had become a source of support for several of the women. Lee (1993) echoes this aspect when he explores the issue of seeing the researcher as a friend. Survivors greeted me warmly on the second occasion in every case and often made comments about it being easier this time 'because I know you'.

Survivors conveyed their lack of opportunities for telling their stories. Telling the story may gain support, but it also involved risk. There was a strong sense of stigmatisation here. Whilst what had happened to them had deeply affected their lives, not through their choice, it had concurrently isolated them from 'the norm'; leaving them with the need to deny, or hide part of themselves within most areas of their lives. Though it was deemed appropriate to tell certain, usually close or trusted, people aspects of the story, it was deemed inappropriate to mention it in other situations. This may be compared to how such issues as terminal illness or recent bereavement are handled in our society. Pincus and Dare (1978) argue that any loss involves guilt and pain and in an effort to avoid these emotions people often become inflexible in their reactions to these areas. They see being unable to discuss feelings and 'secrets' as ultimately damaging. If dealing with loss involves dealing with the guilt and pain surrounding it, survivors within a society which practises avoidance of painful issues are in a double-bind. They are dealing with their own loss, and that loss is being compounded by further losses of support or trust while they are dealing with it. Not only are the survivors dealing with their loss, they are also constructing meaning from the events that surround it. These meanings, in turn, become structured into their stories and, if they become challenged by people or subsequent events, are in themselves potential sources of loss.

Paradoxically, even in disparate contexts, growth and learning can be seen to involve pain and loss (e.g. Pedler 1986, in relation to management learning). Arguably, therefore, some of the subsequent losses survivors undergo may also be perceived as gains, and in some of their stories this can be seen. Survivors talked about the need to structure their stories differently for different purposes. They perceived themselves as being open to blame, judgement or discrimination, and needing to be wary about precipitating such reactions.

Those who might react adversely could be family, friends, employers or care professionals. Survivors feared that people might think they were lying, overreacting or likely to be unpredictable and damaged. All had experienced at least one of these reactions on occasion and felt the need to guard against recurrences. One survivor described how she applied for 'the stupidest jobs, you wouldn't believe what I've applied for', so that people would not need to ask about her lack of qualifications. I have commented elsewhere on implications within the workplace (Skinner 1999a). Another survivor mentioned that she may have to go to court in connection with her reporting of the abuse to the police and worried about what this might make her boss think of her. There was a worry about being judged when talking to 'health visitors or anything. At first I felt you had to watch what you were saying in case you slipped up and said something.' It is possible that this unwillingness to mention certain details to such professionals may stem from an awareness of the idea of cycles of abuse. Two survivors voiced the idea that people would assume that because they had been abused they might be more likely to abuse. An alternative interpretation may have been that survivors had poor self-esteem or underestimated their own strengths.

There was evidence, too, that information was being shaped for the purposes of the interview when two survivors identified details which they had not intended to mention to me. One commenced by trying to anonymise members of her family but finally used names when she seemed to accept that I would not disclose them. Another mentioned her nervousness about talking to a stranger, adding 'but now I've seen you it's all right, I can talk to you'. The accounts were not only constrained by the details which survivors were willing to reveal to me, or which they considered to be necessary ingredients in the story for this purpose. As Barker (1992) argues, meaning is also constrained by the language available to the teller of the tale and the understanding of the receiver. It is through discourse that they create both memory and meaning.

In constructing their stories, there seemed to be two extremes in the styles of recounting events. At one pole, detail was minimised and reference to feelings omitted; at the other, both were described in great detail. The exception to this was the style used by one survivor who asked questions constantly in what seemed an attempt to assess her own experience against that of others known to the researcher. For me as a listener, it seemed that this survivor had made less sense of her own story than had some of the others. Herman (1992) talks about recreating the flow of the survivor's life through the telling of their stories. Whether their stories contained the actual reasons for events or not, their own healing seemed to have been advanced by the understandings they had achieved. Shepherd (1990) and Parry (1991) have commented on formulating and reformulating the story as an aid to healing. The survivor who constantly questioned stated that she was taking part in the research 'because it might help me to understand' and her story was arguably more disjointed than those of others in the sample.

Elsewhere, there was a real sense that connections were being made during the course of an interview. Sometimes, a question of mine would spark a new perspective on what had happened; on other occasions, a survivor would have a sudden memory or link details together. Hence, within the interviews there was a co-construction of reality when my comments either opened up new areas or closed them down.

Some survivors were interested in my purposes for undertaking the research. The most common assumption was that I had gone through something of this sort myself and that I understood what it was like. I was comfortable with this assumption and it probably helped with rapport. But one woman suggested that I had been abused by my father because I had 'that look'. I found this difficult to handle, as I did not want to restrict the flow of the interview. She was the most nervous of all the sample, so I made what I hoped was a non-committal noise and felt uncomfortable for days afterwards. This was the only interview in which I felt uncomfortable. In the others, which sometimes contained more harrowing detail, rapport was often strong and sustained both me and the speaker. This was also the only interview in which there were tears. This survivor broke down when talking about her son, who has currently challenged her about her promiscuity while he was a child. The other interviews often included shared laughter, which lightened the atmosphere for both participants. The impact of what had been said often affected me after the event rather than during it. This made it difficult for me to return for a second interview: I had to feel strong enough to cope with another session. Although every survivor greeted me warmly on the second occasion, often commenting about it being easier this time.

My own style was related closely to the ease with which survivors talked. In four of the interviews, I said very little, though I was aware of the extent to which I used paralinguistic devices – such as 'mmm', 'uh-huh', nodding and body language to convey active listening. The other three interviews were shorter and more dependent on my probe questions suggesting that certain areas might be described more fully or further explained to me.

Stories are a continuing process of attributing meaning to events for the survivors. Some of the issues from the first interview arose again in the second interview; other incidents were omitted or told for the first time. Whilst different levels of coping were apparent, there was little question that their stories continued to affect the survivors.

Family life for the survivors

The survivors in the sample came from a variety of backgrounds, which they conveyed in different ways. Areas which arose in the interviews involved how survivors described their background, how they perceived normality, the sort of meaning they attributed to events and how they coped with the differing realities of their family lives. They commented on their parents, their siblings and the people to whom they felt closest. Issues of conflict, communication and power are implicated in their stories. It would be impossible to address how memory had affected the issues which are described.

Several researchers have commented about how abuse can damage memories which may once have been happy (e.g. Hall and Lloyd 1993). These survivors provided for the purpose of the interview a snapshot view of how they felt their families had affected them. Had the interview taken place on a different day, or in different circumstances, aspects of their stories may have changed. In addition to talking, two survivors also provided material they had written at an earlier date; it was felt that this might 'fill in the background'. Whilst two claimed that until recently they had had few memories, the others suggested the reverse. For example, one said: 'There's nothing that I can't remember…nothing, down to the punishment me father used to give us.' And another: 'I just cannot forget. I mean that's one of the things I've found in counselling when people say they forget – well, how can they forget? I can remember everything, I can't forget anything.' One of the two who had used denial as a coping mechanism was able to describe the good memories she had once had of her family, all of which she found she had to reframe after her own acknowledgement of what had really happened.

The fathers of six of the survivors were regularly in work. Three of them commented that their abusers were well respected in their respective communities, and one added that even though none of her siblings had been able to remain in employment because of problems stemming from their abuse, her father had 'never missed a day of work for 40 years'.

How did survivors conceptualise their experience of their families? Whilst aspects of the family backgrounds described by survivors might be perceived by the majority as abnormal, the debate about how to define normality in families is ongoing. Surveys (e.g. Newson and Newson 1989, on physical punishment; Smith and Grocke 1995, on sexual behaviour) have explored different aspects of behaviour. They have found that views of 'normality' are subject to change and include behaviours that may be regarded as indicators of abuse. Normality for the survivors comprised different things. What is deemed normal at an individual level may not coincide with what is seen by society as normal. Whilst this is a dilemma for child protection professionals (Smith and Grocke 1995), children who have no way of differentiating are left to construct their own meanings for the situations they find themselves in. One survivor who had been subjected to multiple abuses from the age of two did not challenge the normality of her situation until she was in her twenties. Another described her father's regular violence towards her mother as the norm in her family.

Attributing meaning to themselves within the context of the family was an overt issue for six of the women. Herman (1992) notes that survivors need to explore the questions 'why?' and 'why me?' in order to reconstruct themselves and restore their own sense of self-worth. Part of the discussions on their family background involved women contextualising themselves within it. Six of them claimed they were treated differently within their families and linked this to such factors as:

- *their appearance* – one looked like her mother, another like her father;

- *their behaviour* – one commented that she was quiet and withdrawn, another that she asked questions and challenged things;

- *their gender* – one felt she would have been treated differently had she been male;

- *their ability* – one considered that she was regarded as less intelligent than her sister.

This could imply that survivors felt some sense of unwitting responsibility or guilt for what had happened to them. As noted, Finkelhor and Browne (1988) include both powerlessness and stigmatisation within their four-factor model of the effects of sexual abuse. If it is viewed in the light of transactional analysis, another, not incompatible, reading would suggest that survivors had been provided with this 'script' by the conditional messages within the family. They had been given a sense of being 'not OK' because of certain aspects of themselves which were outside their control. In terms of attachment theory (Bowlby 1988), they had not been provided with the confident sense of self which stems from secure attachment, but rather were anxious, or unsure of how they would be treated. The seventh survivor strongly differentiated between the treatment she received from different members of her family and depicted a sense of secure attachment to her mother and later to her stepfather.

Four survivors described their fathers as alcoholics and one of these said that her mother had a similar problem. Several studies have noted the likelihood of a link between alcohol abuse and child abuse (e.g. Finkelhor 1986; Horton *et al.* 1990). And as Hall and Lloyd (1993) discuss, the presence of such problems within the family exacerbates the other difficulties they face. In each of these cases the parents described as alcoholic were also responsible for sexual abuse. Hooper (1992) notes the addiction model as an explanation for abuse itself, as well as for the other conditions which often accompany abuse.

Five survivors described their fathers, or in one case stepfather, as violent towards them. Of the remaining two, one father was not the abuser and the other, though not classified by his daughter as 'violent', 'always seemed to be smacking' her. Three of these fathers, and the stepfather, were also violent towards their wives and others in the family and were perceived as a threat. This finding links with the inequalities of power often characteristic within families in which abuse is present. Hooper (1992), for example, points to the paradoxes between a mother's relative powerlessness towards her partner and her comparative powerfulness towards her children. The four survivors who saw their mothers beaten had differing reactions to their mothers. By merely describing that they were beaten they demonstrated some awareness of the problems their mothers faced. In two of these cases, survivors described how their mothers tried to protect them from their father's violence, but only one saw her mother as having done as much as she could given the situation. In the light of the psychoanalytic perspective, it may be that only one of these four survivors had a relationship with her mother which was long enough or close enough to provide her with the opportunity to resolve her conflicts with her mother, and to come to see her mother as a person rather than an ideal (Honess and Lintern 1990). However, this survivor did describe her relationship with her mother in terms which suggest it was more supportive than that experienced by others. As Esparza (1993) argues, a mother's ability to support her child during a crisis may be crucial in optimising the child's ability to cope.

As has been discussed elsewhere, there may be factors other than the sexual abuse within family backgrounds which diminish a child's ability to trust, or depend upon, his or her mother. Alexander (1992) has looked at some of the attachment characteristics which may make a child more vulnerable to sexual abuse. Wyatt and Mickey (1987) have noted the need for a good relationship with a trusted figure to ameliorate the effects of abuse and develop resilience. The backgrounds of those in the sample, and their early attachment styles, seem to have been predictive, in some measure, of their ability to deal with their abuse.

Spaccarelli (1994) warns of the danger of assuming that individual factors are responsible for a child's reaction to abuse. He posits that this is particularly problematical in studies based on retrospective accounts by adults. As has been argued, survivors would have constructed their stories in particular ways. In this study, with one exception, they had received counselling. This, I would suggest, had caused them to re-explore their notions of what their families were like and to reassess the responsibilities. On occasion, phrases such as 'she was my mother, so she was the adult and I was the child' had a borrowed feel to them, as if this explanation was being grafted on to a survivor's experience rather than being devised by herself.

Five survivors made comparison to other families when describing their own. This was another device which, it seemed, had often been modified by subsequent experience or awareness. One survivor, who had earlier commented on how she had been forced to review her 'fantastic' family when memories of abuse had resurfaced in her twenties, commented on the differences in treatment between her own family and that of others, stating that her brothers and sisters were always filthy and uncared for. Others described incidents which seemed more immediate, as when one described how she could not believe how a friend's parents acted towards each other and dared not look them in the eyes in case she caused them to change. This conveyed a sense of how fragile were moments of calm in the relationships she knew best.

Five survivors had people who were important for them – in one case, the friend's parents described above. Four others had family members who were important to them. For one, this was a grandmother: 'I used to sit for hours with her she taught me to knit and to sew and to embroider and she'd sit on the chair in the living room and I'd sit at her feet and she'd lay there stroking me hair for hours'; for one, her non-abusing mother mentioned earlier; for another, her father:

> My father was the most placid person – grandma always said he was a gentle person and a gentle man. You know, he was so soft and placid he wouldn't…er…it was very rare you would have heard him raise his voice. He was a lovely man he had so much love to give; I mean, we were really close you know.

For another, an uncle:

> I remember him having a kind smile that reached his brown eyes. I remember once getting something in my eye and couldn't get whatever it was out. He tried for ages to get it out and was very patient. He asked his wife to take me to the doctor's, and the doctor couldn't get it out so I had to go to casualty. I remember panicking, thinking I was causing too many problems for them, but they were great – actually worrying about me and reassuring me. When my mother found out she went mad, calling me a bloody nuisance.

Whether such incidents would have been as memorable to those who had easier passages through childhood is debatable. What is notable is the comparatively trivial nature of the kindnesses which have taken on significance for these survivors and the contrast between such incidents and what they were facing at home. Despite the frequent perception that conditions at home were 'normality' there does seem to be some recognition that not all 'normality' is the same. It may be that those who have never had cause to explore their 'normality', are those who are most likely to be experiencing it – once it arises as a question it is unlikely to be resolved easily.

The 'special' people survivors mentioned were those on whom they could depend to some extent. They provided them with some sense of security and value, although none, apart from the mother mentioned earlier, were subsequently informed of the abuse or in any way protected the survivors. Rather, they seemed to be some sort of oasis for them. How these people are described indicates some ability in the survivors concerned to differentiate between people. This may indicate that theories based around cycles of abuse may have to query victims' inability to discriminate between people as a factor in causation. However, what these survivors described would suggest that a feeling of stigmatisation or poor self-worth may be more likely than inability to discriminate to cause any unsatisfactory relationships they find themselves in.

Two accounts made no mention of people to whom survivors felt they could relate whilst they were children. In one case, the survivor has subsequently found this support in a partner; in the other, the search continues.

The actual composition of the families involved raised some interesting points. In three of the seven families, the natural parents had divorced; in the remaining four, the parents were either still together or, in one case, had died. In two of the families which had experienced divorce, the mothers had remarried, and one of the stepfathers was the abuser in that situation. In the four families which had remained intact, three included parents who were also abusers; and in two of these three cases, survivors had reported their abuse to the non-abusing parent. The family in which the stepfather had abused was similarly still together despite disclosure to the mother. Whilst feminist researchers (e.g. Carter 1993; Hooper 1992) have warned that survivors may assume a mother knows about their abuse when in fact she may not, the three survivors whose abusers were still with their mothers all reported actually telling their mothers what was happening or had happened.

A further insight into their lives was given when four survivors remarked on how they were unable to take friends to their homes. In one case, this was because other mothers did not want their children to mix with them; in another, because they were unsure of whether friends would be made welcome; and in another, because home was seen as a place to eat and sleep but friends belonged to school or out of doors. The survivor who was abused by her stepfather noted that her siblings (the children of mother and stepfather) could take friends to the house but this was not permitted to her.

There was not a question specifically about whether survivors had many friends and whether they came to the home. The information comes, therefore, from those who made specific points about this as a part of their childhood. It is within this limitation that the evidence must be contextualised. The fact that four of the survivors mentioned that they were unable to feel comfortable with friends calling at their homes, or that this was actively discouraged, may point to the experiences of individuals within the particular small sample or may lend credence to the theory that victims are groomed and isolated from sources of support (e.g. Horton *et al.* 1990). It may also be deemed a form of psychological abuse (Briere 1992), as the child is deprived of contacts beyond the family and potentially denied a source of comparisons against which to judge her own experiences.

The question of power and how it operated within the families was one which interested me. There seemed to be a variety of different levels. All of the survivors pointed in some way to their own powerlessness as viewed from an adult stance. Yet within that sense of powerlessness to affect what was happening within the family, all mention occasions on which they did things to try to improve their situation. The notion of victims as passive has been challenged by feminists (e.g. Kelly 1988; Kirkwood 1993), male power at a societal level often being cited as a root cause of violence or abuse of women and children. Hall and Lloyd (1993) criticise the feminist tendency to be too ideological, blaming much of the causation of child sexual abuse on male power within society. This criticism is being addressed in some measure by more recent work with focuses on individual differences within the wider societal context. Kelly (in a preface to Orr 1995) notes the need to challenge perceptions of what abuse is and of who abuses. The whole question of power is shifting from a linear analysis to an interactional one influenced by work such as Foucault's (1981) which links discourse to power. How meaning is drawn from situations is often the dominant discourse on a particular topic. At the family level, this may refer to the status quo or rules of operation. Hence, power may dictate what is regarded as normality in that situation. However, despite Foucault viewing discourse as both an instrument and an effect of power, within this he perceives the potential for resistance and opposing strategies. During the early lives of the survivors, such opposing strategies may not have become formalised into discourse. But I would argue they were incipiently there and formed the seeds of the interpretations or reframing of stories, which allowed survivors to examine alternative views or formulate strategies as they grew.

Early examples of oppositional power include one survivor who mentions staying away from her father when she realised that she was often the precursor to him beating her mother. Another tried to persuade her mother to take her father to the doctor as he was still abusing her. Three survivors openly acknowledged their lack of power to produce a convincing opposition as children, but commented that their abusers seemed not to realise that they would one day grow up and be able to tell their stories, or that they simply would not forget what had happened in their future adult dealings, or lack of dealings, with their abuser.

The degree to which the families involved communicated was an issue which interested me. This has implications for the construction of meaning of certain events for the family and is potentially a different facet of power. Would it be easier for a child to cope if events made sense to her, if she had knowledge power? There were differences in the extent to which families discussed issues or were able to have conversations about their feelings or problems. One survivor felt that in her family nothing could be named. By the time of the interview, she had constructed the lack of information on bodily functions partly as a vestige of her family's religious beliefs but also as a device they used to conceal information. Sometimes knowledge which would have empowered a survivor to realise that parts of her experience were abusive was hidden. The survivor said:

> Everything was silent…we were brought up that all our body bits were…first of all I didn't even know that I had a vagina, I didn't know there was a hole there if you like, and it was so weird because you didn't think about your body – you didn't feel your body was anything in a way, you didn't even know that you had it in a way, and when your mum would go like this and say, well, that's filthy or this is filthy, I think it was like in your mind before you were even…you just closed off those parts of your body, switched off. I think it was quite clever of her to have presented it like that so that when you were abused or damaged you didn't know.

Another survivor told how her mother left her father, and without explaining the situation moved in with the stepfather who was later to be her abuser, leaving the survivor to think they were on holiday for some time. Three survivors said that sex was never discussed within their families and that they were given no information about it or about their own bodies. Only one survivor said that she could discuss this sort of area with her mother; the others implied it was a difficult topic. One noted that she was able to discuss this subject area with her mother when she became an adult. It was not until this time that she was able to say anything about her abuse, as the subject was an adult one and she felt it more appropriate to tell by the time she reached this age.

It was not only overtly sexual topics which proved difficult. In four of the families, emotions and feelings were not easy topics to handle. Five survivors reported that they had no memories of any affection or affectionate gestures from their mothers. The remaining two had lots of affection from their mothers but only one perceived this as support by the time of the interview. Additional messages which families sent the survivors about emotion differed, although common themes centred on certain areas: conformity and compliance on the part of female members (mentioned by six survivors); not making a fuss (likely to attract physical punishment in five families). One explicitly described her skill at reading expressions and responding to them: 'If an adult looked at me with a blank expression, that was normal. If any adult looked at me with a smile, I would frown without returning their approval because I didn't know what would happen or how they would return their friendliness.'

Memories of childhood and of the abuse itself were inextricably linked. Survivors talked of their childhood as a landscape rather than a sequence of events. The landmarks were events which had impacted on them; the contribution of others, unless it directly impacted on them at the time, was viewed from a distant perspective. Often, during the interview, adult reflections on the problems being experienced by other family members were mentioned, but survivors' stories mostly consisted of direct statements about what had happened to themselves.

Four of the survivors described themselves as very quiet children, coping by staying out of the line of fire, not talking in case things became worse. Two commented that they were 'the black sheep of the family' and their coping was through questioning and action. This, they suggested, made their treatment worse than other family members because they did not easily comply with what was happening. The seventh survivor did not classify herself as either good or bad but noted instances of both types of behaviour. Her strategy she described as 'always changing, always trying to change my behaviour'. This she saw as a device to be what her mother wanted, although she felt she never achieved this.

Briere (1992) cites his 'abuse dichotomy' by which a child makes sense of abuse and incorporates it into self-image. This model allows for the child to comply or rebel on the basis of the quasi-logic incorporated in the reasoning. Briere describes six stages:

1. The realisation of being hurt in some way by a trusted adult.

2. 'This is either because I am bad or my parent is bad.'

3. 'Other adults affirm that parents are always right and do things for your own good – this can involve hurting you if you are bad – this is punishment.'

4. 'If I am being punished, it must be my fault.'

5. 'If I am being punished, I must be bad – as bad as the punishment is since the punishment fits the crime.'

6. 'Since I am hurt very often, I must be very bad.'

Briere points to the potential from this scenario both for poor self-esteem and for self-fulfilling prophecy – if I am that bad, I'll be that bad. This incorporation of warped logic into the understanding of self is equally applicable to attachment theory. Alexander (1992) pinpoints the difficulty of differentiating specifically sexual abuse characteristics and those caused by attachment style and parenting. Likewise, transactional analysis notes how the child 'forces his perceptions into the mould of his needs' (Harris and Harris 1985, p.29). Subsequent dealings with people are likely to be affected by learned schema. Bowlby (1987) proposes that basic attachment styles, which predate reason, are likely to be enduring. Herman (1992) suggests that trauma in childhood affects personality development.

This gloomy prognosis is slightly ameliorated by others such as Wolin and Wolin (1995) who say that positive resiliences can arise despite a troubled family background, although these will never compensate entirely for the losses the survivor has endured. Their research looked specifically at substance abuse in families. They cite the presence of rituals such as celebrating birthdays, having holidays together or even eating together as potentially protective devices, if these rituals were performed in a way which allowed them to be positive. In their research, this meant that parents made the effort not to indulge in their habit on these occasions, so that they could be constructed as pleasant family events despite other things that were happening. Osborn (1990) similarly identifies ways in which survivors developed resiliences and Gilgun (1991) suggests that supportive relationships with mothers, or trusted others, can aid in the development of such resilience.

Living with the abuse

Their family backgrounds provide the backdrop against which the survivors coped with sexual abuse. These backgrounds, it will be argued, had implications for them in terms of both recognising and disclosing their abuse.

Two survivors coped with their abuse by practising denial or dissociation. Hall and Lloyd (1993) define this as a strategy of 'learning to deal with the abuse by denying its reality, by dissociating themselves from it or by repressing it partially or completely' (p.76). One survivor described a device she used:

> I remembered the first time he penetrated me like always... always...the first time he done it it was so sore and just ripped through my body and within seconds my mind just went uh uh, I'm not having this and it closed, so that's why a lot of it is. I can't remember a lot of it because I quickly adopted a way to just pull the shutters down in my mind and so when I woke up in the morning it was like that last night never even happened to me.

During the interview, she pointed to many abuse events which she remembered, but expressed her awareness that more lurked in her mind and were yet to surface. Denial allowed her to survive during the abuse, but as her memories were returning, she was faced with unpredictable and often horrific flashbacks, which could trigger buried emotional responses. Often, she described herself as feeling out of control, aware that more would surface but unsure of when or how.

The one other survivor who experienced a comparable loss of memory was currently a medium spiritualist and believed that she had had her experiences returned to her by her spirit guide. This she had constructed as a necessary part of her education to prepare her for the next world and provide her with the degree of knowledge she would require to progress. The rest all had memories of specific events or occurrences and could often put quite precise ages to when these events happened. Whereas one survivor thought that she was first abused at about the age of two, other survivors mentioned ages ranging from four to thirteen. In line with the predictions of theory, the survivor who was 'about four' was the other who practised dissociation.

Both Briere (1992) and Herman (1992) suggest that those subjected to abuse at a very young age are more likely to use this mechanism, as they have fewer other potential strategies at their disposal. For these two survivors, sexual abuse was part of the normality of their existence, whereas the survivor who was thirteen at the time of the sexual assault by her father had been coping with other aspects of his 'violent alcoholic' behaviour since babyhood. That was normality for her, this specific episode was something else. She described how it caused her to change her behaviour – particularly at school – and that this change was noticed by a teacher. Despite this, she was not able to disclose what had happened until she was six years older and had left home.

She told how she was imprisoned by her father in his flat for three days after this incident, but how on her return home her mother assumed that she wanted to live with him and did not provide her with an opportunity to disclose what had happened. This survivor did talk to her close friend but assumes now that this girl was too inexperienced to understand what she was talking about. So, although she was a source of support, she was not able to initiate action. The survivor described how her mother had seen her as a problem because her father had singled her out for special attention. She also commented that she herself felt responsible for her father and would visit him despite the existence of a court order banning him from contact with the family. Given this background, and the lack of real communication between mother and daughter, the mother's assumption that her daughter wanted to be with her father was unsurprising. And the daughter, who often fell foul of her mother's tongue and blows, was probably more likely to use her learned mechanism of avoidance than to add another source of censure to the existing list. This survivor did not use the device of repressing or denying the abuse but used a variety of strategies to attempt to understand why it had happened and to give it meaning. Interestingly, the strategy of avoidance, which her mother had encouraged her to use as a young child when her father was drunk, in a temper or with his friends, was the one which she opted for. After the abuse, she tried to avoid her father, the issue and its potential consequences.

Three other survivors talked to friends at the time of their abuse but all tended to assume that they did not realise what was being talked about. Friends who did not act on what they were told were forgiven much more easily than adults, who may or may not have known what was happening. The finding, mentioned earlier (p.78), that several survivors had problems with taking friends to their homes may also be a factor which contributed to the friends' lack of understanding. Such friends would have had little opportunity to see what was happening in a survivor's home and may have interpreted a survivor's difficulties in the light of their own restricted understanding of family dynamics. Further possible reasons why these friends did not pass information to adults or to others who may have been able to help might have included: the nature of the material involved and the associated taboos; their own relationships with adults and the extent to which they were able to communicate freely; and the possibility that they had been requested to keep the information secret as the survivor was embarrassed or guilty about what had happened and did not want details to be spread. If the information had been passed to an adult, there may have been further barriers to action at this level, including:

- The prevailing myths at the time when this information was given. For example, the child may have been seen as a seductress; Glaser and Frosh (1988) note that this is a legacy from Freud's work.

- Existing assumptions about the child concerned. For example, an assumed predisposition to fantasy; however, researchers (e.g. Driver and Droisen 1989; Kelly 1988) note that children are unlikely to lie in this sort of situation. Here, again, a link can be made with Freud's work, and his conclusion that Oedipal fantasies rather than reality fuelled his patients' revelations. More latterly, 'false memory syndrome' has been used as a counterargument against survivors such as the two in this study who had repressed their childhood memories.

- The standing or status of the adult concerned, based on myths surrounding who abuses. Abusers have, in the past, been assumed to come from certain social classes, or to be ill or misfits. Driver and Droisen (1989) and Kelly (1988) point to such myths. Stanko (1985) identifies an inbuilt unwillingness in society to believe the stories of those who are less powerful.

Any combination of these factors may make information relating to abuse less credible and less likely to be pursued.

In line with Briere's (1989) model of the abuse dichotomy, four of the survivors attempted to ascertain their own responsibility for their abuse. Rather than being able to believe that a parent who loved them could treat them in this way, they incorporated a sense of being in some way responsible for what was happening to them. This is particularly acutely verbalised in one case:

> I was about seven years of age when it first started, and I was having a bath with my sister and…er…my dad was washing my bottom and he did something to me – sort of pushed his finger up me – and I smiled at him.

That smile and her possible responsibility had haunted her for almost 50 years: 'I said to my counsellor, "I don't know whether he thought that was a come-on."' She returned to this theme on several occasions during the interview for her, this was still part of living with the abuse. I would argue that both the image of the 'child seductress' of myth and an impaired sense of self born from the inability to believe a parent could deliberately maltreat her are present in this fear. It is also possible that she enjoyed the physical sensations which this touching provided, and the guilt associated with this realisation might have been exacerbated by her former husband. He had suspected her abuse, and believed their sexual problems stemmed from her search for something she no longer had. She rationalised her subsequent sexual encounters as being symptomatic of this search for another who could touch her in the way her father did.

Two of the four survivors who expressed elements of their own responsibility for the abuse rationalised it in terms of their appearance: one looked like her mother, the other like her father; this was constructed as a reason for the abuse.

Whereas all survivors in this sample described their experiences as abusive, which was what my original letter requested, they did differentiate between degrees of tolerability. The effects of the passage of time will inevitably have had an effect on how the survivors perceived their abuse, and though this chapter deals with the coping mechanisms used whilst living with the abuse and during the process of disclosure, what is said has been coloured by a multitude of factors. This colouring is likely to be particularly noticeable where the four survivors who were abused by more than one perpetrator differentiate between their abusers. While maintaining the argument that responsibility for the abuse lies with the perpetrator, there is clear evidence within one of these stories of choices which the survivor had made.

In this case, the survivor was abused by both her brother and her uncle. She was more disturbed by the abuse by her brother, who ensured her silence by threatening to tell their parents about her bedwetting (which usually resulted in her being punished) – her brother knew this and she 'let him do whatever he wanted to do' to buy his silence. The implication here is that the abuse, although unpleasant, was preferable to the physical punishment meted out by her parents. Her uncle bought her affections with the sweets and buns in his shop. 'He'd sit me on his knee and he'd...um...just sort of like pat you and put his hands up your dress and things like that, but then at ten you didn't think anything of it.' Not until puberty did she rethink, 'because you know I'd started developing and I just didn't want him touching me'. Without any disclosure, she made a fuss which discouraged her uncle, and with the death of her aunt shortly after this incident the visits to her uncle's home diminished and eventually ended. She did not finally disclose this to anyone until two years before the interview took place. She had not, by her own admission, been as troubled by her uncle's attentions as by her brother's. Her sense of being 'a victim' had been a cumulative process compounded by reflection on the number of problems she had encountered during her life. It may well be that the naming or reframing of certain incidents as abusive does not happen unless subsequent life events cause reflection on earlier comparators. Such events may, as Hooper (1992) has pointed out, include the abuse of one's own child.

The idea of one abuser being easier to cope with than another is echoed by three other survivors who were abused by more than one perpetrator. One saw one abuser as giving her affection and attention, although she was unhappy about aspects of what was involved. Another saw her brother's abuse of her as more brutal and violent than her father's, and transiently viewed a stranger brought to the home as more considerate of her. The third saw her father's abuse of her as more of a violation, more difficult to comprehend than the abuse by her uncle. Although she does admit that after the incident with her father she came to believe that every male was a potential abuser.

There is a sense throughout survivors' stories that incidents were just a part of life, to be accepted and coped with, rather than changed.

The question of power and control has been differently constructed. Two survivors specifically mention feeling in control in different ways within situations they faced. These situations suggest that survivors can come to doubt their own power or ability to act, if they are unsuccessful in preventing further abuse or if they are unsupported. In the first case, a sense of control in the initial incident was extremely transitory. This survivor talked of a man who had been brought to the house asking her permission to do certain things to her. The survivor said: 'I felt very in control at that point because he was polite to me.' She refused to comply. However, he enlisted the help of her mother in gaining her compliance. Despite the fact that her father and brother regularly abused her, her anger focused on her mother, who not only failed to protect her, but also was perceived as more devious than her father. It was as if she saw her father as somehow less responsible for his actions; his lust apparently more comprehensible to her than her mother's greed – she had taken payment for her daughter's services. The second survivor described how she barricaded herself in the bathroom of her grandmother's house and 'stopped him from coming in again'. The cases are very different – within weeks this survivor had disclosed, had been believed and was being supported. Her belief in her power to act could thus be more immediately strengthened. Spaccarelli's (1994) insight that a cluster of factors contribute to coping with abuse and disclosure is exemplified here.

In more or less overt ways, each of the survivors detailed her coping, whilst the abuse was being enacted, as involving preventive strategies. They learnt ways of minimising the effects on themselves, or of resisting parts of the behaviour. They watched for danger signs and tried to avoid the situation where abuse might take place. Within the abusive acts themselves survivors pointed to aspects over which they had no control and other areas which they resisted. Three spoke of perpetrators touching them but of their own resistance when asked to reciprocate. Hall and Lloyd (1993) conceptualise these coping mechanisms as strengths that prevent the survivor from being 'overwhelmed by the abusive experiences' (p.93).

If normality includes the concepts that adults cannot be trusted, cannot protect you, or may be at risk themselves, it is unsurprising that coping strategies do not include asking for this help. It can be argued that this in itself indicates resourcefulness. The passivity of 'learned helplessness' is not the experience of these survivors. Indeed, it is argued that passivity can be an active coping strategy if the survivor assumes that the converse would exacerbate problems further. For these survivors, their knowledge was the guide to their actions. Not giving a violent man opportunity to hit them was, in that context, a very positive strategy; as was not telling anyone what was happening if they were going to be blamed or punished for the events, or simply not believed. One survivor details how those in authority, such as the police, were seen as the enemy by her family. This belief isolated her from asking them for advice.

Survivors often saw the coping strategies used at the time of the abuse as different from their current responses to problems. There was a tendency to undervalue the strategies they adopted at the time of the abuse, which may be linked to a remaining sense of their own responsibility for the situation. They saw different aspects as being involved in coping at different stages: during the abuse; whilst disclosing the abuse; with memories of and around that time; when reflecting on issues; and when faced with various 'triggers'.

The process of disclosure

Hooper (1992), following on from Glaser and Strauss's (1964) analysis of how secrets are handled or disclosed, sees disclosure as a process in which 'awareness contexts are maintained or transformed, according to the gains and losses to each actor' (p.54). I would argue that, to a greater or lesser extent, disclosure remains an ongoing issue for survivors, in which this same process is repeatedly involved, and decisions about disclosure have potential for colouring all areas of their lives.

Initial disclosures occurred in different ways. As has been mentioned, several of the survivors told peers about their experiences, often to little real effect. Here I will concentrate more specifically on occasions when survivors dealt with people who could have provided help or support.

Two survivors remembered being challenged by their mothers about what might be happening to them. One recollected that her mother asked her whether her father was doing things he shouldn't to her, but even her assurance that this was the case did not stop the problem. This failure to protect her, she claimed, changed her relationship with her mother permanently. The other was more immediately supported, although she admitted that it was only through talking that she was able to realise that her mother had not been aware of what was happening earlier in the process. This was a telling comment in the light of what others have written. Hooper (1992) has claimed that survivors often believe that their mothers knew what was happening, when in fact they did not. Without communication, or the sort of attachment pattern which has allowed for trust to be possible between mother and child, it is unlikely that a mother will be seen as a suitable ally or protector during disclosure or discovery, when, as Goldstein (1992) suggests, the relationship between them may be particularly fragile and vulnerable. Generally, researchers are increasingly of the opinion that a supportive relationship with the mother will ameliorate the effects of abuse. (e.g. Esparza 1993; Gilgun 1991; Wyatt and Mickey 1987).

Similarly, the mother's response to disclosure is viewed as important (e.g. Beitchman *et al.* 1992). Here, four of the survivors pointed to, at least initial, disbelief. One disclosed to her mother six years after the event and was met initially by disbelief. But her mother did challenge her father and did discover that what had been said was true. One disclosed to her mother and was speedily evicted from home. Another mentioned the memory of several disclosures during her childhood which had made no effect. She now feels that her mother colluded with her father and permitted his abuse of her children to escape the possibility of further pregnancies. This survivor finally challenged the 'normality' of her family life in her twenties, after a break from them, and subsequently pursued police action. The fourth told her mother about her uncle two years before the interview, over twenty years after the abuse; she was not believed. Her sisters who were party to this conversation confirmed that they had had similar experiences, though none had known about the others. This survivor had not discussed her abuse by her brother with anyone except her current husband. A fifth, who had not disclosed to either parent in their lifetime, had used spiritualism as a way of, in a sense, discussing issues with her dead parents, and claimed during the interview that her abusing mother had asked for forgiveness.

The sample is small but there is some suggestion that the sooner the survivor is able to disclose and gain effective support, the sooner she is able to share her explorations of meaning and deal with questions of responsibility, guilt or causation. This opportunity to assess the experience, to be validated as having survived it and to acquire an acknowledgement of the coping skills involved in it can strengthen the survivor at whatever stage it occurs. But it seems from this sample that without support, healing is difficult; and the longer the gap between the events and the disclosure, the less the coping strategies employed during the abuse are likely to be valued.

The meaning attributed to the experience would seem to modify over time. Of the survivors who mentioned strategies they had used in an attempt to ameliorate the abuse, only the one who had disclosed comparatively early actively valued the strategy. For others, there was a process of erosion of their belief that they could resist or change what was happening to them. Parry's (1991) notion of therapy as a means of allowing a new story to emerge is demonstrated here. He argues that too often their own stories harden into objective realities for people. It seems from the stories these survivors told, that how they codified events, the details they remembered, and the metaphors they used, affected the interpretations they placed on subsequent events in their lives.

It is important to acknowledge that these 'stories' encapsulate not only what may be deemed factual information, but also interpretation of actions or motives: associated emotions including pleasure, pain, guilt or anger and the potentially limited or biased information available to the subject about what was happening. The stories are restricted by the language available to the survivor and may be further constrained by an inability or unwillingness to explore alternative interpretations. It is further argued that the power of existing beliefs or myths at the time of the abuse, or its disclosure, may have inhibited action for either the survivor or the recipient of the information.

Responding to the abuse: Mothers and others

The responses of mothers are not simply responses to the abuse itself; the reactions to disclosure may be unexpected. Survivors' knowledge of their mothers predates their disclosure and may be coloured by other factors including grooming by the perpetrator, a sense of the mother's own difficulties, or perceptions of how mothers have responded to other problems in the past, which in turn may include how effective they have been in solving them. Survivors' constructions of their mothers may not reflect the reality of their mothers' situations and, as Hooper (1992) suggests, may assume that they had knowledge of the abuse when this is not the case.

Survivors may also need the support of their mothers and feel that the risk of disclosing something of this magnitude is a risk to their relationship, especially if they feel responsibility for what has happened to them, or are disturbed about other family issues. As already mentioned (p.42), Lovett's (1995) study indicated that many child survivors described relationships with their mothers as warm and supportive, yet under a third disclosed to them.

It is difficult to ascertain what the survivors would have said about their mothers whilst they were still children. On the basis of what they now say, three would have described their childhood relationships with their mothers as good. One describes her current relationship as still good, but the other two have reassessed: one because of her awareness that her mother failed to protect her despite knowing about what her father was doing; the other because of her memories of her mother's participation and collusion in the abuse. Another hated her mother as a child, but now sees some of the reasons for her behaviour, including how she did try to protect her from her father's violence. Nevertheless, she did not feel there could ever be a close relationship between them. One was abused by her mother and associated her with pain and neglect, describing how she wanted warmth but received this only from her father. Two others described their relationships with their mothers as poor, both in the past and currently.

Survivors are unlikely to speak freely if they have been subject to threats about the likely effect on themselves or their mothers following disclosure. As one survivor said:

> My dad had shot my cat and I'd seen him hit my brother and make my mum cry. I knew what he'd do to me if I said anything, but after my sister told mum and mum asked me if anything had happened I could tell her. I knew she wouldn't like what he'd been doing.

Comparably, the survivor who was abused by her mother was terrified of telling her father. She thought he would kill her mother for what she had done, and thus she would end up with no parents. She attributed to her father the feminine, nurturing characteristics normally associated with mothers.

Attachment theory would suggest that the warm loving climate of secure attachment might facilitate disclosure. This does not necessarily chime with the responses of the three survivors who described their relationships with at least one parent as secure. There may be other factors such as grooming or threat which make disclosure difficult even for securely attached children. In the third case, the inability of the mother to act may have been as much allied to the prevailing views of abuse (in the early 1940s) as to this mother's economic dependence on her husband. It may be that these situations can be productive of a more positive outcome if support is given. However, where perceived or existing support is diminished or inadequate, longer-term coping may be weakened. In this third case, the survivor's perception of herself, of responsibility for the abuse and of the reasons behind it, had mutated to accommodate her belief that her father was ill, that her mother was not acting to help him and that it would be horrific to view him as a criminal.

All of the survivors had disclosed aspects of their abuse to mothers or family members, although often this had not been until many years after the events. This was for a variety of reasons. One constructed her reasons for disclosing to her mother as being to explain some of the problems she was facing some six years after the abuse. Two survivors expected help. In one case this was forthcoming, in another it was offered – although ineffective. One of the noticeable differences between the two descriptions of expected help was the amount of communication involved. In one case, discussion had occurred as often as the survivor had felt the need to talk, although she felt that her mother wanted her to talk about it too much initially. In the other case, there had been inability to discuss the issues involved. Despite her regular contact with her parents, this survivor had been unable to discuss the subject. Fifty years after the abuse, she would still like to talk to her mother about it, but her mother and father are still together. She remembered one conversation with her mother which took place when she was 28. She did not broach the topic but her mother had said to her: 'Do you know [X] what your dad did to you, I think about that every day.' Since that, there has been no mention, but the survivor surmised that her mother probably still thinks about it. Another survivor was told she had better leave when she told her mother about her stepfather's behaviour. She finally disclosed to her mother because his demands were escalating and she felt she could no longer cope. The remaining three survivors were not initially believed by their mothers, although some of these mothers investigated the allegations at a later date, or came to believe what was said after their initial shock. However, the general pattern here was for survivors to be living away from home before they disclosed.

In the context of other family members, one survivor described her disclosure to her non-abusing father as being something she regretted, since it had damaged the relationship she had with him. She thought he felt 'guilty' when she did tell him. She described how she used to ring him every week, but they had an argument over a business deal he was involved in and he referred to the abuse saying that she had 'left him with this crock of shit'. She knew that he was 'trying to blame me for something that was not my fault' but his perception of her reasons for telling him damaged the relationship considerably. This for her constituted yet another loss. She now depends on her husband and children and has minimised ties with both her natural parents.

The experiences of three of the survivors who had less secure childhoods would seem to have provided some of them with a wider range of coping skills. One survivor described how loving gestures were seen as signs of weakness in her family and recollects her mother's regular adage: 'Yer don't need people.' Whilst she suggests that she could not rationalise this with her own feelings, from quite an early age it may have enabled her to progress her own search for meaning into exploring the attribution of responsibility with less angst about the impact on her sense of family. Although a concurrent search for the affection she did not have as a child exacerbated problems in another way. Nevertheless, the strengths of those survivors who had found their own sources of support and worked through meaning for themselves, unhampered by the need to view their childhoods as supportive, fulfilling or positive, were interesting and in two cases had moved the survivors into being able to value their achievements. One in particular noted how she had compared herself with other survivors in a group she had attended and had been able to value just how much she had overcome.

Sources of support were not only perceived as people who had helped at the time of the abuse or shortly after it. Support was seen as something which needed to be ongoing over a period of years, which links with Bowlby's (1987) comments on attachment. Six of the survivors mentioned taking control of their own lives and moving forward as a continuing issue. It would seem that to do this they needed to be self-directing within supportive relationships. Three currently had supportive husbands who they felt cared for them. One had a new partner at the time of the second interview and spoke animatedly of how well he treated her and how she was more able to cope.

How survivors value their own coping skills has been questioned by Reis and Heppner (1993). Their findings would suggest that, rather than modelling their behaviour on their mothers, survivors whose mothers regard themselves as relatively powerless are likely to rate their own coping skills more highly than those whose mothers perceive themselves as correspondingly stronger. Herman (1992) suggests that the sense of self needs to be rebuilt 'in connection with others' (p.61). Two survivors spoke of how they tried to be the people their mothers wanted. One was unable to discover what this person needed to be, so constantly changed how she behaved in order to gain approval. The other felt that she could not forge her own identity as her mother 'wanted me to be something I wasn't, to wear all bright clothes and everything'.

The ability to trust others as part of that rebuilding process had not been achieved easily by the survivors and they detail instances which demonstrate both vulnerabilities and insights. One spoke of how she considered she had been 'taken in' by people who seem to be 'really nice' but turn out to be 'just the same'. Whether this implies that her standards are unrealistically high or whether initial kindness fulfils the need for affection which was unsatisfied in her childhood is in question here. This may link to Freud's notion that we search for mother substitutes in our spouses and would seem in this instance to support Gil's (1983) view that to achieve healing survivors may have to cease to search for the parents they never had. Gibson and Hartshorne (1996) note that survivors commonly expect to be hurt or betrayed in subsequent relationships and hence are frequently lonely as adults.

Five of the survivors had been divorced, two had remarried and had formed quite different relationships with their current partners. Two described their first marriages as a means of leaving home and both used phrases implying that this had been 'out of the frying pan into the fire', as both had married brutal men whose drinking was problematical. For another, her husband had had problems with alcohol. She felt he had treated her badly, although 'he didn't hit me'. The one survivor whose only marriage was successful described her husband as very important to her and talked of their shared interests, their discussions and his support as important aspects of her life. This links to the finding by Feinauer *et al.* (1996) that positive intimate relationships could provide a valuable source of support for adult survivors. The two oldest survivors had each been married once, and both marriages had ended in divorce. One felt her life had improved at that point; the other had returned to live near her parents away from the pressures of her husband and children. Neither described these men as violent, although one said her husband could be 'nasty'. This second survivor had had affairs with other men during the marriage, and the former's husband had had an affair which she attributed to naivety.

Four survivors mentioned that they seemed able to spot people who have been through experiences similar to their own, and claimed to be very rarely wrong in their assessments. They suggested that this skill could be more valued by those seeking to deal with abuse than it is. One instanced a girl she met as a room-mate whilst living in the YWCA. The girl had been crying and this survivor had initiated a conversation by saying: 'You're not the only one who has gone through it you know.' The girl had been surprised by this but had quickly confided that she had been abused by her headmaster and that no one would believe her.

When this happened in the early 1980s, there was still a prevalent myth that men who work professionally with children are less likely to abuse them (Driver and Droisen 1989). This myth has been repeatedly challenged in the press recently, with both priests and childcare workers being revealed as abusers. There is a level at which, despite the media coverage, child abuse is still something which, though it is acknowledged as a problem, does not happen to 'people like us'. Stanko (1985), for example, points to the tendency for people perceived as more important or well placed in society to be more likely to be believed by juries. Whilst a shift in this perspective may be occurring now, such stereotypes remain deeply entrenched in the minds of many people.

All of the survivors spoke of the need for survivors to speak out in order to support others. Four mentioned that friends were willing to confide in them because they knew how to listen, although one was amazed by the comparatively trivial issues which many of her friends worried about.

Counsellors were seen as a source of support by five survivors. Two survivors had not received counselling help. Counselling enabled one survivor to realise that she wasn't treating herself like a human being. She notes how 'it had got to the extreme really – I'd look in all the children's shops and I'd look in the men's shops but I never ever looked in the women's sections or anything'. She promised the counsellor that she would do something about this. 'And it was only then that I started doing stuff for myself like buying sort of bubble bath or stuff and aromatherapy and things that I would never do for myself because everyone else came before me.' One perceived counselling as potentially useful, although she did not feel that she had met the right counsellor yet. Another pointed to her experiences of two separate counsellors and noted their diverse styles at different stages in her healing. The first was comforting and empathetic, the second was a survivor herself and was less sympathetic and more confrontational. Within the framework of counselling, the two who had attended support groups viewed them differently. Whilst one survivor felt that a group had strengthened her own valuing of herself, another perceived the group as wallowing and not moving on. This calls into the question the nature and purpose of the groups as well as the people who choose to attend groups. These experiences can be linked to Hall and Lloyd's (1993) adaptation of Worden's (1983) four tasks of grieving into tasks for survivors. Those can be summarised as:

- acceptance of the reality of the loss

- experiencing the pain of grieving

- adapting to life bearing in mind the implications of the loss – perhaps accepting the impossibility of ever having normal relationships with the abuser

- moving the emotional energy bound up in the loss to other areas.

Counselling and group work can attend to these areas but there needs to be a mechanism for conclusion, for moving the survivor from dependence on the counsellor or group into a desire to get on with life as she or he wants to live it. Support which does not adopt this aim ultimately short-changes the client by maintaining a dependency that limits the potential for development. Those survivors who have reached the point of exploring their own needs can value support without feeling controlled by it.

Doctors were perceived as a source of support by some survivors. One praised her doctor's honesty: 'My doctor's openly said to me that she can't really understand because she's never been there, but, yes, she's a good doctor.' In Hooper's (1992) sample of mothers, doctors had not generally been seen as a useful source of support for mothers. Was this also true for survivors? The survivors in my research had varied views on doctors. One stressed the need to find a good doctor. Another had found this with her current doctor, although had experienced problems with doctors in the past. Yet another knew that her mother had found her doctor a good source of support, though she had not sought help from the medical profession herself. A fourth was scathing about the lack of understanding of health or social work professionals in general. The remaining three had found them of little help. Interestingly, the three doctors mentioned as helpful were all women; although survivors who had experienced less supportive relationships with doctors mentioned both male and female doctors.

Support was possible from a variety of sources, but had to fit with individual needs. Two older survivors had some support from their own children. One saw support as coming from her spiritualism. Another was still searching for a reliable source of support and detailed some of the problems she had with men in this respect.

For some survivors, support ultimately lodged within themselves and how comfortable they were able to feel with themselves. If the search for self is perceived as lifelong (Schein 1988), and seen to involve the assimilation and rejection of perceptions obtained during that process, there is scope for change and healing. Rogers (1967) sees the integration of the ideal self and the actual self as important in healthy functioning, both in regard to self and others. The ongoing nature of this assessment of self implies regularly confronting issues, which it is argued are likely to be exacerbated for survivors. Spaccarelli (1994) suggests that survivors probably re-evaluate their experiences at each developmental stage or when they encounter difficulties with particular tasks associated with developmental stages.

What may be intended as support may rankle for some survivors. One survivor noted an instance which particularly annoyed her. Whilst discussing her problems with a male doctor, he had commented that the survivor was lucky to have a supportive husband. The survivor retorted that other people had good husbands without having been abused and questioned why she should be regarded as lucky because she'd suffered as she did and then got a good husband. 'I said to him, was that my reward for being abused then?'

The role of supporters is not a simple one, either in terms of the issues involved or of the qualities required in relation to individual survivors. As survivors have suggested, they themselves may be able to provide support for other survivors. But as Parry (1991) points out, support needs to give survivors the opportunity to validate their own experiences and the ability to move on and take control of their new stories.

The survivors as they are now

Six survivors are mothers themselves, and this provided a perspective I had not foreseen at the outset of the study. All commented about their experience as mothers and these comments added another dimension to what they had said about their own mothers. The comparisons made between their own mothering and how their mothers had behaved had provided some with insights, some with unexplained problems and some with increased anger towards the members of their families who had harmed them when they were so small and innocent.

For three survivors, there was, or had been, real pleasure in the interaction with their children when they were small. In two instances, the children had grown beyond this stage, but one survivor encapsulated the sort of pleasure she found in doing simple things with her own children:

> A few of my friends think I'm crazy really. A few of the times when they'll come round they'll say, 'What are you doing?' You know, and I'll just be doing something absurd with the children. We made this big lollipop, stop and go. I spent hours doing it with them so that when they're on their bikes they'll know what to do and my friends said 'What are you doing? Haven't you anything more important to do?' – and I said 'no' [laughs]. That's much more important to me than doing an hour or two of ironing, it is! As you can see [laughs].

However, her children had made her reflect on what she now saw more clearly as the shortcomings of her own childhood and her mother's lack of care for her. Her youngest child, a daughter, had reached the age she was when her mother left her father to move in with the stepfather who was her abuser. This had focused her very acutely on the demands which she had faced at her daughter's age. It was causing her to revisit the issues which had faced her at this age.

Another survivor, who had been unaware of her abuse when her own child was between two and three, notes that she had real difficulties coping with her child at that age. She said she had felt unable to cope and was frightened for her child, afraid that she might do something wrong. It had only been later that she had begun to remember the details of her own childhood. During her intensive counselling and therapy, it had emerged that it was probable that she had been between the ages of two and three when her own abuse had started.

In a sense, here were different responses to the lack of an acceptable role model for parenting. Neither of these two survivors had had good relationships with either of their parents. The former, whose memories of what had happened were acute, was determined to be different for her children; the latter was frightened about the role she was being asked to play. Interestingly, both survivors mentioned their interactions with health visitors or social services at around this time. The former worried that, because of her past, they might think she was unfit to look after her children; the latter had wanted them to take her child away because she feared she would be unable to cope. The stories of these two women point to issues relevant for other survivors who are mothers. None of the six survivors lived near family who were available to help when they became mothers – not unusual in contemporary life. Four had left home by 16, and five had had a strong desire to make a success of caring for their own children – as a kind of catharsis for their own difficulties. The sixth did not question her husband's decisions on child rearing and had eventually left them with him.

I would argue that a cluster of factors were involved here which can be linked both to Briere's (1989) abuse dichotomy and Finkelhor and Browne's (1988) traumagenic dynamics model. To begin with, their own parenting had not provided them with a model which they wanted to replicate, but it had left five of them with a need to be good mothers. The fact that they too might 'get it wrong' was unpalatable to them. This breaks down further. If, as Honess and Lintern (1990) have suggested, girls are unlikely to see their mothers as people in their own right until they are in their early twenties, the early break from home may have left four of them viewing their mothers in two-dimensional terms – in their cases, as 'bad'. The fifth had been abused by her mother and wanted to protect her own children. The sixth survivor had greater confusions in that her mother had been warm and kind but ineffective – she could not see her mother as bad. The view she was left with was of mothers not being able to make any difference.

At least five of the survivors needed to be seen by their children and others as 'good' mothers. However, the self-image they had been left with as a result of their own abuse would be likely to contain a sense that they were not good enough for this role – causing two of them to worry and not reveal certain bits of information to authorities. 'I felt I had to be careful what I said to people like that,' said one. Two others became relatively dependent on health care and social workers, and were easily disturbed by the differences in professional opinions of how things should be done. Another two wilted in the face of the enormity of the commitment parenthood represented without understanding why they felt like this.

Furthermore, if the parenting they had received was not a useful model for them, what should it be replaced with? What did they perceive were society's expectations of mothers? The questions posed here were not specifically asked, although in some measure survivors began to answer them. There were several ways in which the issues involved were addressed. As has been said, comparison was made with the style used by their own mothers; survivors also commented on how their contemporaries mothered. This often revealed aspects of their own assumptions of what mothering should involve and implied that some had spent time reflecting on what motherhood should mean to a greater extent than had some of their contemporaries.

It may be that by having had to cope with a relationship which did not meet their needs, survivors have had to challenge their own perceptions of what mothering involves to a greater extent than those who have experienced fewer problems. This does not automatically have a positive or a negative potential in terms of their own mothering, but it does alter how they perceive the role. For instance, one survivor admitted to being 'overprotective' of her son. Her worry that he might have to suffer any of what she had faced had caused her to cushion him from possibilities for benefit as well as detriment. She saw this son as being the person she least wanted to know of her own experiences. Ironically, it seemed that there might be future potential in this protectiveness for him to blame her for it without being aware of her motives.

The theme of protectiveness was one which was mentioned by five of the survivors – generally because they felt that their contemporaries were insufficiently cautious about what their children were doing or who they were associating with. Muram *et al.* (1994), studying mothers of sexual abuse victims, found that they were significantly less impulsive and outgoing than mothers whose daughters had not been abused. It may be that this finding is also implicated where victims become mothers. It would certainly seem from the comments of five of the survivor mothers that they claim to be less likely to take risks than their friends. This apparently clashes with the cycles of abuse view (e.g. Vizard and Tranter 1988), which holds that the children of those who have been sexually abused are more liable to be abused themselves. As Hooper (1992) suggests, the reality seems much more complex. Whilst one of the women in this sample knew that her son had been abused sexually by a babysitter, and another believed that her son might have been abused by one of her own abusers, their ways of interpreting this abuse in relation to themselves differed radically. The former held the belief that she was fated to suffer repeated misfortune over which she had little control; the latter speaks of her naivety before her mind revealed what her family was really like and has a far more proactive view of her own ability to prevent recurrences now that she has the knowledge which her dissociation had kept from her.

If the sexual abuse of their children provides a trigger for mothers to remember their own abuse, this, as Hooper (1992) suggests, may in turn trigger complex reactions based on the meaning of their childhoods for them. In reverse as it were, the meaning of their childhoods may affect their perceptions of mothering in equally complex ways, ranging from a quiet determination to be better to their own child and to provide a wider range of opportunities than they were able to enjoy, to a resignation to the inevitability of failure, with a multitude of other possibilities between. This research would reinforce the difference and complexity of responses.

Whilst five survivors mentioned protecting their children, three also wanted their children to be independent and successful people. One had seen her children achieve this and two others saw it as an important aim. Education was seen as important by all of the survivors in the sample, with most implying that they felt their own prospects had been damaged by their abuse. There was a tendency to invest their hopes in their children's future achievements and this, whilst at one level laudable, could be viewed as a potential arena for further loss.

Losses themselves continued to form an important issue for survivors. There was a sense in which the survivors seemed to be concerned that motherhood was not always a positive experience. It seemed that guilt at not enjoying aspects of motherhood was perhaps exacerbated in their cases. This could again be related back to their need to achieve in this role as they had been unable to achieve in other areas of their lives. Loss, meaning and metaphor had a habit of intertwining in their stories. Three of the survivors pointed to moments of insight which have changed their perspective on themselves and their stories, allowing them to move forward in resolving their sense of loss. Others seemed trapped by their perceptions of life as a 'nightmare' or a 'prison'. It seems that how meaning is conceptualised or loss perceived can have important repercussions on coping.

In her study of mothers, Hooper (1992) uses the loss model proposed by Marris (1986), which describes the experience of loss as moving from shock, through distress, to reintegration. Hooper specifically points to the instances within her study of where mothers had been sexually abused themselves as children and notes that the extent to which mothers had resolved their childhood experiences seemed to have greater relevance on how they coped with the abuse of their own children. She notes that those who had most difficulty in resolving loss were those who 'retained idealised images of their childhoods despite accounts which indicated considerable conflict' (p.48).

It seemed from my research that those survivors who were able to assume a greater degree of responsibility for their actions and control over their lives were the ones who had been able to separate themselves from their childhoods. This involved realising that they could improve conditions for themselves and their own children, rather than maintaining the view that because they had been damaged nothing was going to be easy for them. Marris's model indicates that the person's own level of secure attachment in childhood assists their resilience in the face of loss. However, it was interesting to note that one survivor, whose own childhood was far from secure, was coping happily with three small children at the time of the interview: twin sons, one of whom was disabled, and a daughter. She was able to talk of her pleasure in her children and her surprise that some of her contemporaries could become as stressed as they did over losing possessions or being slightly overdrawn at the bank. Whilst her husband was very supportive and important to her, and was perceived by her as a source of security and strength, she had spent time wrestling with both the meaning of her experiences and of her family of origin. There were variations from this aspect of the model in the other cases in this study. The three survivors who described their attachment to one parent as relatively secure had not necessarily achieved easier resolution of their loss.

The second stage of the model deals with the reconstitution of meaning in terms of the loss. Hooper (1992), here, points to the problems involved in defining what the loss has involved. As has been argued before in this chapter, the survivors continue to deal with issues relating to their situations. New meaning is cast on events as they themselves face issues in their lives which trigger aspects of their past. However, it seems from their accounts that meaning has to be addressed at a variety of levels. The first would seem to be the ability to name what has happened for what it is. Though no simple task, in comparison with resolving the emotional understanding involved this would seem to be comparatively easy. Goleman (1996) argues that perpetrators lack empathy – if they were able to empathise with their victims, they would not be able to commit the acts they do. If the survivor has not encountered empathy, or has perceived it only within a context which has been ineffective, the process of ascribing emotional meaning to events and to the motivation of others will be hampered by a survivor's lack of opportunity for developing this skill. This, I suggest, may account in certain cases for some survivors' tendency to blame mothers rather than to empathise with the situations they faced. Just as in some families the linguistic base available is limited, it is argued that here the emotional base may also be restricted, both in terms of the availability of language to describe what was felt and in terms of the range of emotions accepted as constituting normality. One survivor, for example, described her early wariness if people smiled at her. In a sense, though it has modified, she saw a continuing problem in this area, in that she cited frequent examples of being disillusioned by people she initially thought were 'wonderful' and who turned out to have failings.

The third level of Marris's model discusses the preparation for loss which people have available to them and notes how lack of predictability may disrupt the whole structure of meaning. It would seem from the stories of some of the survivors that realisation of the losses involved in their childhood post-dated that period. Two survivors specifically commented that what they were experiencing was 'normality' for them. Their realisation of the losses involved came later. Whilst disintegration of meaning may arise with the realisation of the loss, it is argued that Herman's (1992) model of complex post-traumatic stress, which notes alterations to aspects of self and situations, may be implicated here. Not only are survivors liable to suffer such impairment as young children, they may also suffer further disintegration as part of Marris's model when they confront the loss they have suffered.

The final stage of Marris's model indicates that events after the loss may either assist recovery or impede it. Here, the model provided support for the experience of these survivors; although it was not simply experiences that were implicated, it was how experiences were interpreted or incorporated into a whole. It seemed the metaphors incorporated into different stories affected self-perception and the attribution of responsibility for healing.

Herman (1992) has talked about how women and children in abusive situations are often captive, mentally if not physically. The metaphors of captivity and freedom were common in the stories the survivors told and had varying implications for their current situations in all cases. Three survivors saw themselves as trapped in differing aspects of their own lives, three others emphasised their increasing freedoms and growing strength, while one had not allowed herself to perceive the chains. The potential for coping and healing which resides in the framing of survivors' stories was demonstrated within my study by the juxtapositioning of their stories. It seemed that survivors who had taken control of their own stories and who made comments such as –

> I think...um...it affects everything you do, yeah. Your confidence and your strength and your willingness to do things and oh everything really and like I say I've felt safer for the six months now but had I been like this, feeling this good from the age of five, what could I have done? So I'm not ever going to shed that aspect of it. But I'm now getting on with the rest of my life.

> This is the hardest thing I've had to deal with by a long way. Compared with the average person I've had a lot of difficult things to deal with really. I mean we've actually had two suicides to deal with in the family, and then I've had to deal with having a son with special needs and...um...there are other things as well. A lot of people would sort of be at break down point with it...um...putting it in perspective, it's

made a lot of other things seem menial really, that I mean in one sense
that's pretty good. I mean that's the good thing about it and I get
frustrated with people like the car exhaust's fallen off and it's the end of
the world

– had attained a stage of understanding which enabled them to function
more effectively in some areas of their lives, although that is not to minimise
either their losses or the continuing potential for harm which the abuse
holds over their lives.

The three survivors who articulated their own progress towards healing
and control admitted that their resilience was fragile, but each in some way
indicated that their own recognition of their strengths, in achieving what
they have, was an important component within recovery.

Meaning for all those interviewed was often constructed around the
device of seeing patterns in aspects of their own experiences. Such patterns
could form both explanations and traps. One survivor saw her son's brain
damage from a difficult birth and her early hysterectomy as yet more
problems associated with 'that area' of her life – an awful irony, in her
judgement. Another saw an enjoyable afternoon out with her son as a link
into some of the horrors associated with sunny days in her own childhood.
And a third mentioned looking at her father's handwriting in a book as
taking her back to when she was eight and the sort of things which were
happening to her then. There is potential in these connections for further
losses which can be added to the original abuse or opportunity for survivors
to disentangle the specific events of that period in their lives from other
disparate events.

Three survivors raised the question of whether their perpetrators ever
thought that they would have memories of what had happened when they
were adult. They felt that one day any abused child would realise that what
had happened was wrong, even if it was part of the normality of their
existence at the time when it happened. Only one survivor claimed to have
forgiven the perpetrator and expressed her horror at how anyone could
report a family member to the police or authorities for something like this.
The meaning she had constructed around her abuse allowed for similar acts
to be viewed differently if the perpetrator was a stranger. In her view, a
family member must be ill to do something like that. This issue of motivation
had been part of the stories of others in the sample, although usually they
had pointed to the time when they realised that their abuser had known
what he was doing and their concurrent release from their own feelings of
responsibility for the act. Two of the survivors had reported events to the

authorities as adults because they perceived the possibility of threat to other younger members of the family. Two others mentioned feeling glad that their own children were not in contact with the perpetrators as they would have to be wary of them.

The survivors' stories varied considerably. None had emerged from the abuse unscathed, and all were still coping with aspects of its aftermath in their present lives. Most of the survivors mentioned areas which still provided problems for them; their underachievement in education was an issue for four of them, all of whom hoped to remedy this eventually. Other general areas which they found problematical included the mistrust of people until they have been known for some time and a tendency to depression – three of the survivors mentioned taking, or having taken, antidepressants. Some talked of their lack of self-confidence or the ease with which they could be upset or embarrassed. One mentioned that she had problems if people are shouting, and another was hampered by her inability to confront her parents about issues – even though she would like to. Yet another had difficulty with sleeping in a bed, preferring to sleep on the couch. She had a system of double- and triple-locking doors, as she was still afraid of retribution from her family.

Support which is available but does not restrict growth or dictate courses of action, time to resolve issues and to develop a voice, the determination to take responsibility for their own responses, and the opportunity to recognise and build on their own resiliences would seem to be important issues for these survivors.

Summary of issues for the survivors

The issues identified by the literature as likely to be of importance in this study include conflict, coping strategies, power relations, gender differences and communication. This chapter has explored these themes in connection with the issues raised by the survivors.

Conflict has been an aspect of survivor experience both at an individual and an interpersonal level. Such conflict has been caused not only by difficulties with relationships or aspects of disclosure but also by the effect of myths on the perceptions of abuse by those involved and ensuing questions of the responsibility for it, as detailed earlier. There was some suggestion that when individual issues were explored by survivors, usually in this sample in conjunction with their counsellors (3) and/or close family (4), that a measure of resolution had been reached. The survivor who had been unable to find anyone to answer her questions and who wanted to discuss issues with her mother but felt unable to do so was the least able, during the interview, to give meaning to her experiences.

In the light of Worden's (1983) four tasks of grieving, as adapted by Hall and Lloyd (1993) (see p.96), it can be argued that survivors have achieved different stages in dealing with the psychic conflict involved in addressing their losses. Individual survivors will not be referred to in this discussion, but it can be shown from the interviews that survivor descriptions of their own positions in dealing with the issues involved range from one who had an incomplete resolution of the first area – acceptance of the reality of the loss – to one who had made a deliberate decision to move her emotional energy into other areas and had thus reached the final level of this process. The remaining five were dealing with aspects of the third and fourth levels, adapting to life or moving their emotional energy elsewhere.

Such resolution of conflict links very closely to coping skills. Spaccarelli's (1994) exploration of the issues which might be implicated here involves starting from areas described by those within the situation as difficult, rather than looking at theoretical indices of stressors. The question posed during the second interview about the relative difficulty of coping with the abuse and dealing with other problems they had faced indicates that for most of the sample this had been the most difficult thing they had ever faced. This was so despite some of them facing the death of family members, serious illness and divorce – commonly ranked as highly stressful on conventional scales of stressors (e.g. The Life Events Scale devised by Hawkins, Davis and Holmes 1957).

Hopson's (1981) Coping Skills Questionnaire incorporates eight factors involved in coping with personal transition. These are:

1. knowledge of self

2. knowledge of situation

3. awareness of sources of help

4. ability to learn from the past

5. ability to care for self

6. ability to let go of the past

7. ability to set goals and plan

8. ability to appreciate personal gains.

There are indications that survivors used these strategies and that such skills may be implicated in healing, but such strategies were less applicable, or available, to them as children. It is here that the base from which survivors begin to cope has to be valued and reaffirmed, as a number of the issues in this model assume a level of basic equilibrium, which some survivors have had to discover *ab initio* for themselves. As Hall and Lloyd (1993) emphasise, it is important not to underestimate what survivors do achieve and how they do cope. Those survivors who have been enabled to value their ability to cope, and who have been supported by people who are important to them and upon whom they can depend, would seem to be those who currently exhibit more of the skills identified by Hopson (1981).

My study suggests that it is not only early attachment patterns that can produce this degree of resilience, though it does appear that the sooner such a figure is involved in assisting survivors the less complicated is the effect of additional losses or problems upon the survivor's construction of self or of the meaning of events. The presence of such relationships seems to allow the survivor the space to construct a sense of self which is separate from the abuse. The study would endorse the finding by Parry (1991) and Shepherd (1990) that the ability to reinterpret events and reframe meaning is an important part of healing.

Power and empowerment issues were also important for the sample. Few actually mentioned their powerlessness within their childhood situations, although two implied it. Generally, comments centred on when they did feel some measure of control, or detailed areas in which they had been able to resist. In some cases, these strategies and their attempts at positive action had been devalued by them with their later realisation of their own vulnerability. Some were able to reframe this into anger at the abuses of power within their families, whilst others did not react in this way. For four, the development of their own sense of self had been aided by reducing or discontinuing contact with their original families. Five had the view that they had to be responsible for coming to terms with their own issues and to take charge of themselves. One had been 'given strength' by her religious beliefs, and one was still searching for a key to her own understanding.

Gender issues surfaced in a number of contexts, which suggested that for several survivors there were ongoing difficulties in this area. These ranged from one survivor's comments that she liked certain named men but did not trust males in general, to another's fear about the prospect of having a girl when she had been pregnant for the first time. By the time of her second pregnancy she was sufficiently confident in her ability to parent not to be concerned about the gender of the coming child.

Another survivor saw her brothers' initiation into abusive roles when they reached puberty as her mother's way of dealing with their sexuality. Her younger brother's suicide was linked by her to the greater difficulty he would have had in acknowledging his own abuse. Another considered herself to be 'better off' without men, although, interestingly, her spirit guide was male and her descriptions of her non-abusing father used the sort of nurturing terms elsewhere associated with mothers (soft, kind, gentle). A differentiation seemed to operate in all the cases between the known and the unknown. There were patterns of thinking which produced generalisations about gender issues, although when specific cases were cited these frequently contradicted the stated pattern.

There were links between communication and gender. Those who had currently supportive partners spoke of their ability to talk to them about a wide range of issues. It was noticeable that when survivors talked of those who had been kind to them in their childhood, these people had spent time with them, talked to them or shown them how to do certain things. There was a sense that at least some of their problems had been resolved through communicating with others and through the development of sufficient trust to allow them to discuss difficult issues; although most spoke of certain people in whom they regretted having confided. The choice of who and what to tell was an ongoing issue for most of them.

The process of constructing meaning from the events of their childhood was still an issue for the survivors. They were all aware of the extent to which small and apparently insignificant triggers could affect them. Several were still in the process of remembering and reassessing their childhood, with the possibility of legal action being a current issue for two. The one who had completed this process, which had resulted in a guilty verdict and criminal injuries compensation, felt that her father had not got his just deserts as 'he was not even put in prison, nothing really got done about it and the money didn't even come out of his own pocket. Anyway, money isn't everything – it doesn't take it away, it's still there.' Two others knew that they may have to face new losses if such action was unsuccessful.

Survivors were willing to explore ways in which others might be helped. Here, perhaps, the two most important issues which emerged for them were the easy accessibility of sources of help for current victims and the need for people to value the experiences of survivors themselves when it comes to helping others. They felt that their knowledge and experiences were something about which professionals should be aware. Most saw training or preventive education as in need of input from survivors who might be both more acutely aware of who was suffering and less likely to underestimate the impact. The issues of the role of the school and the support that might be provided for survivors will form the basis of separate discussions in conjunction with the responses of the other two groups.

CHAPTER 5

The Mothers

The stories of the mothers who took part in my research form the basis of the current chapter. Their stories will be explored in order to assess the problems they faced and the situations they dealt with in coping with the sexual abuse of their children. Whilst comparison with the survivors will be made in terms of some of the issues raised, such comparisons will not form the primary purpose of this chapter. Rather, it will deal with how the mothers perceived what happened to them and their children whilst coping with the discovery or disclosure of the abuse.

The sample consisted of seven mothers, whose ages ranged from 30 to 54 at the time of the interview. The abuse of the children involved happened during the last 20 years. The abuse of the oldest woman's child took place in 1980, and the children of the youngest mother in the sample were last abused, to her knowledge, in 1993. Hence, in comparison to survivors from the sample, though there is chronological overlap with the youngest survivor, in general the abuse events reported by mothers had happened more recently. Mother blaming was, and to some extent is, an issue for these women; but, in comparison with some of the survivor group, none of the children involved were seen as responsible for the abuse events. The ages of the survivor children of these mothers, at the time of interview, ranged from 6 to 25 and included both males and females. In four families, more than one child had been abused. In all, this sample reported on the abuse of 13 children. The perpetrators involved were all male and in three families were the biological fathers of the children involved – none of these men was still living with the mother concerned. In the remaining four cases, perpetrators were family friends – in two instances neighbours, and in two others long-standing babysitters.

In five cases the child, or one of the children in the family, had disclosed to the mother before any outside agency had become involved – if indeed this had happened. Four mothers had contacted the police after their child's disclosure. The other had had a long-running involvement with police and social services because of her husband's brutality. Whilst she still suspects him of sexually abusing her daughter, her overt reason for taking part in the research was to talk about the sexual abuse of her son by a neighbour. Her son was in his early twenties before he disclosed this to his mother, and by his choice no external agency was involved. However, this mother had talked to professionals about him whilst discussing her fears about her daughter – hence she is regarded as dealing with professionals about this topic area. In the remaining two cases, mothers were informed of the abuse by protection agencies – in one case the police had wanted to question her child because of a complaint, and in the other social services had removed her children pending enquiries.

The women were from a variety of backgrounds, and had noticeably better educational qualifications than the survivors. Two were graduates and three were involved in, or had started, higher education courses. The sixth had served as a local councillor and the seventh had secretarial qualifications. Of three other mothers who contacted me, but did not continue to the interview stage, one was a graduate. Despite the small size of the sample, this difference in backgrounds was interesting. My letter to local newspapers had mentioned both mothers and survivors so that the sources from which the sample was drawn were similar, but the respondents to each request were noticeably different. The mothers described by all but one of the survivors were not professional women. It may be argued that this was because fewer mothers had careers at the time most of the survivors were abused. However, the survivors did not describe their mothers as generally communicative towards them. The mothers cited numerous examples of trying to work with their children to address various issues which surrounded the abuse. They described attempts to obtain help for their children from different sources and appeared to be a relatively proactive group of people.

What were the reasons for the tensions between the accounts of these groups? How did they relate to differing purposes for taking part in the research? Had six of the survivors responded because they had also had to survive a poor relationship with their mothers? Had they based their stories or comments on an assumption that a poor relationship with the mother was a factor in sexual abuse? Had the mothers responded because they believed their relationships with their children had not been noticeably poor and were unable to reconcile this with the responsibility they now felt for the abuse? Was one of their assumptions that all mothers involved in this sort of situation would have difficulties with the issues they found problematical? Was part of their willingness to talk based upon the fact that they felt they could articulate their stories because the current climate allowed more discussion of sensitive issues? The juxtaposition of these two groups presented me with primary evidence of the contradictions to be found in existing theory about the characteristics of mothers of sexual abuse victims, and a further indication of the complexities within the individual experiences of those affected by abuse.

Two mothers had been abused themselves as children and both pointed to how the abuse of their own children had reawakened issues on this for themselves. This issue has been debated in the literature by those who favour 'cycle of abuse' theories (e.g. Reis and Heppner 1993; Vizard and Tranter 1988) with their emphasis on mothers maintaining conditions in which abuse becomes more likely; and by the feminists (e.g. Kelly *et al.* 1991) who argue that, given the prevalence of sexual abuse, it is likely that some sexually abused women will become mothers of sexual abuse victims without this being a causative factor *per se*. Kelly (1992) further argues that such models of causation 'embody a determinism which is dangerous to practice' (p.iii): dangerous because the removal of a child from a family might be damaging if some of the child's relationships with other family members were loving and secure.

Another factor of interest was that the range of abuse described by the mothers was different from that described by survivors. Here, the abuse by males who were not the biological fathers of the children involved was more severe than that perpetrated by the fathers in the sample, yet the behavioural problems mothers ascribed to their children, which they linked to the abuse, were worse where the father was the perpetrator.

Telling the story

The mothers had various reasons for involving themselves in the study. There was a sense in which telling the story was a greater risk for them than for the survivors. Gudykunst (1994) argues that a major reason why we do not communicate with others is that we do not see their reactions as predictable. Fineman (1993) talks of our need to get it right, to conceal and to adopt acceptable masks. Two or three mothers in this study assumed support from others at an early stage after discovery but had revised this opinion subsequently. This was hinted at through the words of one of the mothers:

When [my daughter] told anyone what had happened to her I felt that people were sorry for her. When I said anything I felt that people thought...I...it was my fault. I should have known what was going on. It's taken a lot of counselling for me to realise that perpetrators are clever and devious and that just because I was her mother it didn't mean I would know automatically if something was wrong.

Mothers described a tension between what they had achieved as mothers and the coexistence of the abusive situation. This would support the sort of comment noted earlier: 'I thought well that's it all gone for nothing. I can't be a good mother now when something like this has happened.' (Dempster 1993, p.65.)

Gerwert et al. (1993) have argued that the disclosure of a child's sexual abuse presents mothers with a multiple crisis involving them in having to reassess themselves, their relationships and their situation. Hooper (1992) suggests that women experience a number of losses in connection with the abuse of their children and posits that these can be ongoing. One such loss is concerned with their own self-image as mothers. An act such as the telling of the story has the potential for adding to losses, in that either further connections are made to memories that can produce new senses of loss or guilt or responsibility, or the recipient of the information responds in an unpredicted way and undermines the reasons for telling the story. It seemed to me that the mothers in this sample had been made acutely aware that some of those to whom they had told their story believed that they were at least partially responsible for what had happened; or in one case that the mother concerned had fabricated the information for her own purposes. Such reactions had ranged from a GP's well-intentioned but dismissive comment that one mother should not blame herself for the abuse, but that she must have been 'rather naive not to have realised what was happening', to a husband's initial reaction: 'You're the one who's at home all day with nothing to do but look after the bloody kids. How did you manage to let that happen?' All of the women could point to incidents of this nature. All of them had been challenged either obliquely or directly about their own responsibility for the abuse. All had found this particularly difficult as their potential responsibility was an issue which troubled them and was one which was acutely bound up with their own image of themselves as mothers.

Four of the mothers had found that their child's abuse had caused them to focus on what they felt they had done wrongly in terms of their mothering. These ranged from one mother's feeling that she had allowed her children to be too trusting of others – she blamed herself for not preparing them for nastier aspects of society – to another mother's self-blame for her lack of understanding of her child's awkward behaviour at bedtime. It seemed they were trying to convince themselves that if they had got these things right the larger problem might not have been able to happen. Within the literature on bereavement, Weinberg (1995) has pointed to the tensions between the just-world theory and self-esteem theory. The former suggests that when a fundamental tenet of society is breached for an individual, a new search for meaning is initiated, which sets up a state of disequilibrium in the individual concerned. This may result in self-blame. This, Weinberg argues, self-esteem theorists see as destructive and undermining of self-worth. However, Weinberg goes on to say that if women move from this into a process of making amends, this assists them in restoring some control and repairing self-esteem.

This seems to echo the way in which women were trying to come to terms with their child's abuse. The women tried to find areas, potentially within their control, to somehow explain why this unpalatable event had happened. It seemed that they tried to blame themselves to make the larger picture more comprehensible and so more possible to control.

If this tendency is identifiable as part of women's own search for meaning within their situations, it is also apparent in the responses of others, both professional and lay. Unfortunately, these may exacerbate the negatives of Weinberg's model. Whilst feminist writers have noted the tendency to blame mothers for their shortcomings in relation to events, abusive and otherwise, which befall their children (e.g. Caplan 1990; Jacobs 1990; Sommerfeld 1989), it would seem that at a variety of levels, both overt and covert, society continues to assist women in their quest for blame. Sometimes, causes of guilt or blame are apparently trivial. Ribbens (1994) described respondents who invested the family activity of playing board games together with importance and felt guilty that they did not always enjoy this activity. Elsewhere, the conflict between societal expectations of mothers and the reality of their need to work is located by Richardson (1993) at the centre of the dilemma mothers face. Coupled with this potential for blame, Hunt (1993) suggests that in a number of studies of people's attributive reasoning the compelling, if naive, belief in a just world prompts them to ascribe others' misfortunes to their perceived carelessness or risk taking. He claims that, often, the worse the plight the more this style of attribution is brought to bear on those involved in the particular predicament.

Studies of bereavement and its links to depression have frequently shown a link between feelings of guilt about the loss as a cause of depression (e.g. Braun and Berg 1994; Trolley 1994). Trolley pursues this link into comparisons with other traumatic life events. Indeed, such links are well argued in the literature connecting models of the effects of child sexual abuse, or victimisation more generally, and response to trauma (Finkelhor 1988; Patten *et al.* 1989; Wolfe *et al.* 1994).

Whereas a common reason for survivors in the study to tell their story was with a view to helping others in the same situation, the mothers did not envisage the same outcome. Their motivation seemed to be the desire to tell their stories to someone prepared to listen rather than judge. Whilst two assumed that it might be possible to gain support from others who had experienced similar events, none of this sample had deliberately sought to meet other mothers in this situation, although one had used a helpline and two others knew of the existence of mothers' groups. One, whose neighbour had recently discovered her own child had been abused, in fact expressed her fear of talking to this woman in case 'anyone' thought she had tried to influence her. Indeed, this mother pointed to instances in her own experience where her barrister had advised her not to contact self-help groups or helplines in case their advice damaged her case. This served to isolate her further within a situation where she felt unsupported. Despite telling her story for the purposes of the research, she was unsure whether anything she could do or say would really help anyone.

The message that I received from the mothers was that I could present to others what it was like to be a mother within this situation. The unspoken message seemed to be that these mothers needed someone to talk to who would just listen to them without judging what they had got right or wrong. Hooper (1992) noted the tendency in the mothers in her sample to want somebody whom they felt to be 'on their side'. Their experience suggested that official agencies tended to locate them as part of the problem and not people emotionally involved in it. As one mother commented:

> But the court system, the judges, the barristers, the solicitors, the lot of them, it's just a load of whitewash. They need to go into more depth about how people feel about how it…like people who have been through it and understand. They should use them before they make decisions.

For the three women who had left the partner who had abused their children, there had been the additional implication in the telling of their stories that this might be some sort of reaction to the end of a relationship. All three of them had had this suggestion raised to them by the legal profession and found it both devastating and demeaning. As one mother commented 'There are other ways of getting revenge than involving your kids, and anyway they were with me and I was away from him. Why would I want to make something like that up and rake up all that trouble?'

Kirkwood (1993) has pointed to the 'web' which entangles women within an abusive situation, and has suggested that sometimes this web is not visible until women move away from it, as one of her sample commented:

> It would be as if when a spider weaves a web you don't see it very clearly. It's when, it's on two trees and the sun is shining through it, there's dew on it, that you can really see the outline...if you could take a can of spray paint and spray it so that you could see all the linking things that make it manipulative, and what it undermines, and what it's attached to, what string pulls it. (p.61)

Whilst the web metaphor encapsulates the process of entrapment and the levels of disentanglement needed to perceive a situation more clearly, there is also the sense in which mothers described a reassessment of a series of patterns as part of the process of discovery. Here, the metaphor of the kaleidoscope can illuminate aspects of constructing a story around events of which a mother may have only limited awareness. Viewed in one way, events appear to fit into patterns suggesting a certain range of explanations; but, with the addition of different perspectives, alternative explanations have to be found or may suggest themselves. This is clarified by the story one of the mothers tells. She describes how she knew certain things about her husband and how he treated the family:

> It was strange. I knew he had a bad temper and drank too much. If the two came together I would try to keep the children away from him, although this wasn't always possible. I thought they were frightened of him because of his unpredictability. Even though he could do some strange things sexually to me I never imagined he'd do anything like that to his own children, but when they told me I immediately believed them.

However, it is not only the mothers' own constructions of stories that are at issue here. They tell of how they have sought to understand things that their children have done or have told them. They instance how friends, family and professionals have reacted to the aspects of their stories that they have revealed. All, without exception, express ways in which such reactions have modified what they disclose and to whom.

One mother took her early concerns to her GP and was referred to social services:

Social services sort of decided that no action was to be taken and the sort of feeling that I got off them was that I was being paranoid and getting upset about nothing, and really when I look at what…er…and when I think rationally if…er…how [my daughter] was, could be interpreted in other ways. Then I sort of pushed it to the back of my mind. I decided well if everyone else was telling me well there's nothing…that there was nothing to worry about so I just carried on as normal.

However, this mother's concerns did not disappear, but her responses were affected:

I was in that frame of mind, I suppose, because of what social services had said…you know, that it could be just myself and I could perhaps be making a mountain out of a molehill. I didn't tell anyone and at that stage I hadn't told my parents either, so I was in a situation where there was nobody to talk to about it and the only thing that I was looking to, I was looking to him for reassurance that it wasn't happening and you know, I was isolated, I was honestly isolated, like there was nobody to turn to, nothing that could make it better really.

Not all of the sample took their concerns to the authorities immediately; for some there had to be certainty that their suspicions were founded before they took action. Another mother took her worries to the school her children attended. She did not disclose what her suspicions were but on two separate occasions asked teachers whether her children were behaving differently at school. The first teacher she asked assured her that there were no problems with her children and added a comment to the effect that she wished others were as well behaved. A second teacher was more suspicious about how well behaved the children were, and asked the mother about the nature of her worries. This second teacher was more ready to accept that their exceptionally good behaviour might provide cause for concern.

The issue of choosing a recipient for their stories was central for the mothers. Often, the ability to discuss feelings and worries about a child with someone outside of the family seemed to be an essential ingredient in determining what was to come next. There was a strong indication that women needed someone else to validate their sense that something was wrong before they could move into more definite action, or seek confirmation of their views from the child.

There were a number of differing reactions when the need to tell their story became an issue for the women. Two women who had not been told of the abuse by their child but had discovered it from other adults – in one case the police and in the other social services – expressed more of a sense of disbelief at the news. This moved quickly into self-doubt and feelings of guilt or blame. Four of the remaining five expressed their first reaction as horrified belief, or a flash of connection, which made sense of what had happened. These women described anger as driving their subsequent actions before the self-doubt and questioning of their own responsibility came into play. The final woman was told of his abuse by her son only when he became an adult. This was the longest gap between the events concerned and disclosure. Whilst this woman was angry with the situation, there was a sense in which she assimilated this latest 'horror' into a long list of horrors that had befallen her, rather than linking it to increased understanding of her son. She said:

> Some people aren't so fortunate, some people go through life and think things'll never go right for them and I feel I'm one of those people. Yes, there may be positive things that happen but nobody can expect somebody like me, or anybody else in a similar situation, to think positive when so many negative things have happened and still keep popping up round the corner.

Only this woman, of the seven mothers, actively linked her own story to fate. It is interesting that of all the survivors and mothers in this study, she is the one whose storytelling style meshes most closely with Klein and Janoff-Bulman's (1996) findings that child abuse survivors tend to focus on the past and to underestimate the role of the self. This may imply that their findings can be extended to what happens to mothers in a child abuse scenario, but it may also indicate that the strategies they outline are not broadly generalisable, even within the original group they studied. This woman revealed during the interviews that she was, herself, a survivor of child sexual abuse, but she was not the only mother to whom this applied. What seems to be of importance here is that there is a link between ownership of one's life story and belief in one's coping ability, but this may be more broadly based than Klein and Janoff-Bulman's study implies.

There is one further important issue in terms of the mothers' stories. It was apparent, in listening to the mothers' descriptions of their experiences, that they were not telling only one story. Whilst what they were recounting was their story, this story had a complication that was not apparent in the way the survivors related their experiences. The mothers were not only relaying what had happened to their children, they were also talking about what had happened to themselves. Sometimes, the needs of these two main characters in the stories they told were incompatible. Hence, mothers not only spoke of their own emotional response to events, but frequently linked this to other factors. Four mentioned their need to hide feelings or information in order not to upset the child involved. Two mentioned how they had had to reveal to the authorities information the child had wanted to keep confidential – this had made them feel uncomfortable and had led to problems with the child. One woman could not bear to mention the name of the neighbour who had abused her daughter, even at the time of the interview, some 15 years after the event. Her daughter did not share this problem. There was, therefore, a sense in which the issue of telling the story was coloured by the question of ownership and the need for separation of those issues which belonged to the abuse itself and those which belonged to its impact on the mother involved and her perception of the situation surrounding it.

Neate (1992) has noted the need for mothers and children to move towards mutual understanding of the abuse through discussion of issues where blame might be attributed to mothers. Such issues of primary and secondary victimisation have been addressed (e.g. Remer and Elliott 1988) in terms of the effect of trauma on different family members. Such effects would seem to be an important issue in the relating of information or feelings about child sexual abuse. It may also be, as family systems research has suggested (e.g. Furniss 1991), that where a family has had to accommodate dysfunctional behaviour from one member that others have formed alliances or groupings which interfere with parent–child or adult–child boundaries, some families thrash out their problems whilst others deny them. In these instances, as Ann C. Miller (1990) has suggested, it may be that various family groupings, as well as individuals, need to restructure the meaning of their experiences. As Parry (1991) discusses, stories may be restructured for different purposes, and when requested to narrate aspects of their lives people choose what incidents they will relate. If the reframing of individual stories is of benefit to individuals, it follows that the restructuring of a family experience by those involved has benefits for them as a group.

Four mothers had some experience of family therapy but most felt that whilst this had uses it was insufficiently supportive of individuals. One commented:

> We went to family therapy on about four occasions and it ended up making me feel worse rather than better. I wanted someone to listen to me – not to feel that everyone blamed me for things. I was already making a good job of that.

This would link with similar comments made by Sgroi (1982), who points to the need for individual work in order to provide people with sufficient confidence to explore stories together as a family. Unfortunately, such insights did not seem to be reflected in practice in the experience of this sample. Too often they were pawns in their own stories rather than controlling narrators. It seemed that the story for them was ongoing, that the present could still be affected by the past, and whilst mothers could point to areas of growth in understanding, none felt she could ever finally resolve the loss. Despite their own awareness that responsibility lay with the perpetrator, their experiences had not convinced them that others shared Liddle's (1993) view of child sexual abuse as 'the product of an individual failure to be self-directing and autonomous' (p.121).

As in the case of the survivors, how mothers understood the stories in which they were involved and how they coped with events was located within their own experience of family life.

Family life for the mothers

There were difficulties in ascertaining what family life was like for the mothers before the abuse of their children. Hooper (1992) has pointed to the effect on memories of discovering the abuse of a child and to the process of reattributing meaning to past events. None of the mothers or the survivors could talk of a time without the abuse, as it had coloured past and present for them all. I will, however, seek to provide an overview of family issues which were not directly related to the abuse itself, whilst acknowledging the constraints imposed by hindsight.

All of the mothers were, or had been, married women. Whilst one was now a divorced single parent, the others were currently married. Only one still had any regular contact with the abuser, and in this case the children were also still in contact with him. There were four families in which the abuser had been a friend or neighbour. In these instances, two women were still married to the husband who had supported them at the time of the abuse, but only one of these men was the father of the child concerned. In one of the remaining three cases, the abuse was disclosed after the mother had remarried. Divorce had followed disclosure for the remaining two mothers. In the three families where the father had been the abuser, there was a background to the marriages of either overt violence or threat. Two of the three men had alcohol problems, the third was 'heavily into drugs'. Such links with violence, alcohol or drugs have been well documented (e.g. Deblinger *et al.* 1993; Goddard and Hiller 1993). Hooper (1992) notes links between addictive behaviour and abuse, pointing out the addict's capacity for secrecy and denial as well as rationalising of behaviour, or blaming others for what was happening. This has resonances in the stories of the women whose husbands were the abusers of their children. There is a sense in the stories of these three women that they were

- aware that their husbands had problems or faults and were prepared to make allowances for them. 'I knew he could drink too much but he could be very loving. I learned to watch for the signs and I think the kids did too. I just didn't imagine he'd do anything like that.'

- prepared to endure difficulties. 'It was like living in a nightmare, you know, and he kept trying to blame me for things. Like I had a twin brother who died and he kept saying I was mad because of that and he was making out, like, that these bad things were all coming from me because of that trauma and I sort of believed that.'

- aware that marriage was not going to be without difficulties of its own. 'I was prepared to work at it. I didn't expect a bed of roses but I did sometimes feel that it was me that was putting the effort in. Like he wasn't very good with money and I had to look after that, but he'd often get us into debt.'

Barrett (1993) argues that whilst such behaviour has often been perceived as contributory, the point is often that such mothers are holding on in order to survive and to protect their children by maintaining the economic security of what may be a poor marriage, rather than knowingly contributing to abuse.

The mothers whose children were abused by friends or neighbours described their marriages variously. Two had experienced similar problems with husbands who could be violent or drank heavily – these two were no longer with these men. The one who had been married the longest pointed to difficulties with her husband – he did not talk to her much about what had happened. This she saw as a characteristic of his which had been there throughout their marriage, but it was contextualised in the present. She remarked that his attitude was that she 'ought to be over it by now' and she did not feel that she ever would be. She may not have commented on this sort of behaviour had it not been for the abuse of their child.

Five women admitted that there were some communication problems with the men in their lives, though they seemed to hold the view that this was part of masculinity. Another woman pointed to the difference between the husband who had abused her children and her current husband who could talk about feelings and was willing to listen:

> With my first husband I'd try to get him to talk about things, about feelings and stuff like that, but he'd say, 'I don't know what you want me to say.' It was as if he hadn't got the words to express it or perhaps he didn't feel it.

There was also a sense that women sometimes restricted their use of words or discussion of issues because men saw them as 'going on' or found themselves in some way threatened by the women's use of language. Horsfall (1991) notes how such gendered differences in expressiveness may lead to areas of unresolved conflict in families. Three women noted their difficulties if they talked to other men; in one case, if other men looked at her.

There is a strong feeling in all of the stories that their role as wife and mother separated them from contact with those who might give them an opportunity to discuss the sort of issues that could allow them to reflect on their situation; sometimes this was unspoken, sometimes articulated. In one case, a mother admitted that she had started an evening class in sociology but had given it up after three or four weeks because 'I knew if I kept on going my marriage wouldn't last'.

Where women had contact with their families, or the families of their spouses, there were often comments about how information about problems or suspicions was kept from family so as not to upset them. Before and during the period when the abuse took place, six of the women were not living near to their own parents, though three were within easy distance of their spouse's family. One woman mentioned how she had once tried to tell her own mother that she was worried about her husband's temper and drinking, but was counselled that she ought to give the marriage one more try. She spent the next twelve years doing this, at the end of which her mother told her that she had realised there were problems.

This degree of isolation from sources of support seemed to be a common factor in the lives of the women who took part in the study. Partially this was caused by geographical factors, partially by an unspoken code which prohibited the discussion of problems, even within the family. In some cases, it seemed that even the opportunity for reflection on their situations was improbable. In varying degrees, the husbands involved discouraged discussion of issues or contact with others, so that even for the women whose children were abused by those external to the family there seemed to be a sense of isolation from opportunities to talk about intimate or personal issues. It may be, as Sanford and Donovan (1984) suggest, that such isolation impacts upon a woman's self-esteem and causes her to doubt her abilities in other areas. In the absence of the ability to experience emotional intimacy, women become diminished and hence value what they can do less.

The women described their emotional investment in their children. There are frequent references to their love for their children, how they talked to them, and their worries about them. It is difficult to make links to the type of attachment bond between these women and their children as their accounts are subjective and unsubstantiated. Alexander (1993) suggests that secure attachment may lead survivors to be able to talk about positive and negative events in childhood, which may provide a valuable resource in terms of coping with trauma of whatever nature. The mothers' accounts do provide differences from the accounts of survivors, and from much of the literature. The survivors describe mothers whom they saw, in all but one of the cases, as distant or collusive in their abuse. The mothers portray themselves as caring and supportive. The literature on families (e.g. Oakley 1986; Welldon 1992) notes a difference between the stereotypical view of a mother – constantly caring, always available for her children, the emotional hub of the family – and the reality in which women acknowledge their dissatisfactions with the role, with its tedium and demands that coexist with its pleasures and satisfactions.

The mothers in the sample were all still available to their children. Even when these children were adult and had moved away from home, the mothers talked of their discussions, letters or telephone calls. In some senses, it was difficult to assess from their stories what their mothering had been like before the abuse had coloured the picture. There seem to be hints that attachment may have been more secure and communication more open within this group, but that suggestion has to be contextualised within the limitations of the study.

However, there are other strands in this picture. Four of the women described their pleasure in their children and incidents such as birthdays and holidays which had demonstrated this. But they had had to work, or had been studying, when the children were fairly young. This had entailed them leaving the children with their husbands, or with babysitters. The remaining three women had not been in paid work whilst their children were young, though one had been hospitalised fairly regularly through a combination of her own suicide attempts and her husband's violence against her. None of them seemed to admit to dissatisfactions with child rearing either before or after the abuse. It was as if they had to deny this because of what had happened to their children. Perhaps acknowledging such feelings now, if indeed they had had them, would be to acknowledge guilt. There was also the fact that I was a researcher who was looking at the mother–child relationship after sexual abuse; as Silverman (1993) has suggested, aspects of mothers' stories may be constructed to display their reasonableness and responsibility as mothers. There is also the point made by Kohler Riessman (1993) that not only do narratives change over time but they contain changing agendas and modify as perceptions of cause and effect, or power relations, change.

The earlier literature on child sexual abuse found that mothers of victims were often physically or psychologically absent (e.g. Finkelhor 1984; Herman and Hirschman 1981). This study would confirm that in all but two of the cases this could be claimed to be a factor. Johnson (1992) has argued such absence may be outside of a mother's control. Orr (1995) goes further in arguing that work which tries to fit mothers' experiences into the familiar stereotypes neglects the complexities of their individual lives and circumstances. I wish to echo this point and to add that none of the circumstances which mothers described to me were so simplistic that they pointed indisputably to a certain outcome. Indeed, whilst reflecting on this issue, I produced a mental audit of my own acquaintances which seemed to demonstrate that: several worked and had left their children with spouses or babysitters; others had been ill or incapacitated and had been absent either physically or psychologically. To my knowledge, none of their children had been sexually abused. Whilst Johnson (1992) argues that such factors increase risk and should not be underestimated, they do not necessarily create risk or culminate in abuse.

In exploring the backgrounds of survivors and mothers, there was a strong sense of the emotional investment in the stories being told. Not only did the interviews produce a co-construction of the realities of events for each of the groups, they also involved a co-construction of emotions. The feelings evoked for me included the sense that mothers must have known and must have been culpable in some of the cases related by survivors. Reflection suggested that survivors had perhaps maligned very over-burdened and abused women or misinterpreted responses. The range of feelings, from definitely guilty to probably innocent, was similar with the mothers in the sample. There was a sense that they were good mothers who had been coping with difficult relationships or situations and who should not be held responsible in any way for what had happened. Reflection here suggested that some of them did not realise the impact their behaviour would have on the children involved and that often they could have done more.

Unfortunately, such judgements are all too common in researchers and professionals and hinge to a disturbing extent on constructions of meaning based on differing values and experiences, which become entwined with emotion and anger when such a subject is involved. The same case could often provoke both the feeling that there was definitely a guilty party and the opposite view that probably no one was to blame. Orr (1995) speaks of her fear that by telling their stories mothers in her study might attract more anger, and of her worry that this fear might also act to silence the voices of these women.

The lives of these mothers would not bear scrutiny against the myth of motherhood depicted, for example, in Bowlby's (1965) early work; but it is arguable that no mother could achieve this ideal. However, in five instances, at the time of the abuse the families presented a facade of respectability – two parents, earning more than the average, apparently bringing up their children correctly, not known to social services. This accords with the findings of Walker's (1992) study.

The whole picture was complex. Mothers were coping with their individual lives in varying ways. The events which befell their children changed their lives and cast doubts on their ability both to cope and to mother.

Living with the abuse

The mothers did not move from ignorance of the abuse to full knowledge of it. In fact, two argue that they will never know the full story of what happened but have acquired information about different aspects of it at various times.

As Hooper (1992) describes, discovery was a process which moved through a variety of stages as awareness grew or was tested. For three of the mothers, that process was short-circuited; for one, in some senses, it was comparatively short; and for the other three, it was of longer duration. One mother learnt of her daughter's abuse by a neighbour from her elder daughter, who interrupted him in his assault upon her sister. Another mother learnt of the suspected abuse of her children when they were removed from her home by social workers, who informed her that her long-term babysitter was a known paedophile. A third mother was informed by the police that a neighbour was to be charged with buggery on a number of local children, one of whom was her daughter. This child had been having bowel problems, the doctor had reported his suspicions to the police, and they had made the connection with the neighbour before informing the mother. The doctor had not mentioned his concerns to her. The mother for whom the process of discovery was comparatively short had had suspicions about her husband which she reported to social services. Unfortunately, they did not share her concerns and her husband played on her vulnerability by trying to convince her that she was imagining things. In her case, at the time of the interview, the legal battle continued, with her suspicions still unaccepted by the law as her children had confided only in her, refusing to talk to anyone else.

In the remaining cases, women described suspicions which grew and receded and events or conversations which made strange half conversations or hints click into sharp focus. One mother said:

> A number of things came together when she said that. I remembered how she hadn't wanted to go out with her father when he came to visit. She'd said that he'd have to change a lot before she would trust him. I'd thought it was about his drinking and his temper but when she said that I had to believe her.

The stories the women told seemed to demonstrate that they did notice changes in their children and were concerned when they seemed to be having problems or difficulties, but that they did not understand the cause of these problems until they had further information, or some sort of confirmation, from the child concerned.

The mothers constructed meaning for what was happening around their perception of the factors involved in the family situation at the time. This may have involved 'problems at school', 'feeling off-colour or tired' or just 'going through a funny phase'. It is interesting to note that none of these mothers mentioned disbelief as their reaction, although in the survivor sample this was a response attributed to several mothers. Whilst mothers in this sample may have suspected that something was wrong, and perhaps even had odd hints of what might be the real nature of the problem, disclosure moved them into the role of having to act, and having to cope.

Gudykunst (1994) locates our behaviour within our culture, and our notions of the rules and norms of this culture within our families and acquaintances. Though there are norms for how mothers should behave in a wide variety of 'normal' situations, we do not know what role to play when something outside our experience happens. This can be compared with reactions to death. Rosenblatt et al. (1991) suggest that a death entails those affected in coming to terms with 'new realities' (p.121) and that this can challenge existing relationships. Thompson and Range (1992), researching support for those bereaved by suicide, indicate that well-intentioned support may fail because it is inappropriate in some way.

In relation to my research, support given by mothers to their abused children may not meet the child's need, and support of others to mothers may not encompass their needs. Insights from research on primary and secondary victimisation would indicate that mothers and children are likely to be at different stages of dealing with the situation concurrently (e.g. Remer and Elliott 1988). Needs may change abruptly and explosively and as Goldstein (1992) has suggested, the relationship between mother and, child, at disclosure, may be particularly fragile. However, the mothers all maintained contact with their children and described their processes in maintaining the emotional bond between themselves and their children. Giarretto (1982) proposes that the maintenance of the emotional bond between mother and child is of crucial importance in dealing with child sexual abuse.

Spaccarelli (1994) identifies several factors involved in coping with child sexual abuse. The model he develops is based on a transactional framework and on his acknowledgement that there are implications for coping abilities at a variety of psychic, environmental and interactional levels. Whilst, in this model, the mother can be seen as one of the elements in the interactional or environmental levels and, as such, can have positive or negative impact upon the child, I would posit that a comparable process is going on within the mother. She has to:

- process her own stress about the abuse and the disclosure

- fit this event into existing schema about family life, the abuser, the possible effects on her situation, and any concurrent family problems

- activate coping strategies

- deal with her emotions and her reactions

- deal with the effects on her child.

Mothers spoke of the complex and conflicting nature of the demands they faced when abuse-related issues began to emerge. There are several corollaries to this. It may be that survivors interpreted some of the early misunderstandings made by mothers as disbelief, or saw them as making excuses for what abusers were doing. Two mothers in this study commented that in conversations a considerable time after initial discovery or disclosure, their children mentioned that they had believed their mothers knew what was happening. Here, children had greater awareness of the reality of their own situation than mothers did. Although, I would argue that, in line with

Briere's (1989) abuse continuum, a child may tend to assume that its parents know what is best for it and hence what is happening to it. Osborn (1990) has suggested that children still at the stage of 'magical thinking' may assume that mothers know all that is happening and hence harbour persisting hostile feelings towards them. Hooper (1992) notes that the belief that mothers know is common, but also mentions that children may go to elaborate lengths to keep such knowledge from their mothers. Whilst communication between mother and child seems to be of central importance both in discovering and dealing with abuse, there are well-intentioned mechanisms, which either party may employ, that distort understanding. In my study, three mothers spoke of their children not telling them about the abuse for quite specific reasons: 'She said she hadn't told me because she knew I had enough problems already.' 'She told me she thought he'd only hit me again if I'd asked him about that.' [X] just told me he said he'd kill me if I told anybody.' There were more practical considerations to children's reasoning too. Some perpetrators had outlined the consequences to the family of disclosure, mentioning that they may have to go to prison, or that Mummy would leave or not love the child involved any more.

Hooper's (1992) observation that losses are multiple and ongoing is echoed in the comments of these women, although, within the concept of loss, some of the sample also saw areas which could be viewed as gains. What they describe encompassed differing areas of their lives. None of the women currently lived in the area where the abuse had taken place – for one, the move had been to another part of the same city; but for others, greater distances were involved. For four, it had involved a reduction in their standard of living. It had involved loss of friends and contacts, but had also removed the children from people who knew what had happened and provided a different start. This point can be linked to how women felt friends or families responded – a further area of loss for some, in that they felt unsupported by those they had believed close to them and, in some cases, surprised by those previously seen to be less close.

Loss of face was an issue specifically raised by two women. Their beliefs about abuse and abusers had been challenged by their own involvement in this situation. One spoke of her own close sexual relationship with her husband and her prior belief that 'this sort of thing happens when women don't fulfil their husbands'. Another said that she had been quite particular about her children's contacts and felt herself to be more cautious than others in the area where she lived. That a neighbour she trusted should have been involved in this way shook her belief in her own judgement. Braun and Berg

(1994) suggest that 'a crisis occurs when the social stock of knowledge does not explain the event satisfactorily' (p.108).

It seemed that, in the middle of the morass of reactions attendant upon discovery, several women also suffered losses in terms of their own belief in their coping abilities. Reis and Heppner (1993) point to mothers of sexual abuse victims having reduced coping skills and being ineffective within the family group. What women in my study describe supports the finding that women do not trust their own coping skills as much after this experience, but refutes the suggestion that they do not exercise a wide range of coping skills and strategies. This suggests that Reis and Heppner's findings underestimate the coping skills that women do use in dealing with the abuse of their children, and concentrate only on the women's own assessments of their coping.

This may be connected to my particular sample. As discussed, these women seemed to be a proactive group and different from the mothers described by survivors. It seems possible that survivors mothered by women who do take more initiative may not respond to studies such as this as adults, because more of their issues have been resolved. I may have attracted survivors who were poorly mothered and mothers who felt that despite their efforts this had happened.

However, whilst these mothers described a variety of coping skills, they did not feel that they had done sufficient to resolve problems inherent in the situations they faced. This loss of self-image, coupled with reframing of events from the past, had caused them to doubt whether it was ever possible to produce satisfactory outcomes. As one mother said:

> I see it as rather like patching your children up. When they are little and they fall over, you can put a plaster on their knee, or give them a cuddle, and it's better. With something like this there isn't a plaster, a cuddle can be misinterpreted and part of it has to be time for you and them to heal. Knowing you can't make it right is the most difficult thing. It's always there even when it recedes.

This point is echoed by Trolley (1994) when discussing the linkages between death and other traumatic events. Trolley speaks of both the difficult process which secondary victims of trauma experience and the need for them, and the primary victims, to have time and permission to grieve and to accept that recovery takes time.

Mothers have to cope not only with their own reactions but also with the reactions of their children and those of others with whom they discuss the abuse. Finkelhor and Browne's (1988) traumagenic dynamics model has been applied to mothers by Dempster (1993). Here, four effects of child sexual abuse are noted:

- *stigmatisation* – feelings of guilt, shame or badness related to the abuse

- *powerlessness* – the feeling of invasion against one's will and the perception of increased threat if attempts at disclosure fail

- *betrayal* – the response of being cheated or manipulated by a trusted adult

- *traumatic sexualisation* – how sexual behaviour is viewed: perhaps as a way to gain affection, perhaps as something to avoid.

Stigmatisation

Mothers' perceptions of their feelings of guilt and of having failed as mothers have been discussed earlier in this chapter. This sense of guilt or badness was exacerbated by reactions which they voiced in terms of how they were subsequently dealt with by friends, family and those in authority. This sample referred to such effects most frequently in relation to social services and the legal profession.

Powerlessness

Powerlessness was enmeshed with stigmatisation. All of the mothers had had dealings with both social services and the legal profession, although in one instance this had not been directly about the child's abuse. They had felt devalued within this process. The women who had been informed of their children's abuse by the authorities had felt that they were being blamed for some unexplained role within this situation. The women who had reported the abuse of their children to the authorities had felt that they were being interrogated and assessed as if they were responsible, or as if they had a secondary agenda for making such allegations. Rando (1986) suggests that there is no other role with as many socially assigned, or personally assumed, responsibilities as that of a parent. Crises serve to exacerbate this role overload.

The woman whose son did not disclose until he was in his twenties referred the matter to the authorities when she had suspicions about her ex-husband's behaviour towards their daughter. She was convinced that he had been complicit in what happened to her son and mentioned this to social services. She was depressed by their responses: 'They had no answers, none,

none whatsoever. No, you're in a no-win situation, you are, you're in a no-win situation. I think so anyway.'

Betrayal

Betrayal for mothers encompassed multiple sources. They had been betrayed by the spouses or neighbours who had abused their children. Strand (1991) perceives mothers as feeling betrayed by themselves. In my study, mothers frequently felt themselves to be betrayed by their own memories of happier times, which now had to be viewed differently. The kaleidoscope had been shaken and what had been constructed as a complete meaningful image had to be revisited and differently perceived.

Traumatic sexualisation

The effect of traumatic sexualisation on the mothers was both personal and interpersonal, involving their perceptions of men, of sexual relationships and of their children's behaviour. Mothers spoke of their difficulties in trusting men, including their own husbands where they were not perpetrators. One said:

> It had a strange effect on me really. I couldn't bear to be by myself in a room with a man – even if I knew him. It made me feel threatened because I'd thought I knew [X] and he'd done that.

Another mother spoke of her difficulties with her husband:

> We'd had a good relationship but I couldn't bear him to touch me after that had happened, even though he didn't have anything to do with it. It was the idea of sex being used like that that put me off it altogether.

The mothers all mentioned incidents of this type, ranging from a lack of trust in men in general through to effects on their personal sexual relationships. One mother commented specifically on the stress she had felt at having to discuss intimate sexual details with the authorities:

> I found having to talk about sex to the police and the social worker very hard. In court it shocked me that the barrister used such precise terminology without being embarrassed. It made it seem unreal and like a game and that was horrible.

In addition to personal issues, they were forced to cope with their children's behaviour, which sometimes involved sexualised activities. Three mothers spoke of incidents in which their young children had tried to touch men inappropriately. Two other mothers worried that their teenage daughters were in danger of becoming promiscuous, and another mother commented that she had been told that her daughter would probably never be able to have a normal sexual relationship. The final mother said that her son had become homosexual, which she saw as a direct result of his abuse by a male. Although she said that this did not make any difference to her love for him, she was convinced that his sexuality had been altered by the events and noted that she had been forced into taking a mediating role between her partner and her son in connection with her son's sexuality.

The study seemed to suggest that mothers had a strong tendency to assume that their children were bound to be adversely affected by the events which had befallen them. In some measure, all of them interpreted differences in their children's behaviour as related to the abuse. The mothers coped with this in different ways. One strategy was to attempt to protect the child from any further harm. Three women said that after they heard of the abuse they wanted to keep their children safe. They found it difficult to let them out of their sight, were unwilling to let them visit friends or neighbours or stay away from home. Sometimes, children resented not seeing their fathers, even if they had been perpetrators. This was an additional source of problems for the mothers. Jacobs (1994) has noted the tensions inherent in a 'normal' mother–daughter relationship and comments that sometimes an absent perpetrator may become idealised by a child when there are such tensions. One mother had experienced this with one daughter, although she described her relationship with a second daughter as very close.

The repercussions from what mothers perceived as protective strategies were often that the children resented the increased restrictions on them. One woman mentioned that her daughter had seen this as a punishment on her after what had happened, saying that she had felt that it was her fault that she was not allowed out on her own. Mothers, therefore, could feel blame from the authorities for their part in giving a child a measure of freedom which had led to the abuse, and blame from their children for trying to enforce measures which restricted them too much. This feeling of being caught in the crossfire was one which seemed to encapsulate mothers' responses to a number of issues in relation to the abuse. In this study, these are outlined in Table 5.1, which illustrates the range of situations that those in the sample described as problematical.

Table 5.1 Issues dealt with by mothers in the sample

Area of potential conflict	*Number reporting this issue*	*Conflict with whom?*			
		Survivor	Family	Friend	Prof-essional
1. decisions about leaving the abuser/ending contact	3	3	1		2
2. decisions about leaving the area	3	3	2		
3. decisions about telling others such as family or friends	3	3			
4. decisions about reporting matters to schools, social services or the authorities	4	3	2		
5. decisions about seeking help for herself or the survivor	2	2	1		
6. adopting strategies perceived as helpful to the child	2	1	2		
7. talking about the abuse when a survivor did not want to	3	3			
8. not wanting to talk about it when a survivor wanted to do so	4	4			
9. offering opinions about courses of action to survivors	3	3			
10. not offering opinions about courses of action to survivors	2	2			2
11. expressing feelings or showing emotions about what had happened	5	3	2	2	3
12. not expressing feelings or showing emotion	3	2	1		1
13. discussing what had happened with certain family members	7	4	3	2	

Area of potential conflict	Number reporting this issue	Conflict with whom?			
		Survivor	Family	Friend	Prof-essional
14. not discussing what had happened with certain family members	7	4	3		1
15. obtaining alternative opinions about how to act	5				5
16. negotiating further contact with the abuser	3	3	3		2
17. determining to what extent to make allowances for a survivor	4	4	2	1	2
18. determining personal survival strategies	4	2	3		2
19. reassessing behaviour in the light of what 'normal' children might do/be permitted to do	3	3	2		3
20. determining sanctions for undesirable behaviour by survivors	4	3	2	2	3
21. dealing with communication or contact by abusive fathers	4	4	3		2
22. dealing with demands for renewed contact with abusive fathers	4	4	3		
23. dealing with questions about family life before the abuse	4	4			
24. dealing with survivors' feelings for absent abusive fathers	4	4			
25. dealing with rebuilding and moving on	2	2			
26. adjusting to new relationships, whether personal, social or professional	7	3	4		

Table 5.1 continued

I would argue that Table 5.1 demonstrates that these mothers were able to devise a range of strategies, but that the potential for conflict with others who were involved in the situation was increased. Further, because emotional responses to the situation are likely to be triggered in all who are involved in it, there is a heightened likelihood that people may overreact or overcompensate. All those involved in a traumatic situation are attempting to construct meaning from it, both for themselves and for others.

Trolley (1994) notes several factors which may be brought to bear on the reaction of family, friends and professionals who become involved in a trauma. She notes that parents may blame each other. Children may become disoriented or disillusioned. Social relationships may be coloured by fear and anxiety, with victims and their families being treated as if they are contagious. Professionals may resort to such devices as blaming or stereotypical labelling. When such reactions occur to a mother who is coping with her own responses, it seems unsurprising that she may find difficulty in accepting that any of her coping strategies have been successful. Thus her self-image is likely to become further devalued. Whilst these mothers had resumed their lives, none claimed to have emerged with better self-esteem.

Dealing with the authorities

The mothers experienced interactions with those in various positions of authority. For the purposes of this chapter these will be defined as:

- *health professionals* – health visitors, GPs, counsellors, psychologists, psychiatrists
- *school professionals* – teachers, headteachers, school psychological service
- *child protection professionals* – social workers, police
- *legal professionals* – court welfare officers, solicitors, barristers, judges
- *other professionals* – vicars, priests.

Table 5.2 indicates the contact individual families had with these groups and notes whether mothers perceived the intervention was focused on their needs or on the needs of the child(ren) involved.

Professional group	Health professionals		School professionals		Child protection professionals		Legal professionals		Other professionals	
Recipient	Mother	Child	Mother	Child	Mother	Child	Mother	Child	Mother	Child
A	Yes	Yes	No	Yes	Yes	Yes	No	No	No	No
B	Yes	Yes	Yes	Yes	Yes	Yes	Yes	Yes	No	No
C	Yes	Yes	No	Yes	Yes	Yes	Yes	Yes	Yes	Yes
D	Yes	Yes	Yes	Yes	Yes	Yes	Yes	No	No	No
E	No	Yes	No	No	Yes	Yes	No	No	No	No
F	No	Yes	No	No	Yes	Yes	Yes	Yes	No	No
G	No	Yes	No	Yes	Yes	Yes	No	No	No	No

Table 5.2 Professional intervention received by mothers and their children

Mothers in the sample had experiences with a range of professionals, sometimes as a result of their own attempts to obtain assistance with problems the abuse was causing them, or their children, and sometimes because these bodies intervened as part of a legal or child protection process. Mothers, as mentioned earlier, were divided between those who initiated contact with the authorities and those who were informed of the abuse by the authorities. However, even mothers who initiated contact described how the processes involved in official dealings with child protection swept them into situations in which they felt powerless. One mother had had her children taken away from her home by social workers pending the investigation of her babysitter's involvement with them; another had been informed about what had happened to her child by the police. Neither of the men involved in these cases was related to the children involved, yet these mothers both felt officials believed they were culpable:

> It was as if they thought I'd set it up with him. I'd known him for a while, he seemed a nice guy. He needed money, I needed to work and I offered to pay him to look after the kids. Social services kept them for three days. It was hell. They treated me as if I knew what was going on.

> The police were smashing really, but social workers looked at me as if I was shit.

All of the mothers had had involvement with child protection professionals and such interventions had provoked various reactions. Two mothers who had reported incidents to the police commented that if they ever happened to find themselves in a comparable situation they would not initiate action again because of aspects of the procedure involved. Social workers were perceived to be overworked (3), interfering (4), supportive (2), judgemental (2) and to 'take up a lot of your time when *they* want to know something, but have no time for you if *you* have problems'. This sentiment was echoed by two others. Case conferences had been attended by only three of the mothers and these events had been perceived as stressful and shaming. The question of putting children on the 'at risk register' had been an issue for these women. One was relieved that this had not happened. She had been remarried for over two years by the time this question arose and had reported the abuse of her children by their father as soon as they disclosed it. She felt that her self-esteem and belief in her ability to mother would have been destroyed if the children were declared 'at risk'. Two other mothers had had their children placed on the register. One felt this had been useful, the other was upset that she had not been perceived as an appropriate parent.

All of the mothers had consulted health professionals about their children. Four had had involvement with doctors or counsellors, which they perceived as being to help themselves to deal with the effects of their child's abuse. Four families had had some contact with family therapy – two mothers described this as threatening; one had found it very useful, another was ambivalent. It may be that Sgroi's (1982) suggestion – that mothers need time to explore stories individually before work as a family takes place – is the issue here. Certainly, one mother in the study moved from family therapy, which she found distressing, into counselling help for herself, which she found more beneficial. Four mothers mentioned that they had been offered which she found distressing, into counselling help for herself, which she found more beneficial. Four mothers mentioned that they had been offered antidepressants by their GPs, two had accepted and two had declined. Of these latter two, one said: 'I didn't want anything like that on my medical records, it might've been used against me.'

This sense that their own reactions to situations resulting from the abuse might be used as further sources of blame was common and has links to the making of meaning of the event both for themselves and their children. Some of the discomfort of the situation could be linked to their own understanding of why such situations happened – two mothers whose husbands had been the abusers gave indications that, although they had known there were problems with their marriages, they had assumed that these would have had to be overtly much worse to have coexisted with sexual abuse. Vestiges of myths about collusive mothers or 'problem families' seem to be behind this reasoning. None of these mothers had attended mothers' groups, but if they had they might have found an opportunity to experience the normality or ordinariness of others in this situation and to share issues with those who had had similar experiences. Workers such as Priest *et al.* (1993) note the benefits of self-directed mothers' groups as a tool for empowerment. Even when speaking of doctors or counsellors who had been helpful, three mothers described a continuing sense of isolation in that these people could not ultimately understand as they had not experienced the problem first-hand.

The main issues which emerged from dealing with the legal profession have been mentioned in other contexts within this chapter. The tensions between the human needs and the legal needs of those involved have also been touched upon. In this context, mothers were often dismayed by the legal outcomes of cases that had made considerable emotional demands on them and their children. All the mothers who had had dealings with the legal profession were unsure that the legal system was the most appropriate way of dealing with such issues. There was a sense of being short-changed even when offenders were convicted or criminal injuries compensation was paid.

Similarly mixed opinions were voiced about dealing with school professionals. Two of the mothers in the sample had not mentioned issues to the schools their children had attended. In one of these cases, the child had been pre-school when the abuse took place; the mother did not think that the school needed to know 'in case it made a difference to how they treated her'. In the other case, the family moved from the area concerned shortly after the abuse and the mother did not make any contact with the new school about the issue. The family had left the area because 'after the court case we wanted to have a new start. Everybody knew about it in that small village.' In all other cases, mothers had had contact with their children's schools, although they did not always find this supportive or helpful. It provided another situation in which they felt they were being judged and three of the five who had had dealings with the school felt that assumptions may have been made about aspects of their children's behaviour or achievement. Where children moved to different schools, or areas, mothers described reticence about whether, or how, they should talk to school staff about the abuse. It seemed that they acquired heightened sensitivity to what they heard of how comparable issues were dealt with. One mother mentions such an incident:

> There was somebody I knew whose son was interfered with by an older pupil at the school, and the headmaster took the attitude that this younger pupil had some – well, he was a naughty boy anyway, you know, so that's his sort of attitude anyway, so he'd invited it because he's a naughty boy, you know, he's no angel.

This led to her feeling that whilst she would talk to the class teacher she would prefer the headmaster to have only basic details, and she would not speak to him personally about any concerns.

Two mothers felt that schools had supported them with their own issues as well as dealing with their children's welfare. One felt that the school had been marvellous and had been aware of what she must be going through. She had dealt with class teachers and a year head as well as the school psychological service about her daughter's difficulties. The other had dealt with a school welfare worker who had given her advice about herself as well as her children.

In many ways, professional interventions were seen as a mixed blessing. At one level, mothers discovered that their own agendas became mixed up with those of professional groups and this caused some confusions. A secondary factor was that some professionals seemed to bring personal agendas to the issues involved. Mothers spoke of the differences between the advice given by different members of the same professional group. It seemed to be an issue that, rather than provide time and support for a mother to work out her own issues, advice was frequently offered from a subjective perspective – 'If I were you I'd...' A change of doctor, counsellor, social worker, teacher or solicitor could provoke a radically different set of advice. At another level, there would be differences in whether the advice was slanted towards the needs of mother or child.

seemed more sensitive to the mother's own emotional response and problems. It may be that, as Reid (1989) and others have argued, mothers need a separate social worker who puts their interests first, rather than being viewed as part of the family problem. In addition, as Erooga and Masson (1989) perceive, there is also a need for more awareness of the diversity of mothers within this situation.

The mothers as they are now

As mentioned earlier, there were varying periods of time between the abuse events and the interview. One mother was still involved in a process of trying to gain legal recognition of her problem and had not yet succeeded in her quest to have contact between her children and their father prevented. The longest period between disclosure and the interview had been 15 years.

The mothers had all been affected deeply by the abuse of their children, and all described how they were still dealing with aspects of it. The kaleidoscope of what they described could be shaken in different ways. As Johnson (1992) suggests in the conclusion to her study of six mothers of incest survivors, there were ways in which the mothers could be used to confirm many of the stereotypes about women in this group. As part of a quantitative study, they may have provided evidence for poor self-esteem, reduced coping skills, depression, absence and a host of other negative characteristics. However, reshaken, the pattern changes. The complexity of their lives and situations becomes a continuing process, and one which has been coloured and distorted both by the abuse-related events and by the impact of these events on multiple aspects of their lives and relationships. Their faith in a just world had been challenged; they had had to try to restore equilibrium in a damaged family; had had to operate in an area of life for which there was neither a clearly defined role nor social conventions. As Fineman (1993) notes, most situations we face have a predetermined cultural stock of emotional responses, but one mother in this study articulated concisely what others only alluded to: 'I didn't know what I was supposed to feel.'

The interview style I had used was based upon storytelling, with a loose structure and a number of points which I hoped would be covered. Most of these points arose very naturally without need for probes or questions, but one area that I did raise with the women was centred on the difficulty of this situation compared with other crises with which they had had to deal. Without exception this was seen as the most difficult to handle. Where this situation compared with other crises with which they had had to deal. Without exception this was seen as the most difficult to handle. Where comparisons were made these were to personal experience of such problems as the death of a child, rape and the suicide of family members. Those mothers who did not provide comparators simply answered that it was the worst thing that had ever happened to them. Again, this finding is worth examining in the light of Spaccarelli's (1994) insight that individual perceptions of stress need to supplement existing stress measurement devices. I would argue that popularised measures of stress, such as the Life-Events Scale (see Quick and Quick 1984), which rank death of a spouse as the most stressful event, do not validate the horror of what is involved in alternative situations. Admittedly, this scale is one which seeks to rank fairly common events, but my point is that it is this sort of scale that is generally accessible in newspapers and women's magazines and hence informs a stereotypical awareness of which events should be perceived as most stressful. My argument is not that this perception is new, but that it is perhaps an area which is invisible to the actors in this situation. Marks (1994) argues that the Jewish children who were hidden in order for them to survive the Holocaust needed permission to grieve for their losses because they were perceived as lucky to be alive. I would similarly argue that survivors and mothers of survivors need permission to name what they have experienced as more stressful than popularly recognised stressors.

A related area here was how well mothers felt that they had resolved issues both personally and interpersonally. Here, they made comparisons between their early responses and reactions and current ones. Mothers spoke of early difficulties over when and when not to speak to their children about abuse events; over knowing how much to say or ask; and over what to tell and to whom. Whether these problems had been suitably resolved was not an issue, but what they described was their own resolution of how issues should be tackled. The two who felt they had talked, or asked, too much about the abuse in the early stages now tended to wait for their child to raise the issue. The three who had found it more difficult to talk earlier now dealt with discussions if they arose. Two did not discuss the issue with their children any more. Whether these devices were the most suitable way of dealing with the issues was not a realistic question, when all those involved could not be given the opportunity to express their views. This may be another area in which survivors' perceptions of their mothers' responses can be differently interpreted. Other factors involved here also include the age of the survivors involved;

the proximity of the abuse; and the degree of communication and 'meaning making' which was possible between mother and child.

Effects attributed to the abuse had often changed with the passage of time. Mothers spoke of how they thought the abuse had altered their children and of their fears for possible future impacts. This information, too, benefits from being subjected to the kaleidoscopic lens. As they spoke, mothers may or may not have had recent crises; their children may or may not have faced problems or decisions; situations may or may not have been revisited; anniversary grief may or may not have altered the picture. A myriad factors may have coloured the patterns portrayed and a number of stereotypes may have (mis)informed half fears. One mother spoke of how a doctor had suggested that her daughter may never be able to have a normal sexual relationship after what had happened. This, she admitted, had worried her; but her daughter was now engaged and she was 'sure things would be all right now'. A setback to the couple's plans, or later relationship problems, may cause that mother to reassess what the doctor said – it is unlikely that she would ever dismiss the statement's potential for validity. This incident encapsulated for me how a professional's power to impose meaning on a situation may remain with a mother for years after the event. During a working life in practice, professionals are likely to change their understandings of cause and effect, but those they deal with may remain affected by what was current thinking at the time they sought help.

Other mothers spoke of behaviours which they linked to the abuse. This issue was ongoing for several. The youngest children of the mothers in the study were aged six and seven at the time of interview. Their mother described their behaviour as very aggressive and violent at times, although they tended to be exemplary in school. She added:

> It's very difficult knowing what's related to it. There's a terrible temptation in my mind all of the time to associate it with, oh, it's that and kind of, you know, I've tried to tell myself, tried to work out in my mind what's happened now so that I can deal with it, just with the behaviour as it happens and it doesn't matter what's the cause of it.

Another mother told of how she attributed all of her children's adolescent strivings to assert themselves as linked to the abuse:

> At one time I put it all down to the abuse. Now I can see it as part of what a lot of kids do when they're growing up. I think I changed when I began to be able to see it like that. I realised that it didn't have to alter everything or cause everything.

How this issue was resolved varied between the mothers. One mother fully attributed her son's homosexuality to his abuse by a male and conceptualised events in a fatalistic way. This may have been in part as a result of her own depression at the time of the interviews – during both she made reference to the fact that she was taking antidepressants and listed a number of crises which she had faced in recent years. Other mothers seemed, at the time of the interviews, to be located at different positions on a continuum of thought that ranged from the fatalistic inevitability of poor outcomes in everything to the possibility for change, resolution and growth through the experience.

Anger remained an issue for the mothers. Their anger was directed to a number of areas. All remained angry with the perpetrators of the abuse. Even where the man concerned had been subjected to legal procedures, there was often anger that these had also failed the family involved. Mothers were angry with the lack of help they had received both for their children and for themselves, and remained angry too that their involvement had been questioned – though this was tinged with vestiges of self-doubt. They had not completely resolved issues around the area of their own lack of awareness of what was happening, though all had been faced with the need to reassess themselves and their families and there were indications that this was a continuing process. It was as if the experience of supporting their children through this trauma had sensitised them to future risk and diminished some of their spontaneity. Muram *et al.* (1994) suggest that mothers of sexual abuse victims are significantly less impulsive and outgoing than mothers whose children have not been abused. Whilst it is not possible to assess what mothers were like before their children were abused, my study would seem to indicate that mothers do develop more caution in dealing with a range of situations.

Mothers portrayed their situations as being affected by the dynamics of a variety of relationships. There was a sense that these mothers saw themselves as providing some sort of interface between their children and external events. Where children were still young, this involved them in protecting them from continuing repercussions of the abuse; as they became older, they professed themselves available to talk when appropriate. The mothers whose children were older had, with one exception, evolved a style whereby they discussed abuse-related issues if their child began the discussion but not otherwise.

Mothers in the study had been, and were continuing to be, active in dealing with effects of the abuse; they admitted that they had changed and, in some ways, grown because of it. Nevertheless, however well they thought it had been resolved, it remained for them all the worst thing that life had handed them and they felt it was something they could never forget.

Summary of issues for the mothers

Agyeman (1996) notes the problems of making meaning from the experiences of others if one has not been a full participant in that situation, noting that Reason (1988) has suggested that if one has not lived an experience it is not true. Opposing this, positivists would argue that an even greater threat to validity occurs when one has been a full participant in a comparable situation as this is bound to introduce bias. Steedman (1991) argues that all researchers attribute meanings to situations, however objective they purport to be. Researchers, Agyeman suggests, have power to influence the way in which an issue is perceived.

The dominant discourse about mothers who have found themselves in the situation described in this chapter has frequently been linked to models that perceived them as blameworthy or deficient (e.g. Bentovim *et al.* 1988; Kempe and Kempe 1978; Reis and Heppner 1993). The mothers I interviewed would all take issue with those stereotypes. They did not see themselves as negligent or bad mothers before they found themselves in a situation which was popularly associated with improper care. Feminist work, more latterly, has pointed to the variety of complex situations with which women have to cope and the degree of responsibility which is thrust upon them (e.g. Hooper 1992; Johnson 1992). Featherstone and Fawcett (1994/95) note postmodernist feminism's growing scepticism with the notion that theory can provide universal explanations. The stories of the mothers in this chapter extend the notion of differing situations and shed light upon the complexity of relationships with a variety of others who are, or who become, involved with aspects of the abuse and the official process that follows it. Print and Dey (1992) note that individual mothers will need different degrees of help in coming to terms with their children's abuse. The stories of the mothers in the present study tend to suggest that the provision they encountered was *ad hoc* at best. These mothers had been thrown into a series of changes to their opinions, relationships, physical and emotional situations and self-esteem. All perceived themselves to be changed by the abuse, some seeing only losses, others seeing gains; none underestimated the magnitude of the effects of child sexual abuse on their family.

Arguing for a link between insecure attachment and conditions prejudicial to the effective resolution of child sexual abuse, Alexander (1992) synthesises such attachment with diminished coping skills. Whilst elements of this may be pertinent for mothers in this situation, I would argue that more is involved. In my study, the mothers had not found it easy to obtain help for themselves, and had not always perceived interventions for their children as being beneficial. None felt that the legal process was the most appropriate way of dealing with child sexual abuse. Several in fact felt that their experiences had been trivialised by the process of law and their own emotions and needs underestimated. The general feeling was that those in authority could learn more about what it was like to be in that situation and could value the experience of survivors more than they do. Interestingly, such findings mirror those of Sharland *et al.* (1995), who reported multiple deficiencies in the provision of professional services for families of child sexual abuse victims.

On the basis of the interviews with these mothers, if Hopson's (1981) Coping Skills Questionnaire is revisited (see p.106), I would submit that in some cases there are grounds for arguing that it is not always the mothers themselves who have poor coping skills, or lack awareness of sources of help, it is often society which has insufficient resources and understanding to support those involved. Sometimes, this larger lack of resources is too readily reframed as the woman's own problem when her needs are not being served by existing provisions.

The women in my study had not been involved with mothers' groups and hence had not had the opportunity to make connections with, or give support to, others who had shared their experiences. The links between their experience and bereavement are common in the literature, but only one of the mothers in this study had been supported by anyone who had been through a similar experience – though this support had been questioned by her barrister. Here the analogy with bereavement is less valid as the experience of these mothers is potentially more isolating – it involves a greater taboo than death with fewer conventions for dealing with the issues involved. The mother's potential for assisting in her child's recovery is well documented (e.g. Esparza 1993; Gilgun 1991; Gomes-Schwartz *et al.* 1990), and on this ground alone additional support for mothers has been perceived to be valuable (e.g. Hooper 1992; Orr 1995). The stories from this study lend weight to that plea and to the case for women in this situation to be equally worthy of support in their own right.

CHAPTER 6

The Teachers

The aim of this chapter is to explore the experiences of the teachers I interviewed (see also Skinner 1999b). Their stories also illuminate the complexities that dealing with sexually abused children have produced for them. In some instances, they demonstrate the discrepancies between whatever training or preparation they have been given and the reality of the experiences they faced.

The teacher group was dealt with differently. Whereas survivors and mothers were interviewed twice, teachers were interviewed only once. This was partially in recognition of the probable time constraints they faced, but also because I had sought to attract a sample of teachers who came from different areas of the educational system and eventually interviewed fourteen teachers. As with the other two groups, the interviews were based on a storytelling style.

The teachers, eleven females and three males, came from a variety of educational settings – ranging from nursery school, mainstream primary and secondary schools, to tertiary and higher education. The sample also included those who had had experience in special education, in a school for emotionally disturbed boys, and in a forces' school. Some had had experience in more than one sector of education; this included, in some cases, dealings with sexual abuse survivors in more than one setting. The teachers represented different levels in the organisational hierarchy and two of those involved were the 'nominated persons' with responsibility for child protection issues.

The teachers had had varying levels of training and support in relation to child protection issues, ranging from none to a high level of provision. Sometimes this was connected to the chronological period in which they had to handle disclosure, but not invariably. Between them, these teachers had dealt with a considerable number of children who had been sexually abused. Some mentioned ten or more cases, although others had had knowing involvement with only one child. Where teachers had dealt with a number of children, I had asked them to consider the cases of one or two children in detail in order to concentrate on the effect that dealing with these children had had on them and to give a focus for the discussion of issues.

The ages of the teachers involved ranged from 25 to 60 at the time of interview and the incidents they described had happened from 1976 to 1996, hence overlapping chronologically with all of the mothers and some of the survivors in this sample. No teacher disclosed any personal experience of sexual abuse, although two mentioned how difficult handling disclosure might be for colleagues who had faced such problems personally. One teacher mentioned that she had had problems with violence in a previous marriage and that dealing with abused children had caused her to revisit some of the issues from her own past in that respect. Two teachers were unmarried, all the others were either currently married or widowed.

Some teachers were still in contact with the children they described in the interviews, others occasionally heard about the child concerned. In other cases, where they had lost touch, teachers said they often wondered what had happened to the child involved.

One of my concerns, which is reflected in the literature (e.g. Chamberlain 1993), was that teachers may have preconceptions of those at risk of abuse. At primary, secondary and further education level, the survivors described by teachers tend to be predominantly those who might be regarded as disadvantaged, although more teachers than I had expected mentioned disclosure by boys, which the literature regards as more problematical (e.g. Finkelhor 1986; Waterhouse 1993). One of these boys was additionally a perpetrator himself, which produced particular problems for the school involved. There was a tendency to describe children who were not middle class – only two of those mentioned would fit this description. New (1991) describes her shock, when first working at a centre for sexually abused children, at discovering that one group member was a quiet middle-class girl whom she had taught recently. The teachers from higher education had encountered disclosure from students who contradicted one of the popular beliefs about abuse victims – that they underachieve (e.g. Nakashima and Zakus 1977). Eckenrode, Laird and Doris (1993) admitted to some surprise when their research found that sexually abused children often had considerably higher grades than physically abused or neglected students.

Finally, the teacher of emotionally disturbed children had experienced a school situation where staff had encountered the problem of having to believe that children, who were already violent, manipulative and exhibiting sexualised behaviour, had been further sexually abused by a member of the staff.

As with both other groups, the issues raised by teachers are complex, messy and not accessible to simple remedies or easy amelioration.

Telling the story

The teachers were interested in telling their stories for a variety of reasons. In some instances, the stated purpose was to assist in what they perceived to be useful research. In other cases, they stated that they had never been able to discuss certain aspects of their experiences, and this tended to involve an element of criticism about either the lack of provision for support or how such issues were handled in the various institutions where they worked. Where teachers felt supported, they tended to be less concerned with how this sort of situation had affected them personally. One teacher had identified issues concerning the subject area she taught in further education. She was beginning to believe that abused young people had some tendency to be interested in courses related to the caring professions and had met several survivors in this context. It seemed to me that this interest in discovering more about the areas which had concerned them had links to the inadequate provision of opportunities for help and support for survivors. Whilst some teachers I contacted felt unable to participate in the study because of time constraints, they expressed support for its purpose, often confirming that they had experienced little or no support for the reality of dealing with abused children. Two other teachers who offered to contribute, if required, claimed that they had wanted to talk to someone about how they felt about their experiences for several years. Hence, it seemed that for some teachers there was an element of the same need to be able to talk to someone who was unrelated to 'the authorities' and to whom they could disclose personal issues which had been triggered by dealing with an abused child.

Goffman (1959) has drawn attention to how those in different professions adapt behaviours to support their performance in these areas. As teachers told their stories, I became aware of some of the fronts and roles they had incorporated into their professional lives. One of the sample, who had been involved in the Cleveland cases, spoke of her sense of dissonance and role conflict: 'Social services told us we were the professionals and we knew about children, we'd be able to cope. But we didn't know what to do in this situation, we didn't know anything about it.' When she talked to me, she was some seven years away from the situation she was describing, yet the emotion in this woman's voice gave a glimpse into how out of control she had felt in coping with what had been demanded of her. Interestingly, another respondent from the same authority painted the most positive picture of the support available of anyone in my study. This respondent praised the support and networking mechanisms at his disposal in his role as nominated person for a special school. His experience in this role had post-dated the Cleveland cases and seemed to indicate how the authority had progressed in its handling of the variety of elements involved in child protection.

This story of the support available to teachers in some LEAs threw the experiences of others into sharp relief. In particular, two of the sample who spoke of very recent cases described their personal dilemmas caused by being unsure of where or how to get support. It was interesting that both of these people were working in small schools at the time. Knut (1997) suggests that abuse is less likely to be reported by small schools and argues that this is not because it is never present but rather because the community tends to be closer knit and less likely to make this sort of assumption about those within the group. I would suggest that a teacher in a small school, who acts on suspicions of abuse, immediately becomes more visible. It is less easy for the suspicion to be reported in an objective official way as there are fewer people in the organisation who can act as filters or buffers. The situation thus produced for both the teacher and the family involved would seem to contain a stronger potential for becoming messy, stressful and personally threatening. This sense of personal risk was mentioned by several teachers with experience in primary schools. However, the sort of personal or ongoing support they felt would have been valuable did not seem to be generally available to those in the study, apart from teachers in the 'nominated person' role. It seemed that the teachers in small schools saw 'nominated person' as an extra task rather than a source of expertise and support. This may be a particular dilemma for small schools, but there were few teachers in the sample who would not have welcomed extra support and training in dealing with abused children.

Teachers' stories were located within organisational contexts and there was a sense in some of the stories that the organisation for which they worked affected how they defined the problems which discovering abuse had caused them. For example, one university lecturer had been able to obtain further assistance from the student counselling service 'because I felt that this was an area which was outside my abilities. She needed the sort of help I wasn't equipped to give her.' The teacher had become interested in the difficulties some students faced after they had left home – she regarded disclosing abuse as one of these – and opted to use some of her staff development entitlement to take a preliminary certificate in counselling. Her story links with Easton and Van Laar's (1995) finding that a large percentage of university lecturers are consulted by distressed students. This woman had undertaken further training by her own choice, which again meshes with their finding that support mechanisms for lecturers were 'typically non-existent, or at best haphazard and opportunistic' (p.177).

Elsewhere, as in the smaller schools, the problems of staff cover or financial constraints meant that teachers who might have appreciated further training did not feel that they could be spared to take it, or that it was the most worthwhile use of available funding. Money as a prerequisite of support was a regularly visited theme. However, despite the small size of my sample, one teacher was involved with teaching on a part-time diploma in counselling and was herself a qualified Rogerian therapist. Two others had had some counselling training after coming into contact with sexual abuse survivors in their teaching capacity. Those who worked in larger organisations tended to feel that there were some mechanisms for support available within the organisation, although they could also feel that, on occasion, there was a lack of response to teachers' concerns, or a lack of information available to those who expressed worries about certain children. One had been told: 'Don't worry about [X], we know about her, it's being dealt with.' She felt no wiser about how to deal with the girl should she approach her again, and uncertain of whether what she had heard from the child was revisiting of old information or something which needed further probing. She felt devalued by this response. The child had spoken to her, but her perception was that those nominated to deal with child protection problems had virtually ignored her concerns. This story, although contextually different, had resonances for me with Legge's (1996) description of the stereotypical view of personnel management:

> A sort of motherly type, sorting out day-to-day problems arising between basically sound, but recalcitrant children (employees) and a well meaning, firm but sometimes misunderstood father (line management) in the interests of the whole family (organisation). (p.2)

There seemed to be a similar perception of ordinary staff and those in particular roles within some of the schools described by those in the sample, where set role perceptions precluded ordinary 'employees' from contributing their insights.

An important issue for one university lecturer was that a change in how grades were reported meant that confidential concerns about individual students could no longer be reported to subject boards 'quietly'. The process had become more formal, and concerns which staff could once report to known colleagues in a coded way (e.g. 'serious personal problems') now had to be documented and formalised. The result, she felt, was that certain students with substantial problems would not be given special consideration if they were not prepared to have details of their intimate problems 'broadcast' to strangers who 'sat in judgement' on their results. Briner (1997) suggests that 'it is noticeable how some organisations seem to implicitly discourage, or even prevent, employees from feeling and displaying negative emotions, whereas others seem to encourage them' (p.37).

In the current context, I would argue that this has two corollaries in terms of staff being allowed to involve their feelings when dealing with certain children. If those in authority within a school have labelled a child as 'a problem' which they have 'in hand', it may be easier to concentrate on solving the problem rather than devoting time or resources to the needs of the 'child with a problem'. Or second, organisations may arrange procedures in such a way that difficult or personal concerns are made invisible because broaching the procedures is too risky for the individuals involved.

Several respondents mentioned that they knew of teachers who would never allow themselves to become involved with children's problems, and indeed two expressed their own reservations about further involvement. One teacher said that she knew that several of her students had been abused by a member of staff from the same school but she 'did not want to know' what had happened or any of the details. Though she argued that she did not need to know the details in order to work with the children, it may also have been because the organisational climate was such that too much interest was not deemed to be suitable; or that she had seen colleagues swamped by the sheer mass of difficulties faced by the children in their care; or that she had not been supported in addressing personal issues before doing this sort of work, as Braun (1988) has suggested. Another went further and said that he did not ever want to get involved with dealing with a sexually abused child again, 'because it's such a minefield for the teachers involved'.

These teachers were actively constructing their stories and their responses around mechanisms which allowed them to maintain aspects of their roles, which were rationalised within their personal stories. It seemed that within the work situation some of them found it necessary to maintain certain role boundaries – whilst part of a teacher's role was to deal with particular issues, there were other issues which came outside of this.

There seemed to be an interesting divide between how teachers in the sample constructed their roles. There were some who saw themselves as transmitters of knowledge – subject specialisms were perhaps the most important part of teaching for them. Others saw themselves as responsible for certain tasks within the school environment – in the sample these encompassed responsibility for discipline, special needs, pastoral care, personal and social education, nominated person status or form tutoring. This was linked to a personal expectation that their role would necessitate using a particular range of behaviours towards children and that children might consult them in ways thus defined by their roles. Such role definitions within the stories seemed more common in the secondary school teachers than in either primary or, interestingly, tertiary and higher education. Sometimes these role definitions could lead to teachers wondering why a survivor had chosen to confide in them: 'I teach computing and couldn't really understand why she had chosen to tell me,' one said.

Did this indicate that there was an assumption that those who taught certain subject areas, or who played certain roles within the organisation, would be more likely to be the recipients of certain types of confidences? I would argue that, sometimes, the person perceived to be the 'official' one to contact about a specific area may be one of the last to be consulted. Going to the official person may be perceived as involving more certainty about what is involved, or as a prelude to seeking action. There is a sense in which if you consult a person named 'counsellor' you are admitting to needing a specific kind of help. It is my experience that there are several stages of awareness before this is reached. These move, in the school context, from the child's own realisation that the current situation is a problem that could be helped, to an assessment of who might help and what their possible reactions might be. Just as in the confiding of any other secret, it is likely that the decision to talk to a specific person will be based on a number of factors and will involve a certain degree of risk to the survivor. If a survivor is under severe threat of what will happen if they disclose, it is unlikely, I would argue, that they will disclose to someone with official responsibility for counselling, unless they feel comfortable with that person and have made some attempts to assess the likely response. McGuiness (1995) notes a number of characteristics which people recognise as facilitative in their dealings with professionals. These include: approachability, patience, encouragement, the willingness to listen and the willingness to give time. I suspect these may be particularly relevant in the current context.

In many senses, role mechanisms are valuable for the teacher, and perhaps particularly necessary for the managing of a large school. Continuing to function within a teaching, disciplinary or other specific role allows for a continuation of normality for both child and teacher, although it could be argued that this makes it easier to deny or dismiss the problems which individual children may be facing. In the absence of alternative forms of support, this may disadvantage them or lead to punitive rather than remedial action. Those teachers who saw their role as concerned with developing young people were more likely to want to help and support the individual involved. Research in Canada, focusing on the elementary school sector, indicates that teachers tend to believe children when they disclose and genuinely want to help, occasionally becoming overprotective about the children in their care (Duane and Bridgeland 1992).

With the exception of one secondary school teacher who had dealt with disclosure very early in her teaching career, the stories told by those who had taught in primary schools described a more emotional response to the children with whom they had dealt. Teachers often admitted their personal involvement with particular cases, and their continuing preoccupation with what had happened to such children after they moved elsewhere. Interestingly, when teachers became personally involved with survivors, they often had cause to question school or LEA policy. Sometimes, they described how they had acted in a way they felt to be contrary to such policy, or claimed they had delayed acting in order to assist the survivor in some way before issues became more generally known. The language used to describe such behaviours involved metaphors such as: 'I felt I was putting my neck on the line'; 'The way I felt at that point I didn't give a stuff about school policy'; 'I took things into my own hands. I'd never done anything like that before.'

I would maintain that role behaviour, even when the role was perceived in a child-centred way, disappeared at this point. The teachers who described their reactions in this way were acting from their individual emotional reactions and coping skills rather than calling on a professional mode of operation embodied in their construction of 'teacherness'. For many of them, just as for the mothers, the role prescription at their disposal was not appropriate for dealing with this particular situation. The situation at this point had potential for personal conflict or anxiety, and dilemmas arose over what sort of action to take. Here, unsurprisingly, the nominated teachers had had more training and tended to have better support networks, so that they did not describe this feeling. Indeed, in one case the networking system available to the teacher was outstanding and included regular updates and training.

Several teachers had encountered inappropriate behaviour in the school from survivors or, in three cases, their families. This had been found both personally and professionally threatening. In terms of the telling of their stories, teachers often recounted incidents which had challenged their coping skills and had brought personal feelings and professional roles into sudden conflict.

The American Academy of Child and Adolescent Psychiatry website suggests that the disclosure by a child of sexual abuse may leave adults feeling uncomfortable and unsure of what action to take (AACAP 1996). An American nationwide study (Abrahams et al. 1992) found that a third of the teachers contacted expressed reservations about dealing with this area. The experience of the teachers in my study would illustrate in some cases that this problem does not disappear with disclosure and that there is a need for ongoing support for pupil and teacher in order to deal with continuing repercussions and effects. Crase and Crase (1996), speaking of dealing with bereavement in the classroom, note that teachers need to feel comfortable with the issues they are discussing in order to support the child concerned. I would argue that this insight is equally applicable to the current topic, although 'comfort' is potentially more difficult to attain.

There were two levels of disclosure operating within the stories told by teachers. In some instances, teachers were talking of a disclosure which initiated action by the authorities. In these cases, the child had not previously disclosed to anyone who had taken action to deal with the abusive situation. In the second and more common type of disclosure in this sample, a child needed to talk to a teacher about aspects of personal experience. Though the teacher may not have been aware of the child's history and thus was presented with information that needed to be reported or questioned, further enquiries often revealed that the case was known. Teachers could find this even more difficult, in that support had been provided or assessments made in earlier years, but the child remained with problems which seemed uncatered for by available provision. In a sense, whilst action was apparently being taken, although often stressful for both teacher and child, there was a feeling that 'something was being done'. The child who had been processed by the existing systems and who remained at school often posed more chronic problems, which were less amenable to existing systems – here, lack of money could frustrate teachers. As one said: 'It's so short-term, the thinking. Don't they realise that more money spent when they're still children can save thousands when they're older and they need psychiatric support or end up in jail? Nothing is really being done to help these kids.' Arnold, Rogers and Cook (1990) endorsed the view that early intervention could save on subsequent medical costs, but the recognition of issues and the provision of funding are infrequently automatic.

Even when 'something was being done', it could backfire. Several teachers related a personal sense of desolation when trial outcomes were unsatisfactory. For example, one teacher told the story of a child known to him and produced press cuttings of the trial which demonstrated that the abuser, because of his age, had not been sentenced. This perceived injustice and its effect on the family involved had also impacted on the teacher. He had helped the child to make a disclosure and had supported the family through some of the problems this had produced for them. The father had wanted to take the law into his own hands and deal with the offender personally. The teacher had helped to dissuade him from such action, but had ultimately felt let down by the legal system.

It seemed that some teachers had had to reassess their stories. Existing provisions required them to report cases to the nominated person and to the authorities, and potentially then to attend case conferences or the courts. When these mechanisms failed to provide them with a sense that they had done the best for the child involved, they could be sceptical about what was being demanded of them, and of the children in their charge. Indeed, Knut (1997) isolates low confidence in social services and their ability to respond to problems as one of the reasons for the underreporting of child abuse to the authorities.

The reassessment of stories did not only rest in ultimate outcomes. Teachers spoke of roles which they were asked to play that became untenable. One teacher spoke of how a head had perceived the admission of two badly abused boys to the school as something the school could manage. On discovering the extent of the disruption they caused, the head distanced herself from the problem and handed responsibility for them to her deputy, blaming him when things went wrong. Another teacher was promised support and anonymity if she reported her suspicions about a child to the authorities. She was left to confront an angry mother, who suspected that she had initiated the action, at the close of school on the same day. For further discussion on this case see Skinner (1999a). Whilst some of the sample did not encounter this lack of support, those who did were divided into those who believed that they would act in a similar way again for the sake of a child, and those who had no desire to be involved in such issues again.

Chamberlain (1993) has commented on how teachers conceptualise child sexual abuse and how this affects their perceptions of those likely to be involved and its effects. The teachers in this study, with the exception of the two who were nominated people for child protection, had received varying degrees of training about the issues involved. Some had been given little or even no training; others had been given what they described as useful training about protection measures and procedures, or about the signs to look for in assessing whether a child might have been abused. Some of the training had happened up to ten years earlier, with no refresher course to inform them about more recent research or findings. To take only two examples from the literature, Maher (1988) stressed the importance of regular training, and Oxley and Sanderson (1993) presented guidelines based on practice in one authority for wider consideration. It would seem that neither message has been widely implemented.

This paucity of training led to some comments that indicated that teachers had often incorporated a number of stereotypes into their beliefs about abuse and abusers. It also left some of them making comparisons with events in their own experience – which could exacerbate their difficulties in understanding how an individual child was reacting and potentially predispose them to judgement or sympathy rather than empowerment and support.

As with each of the three groups interviewed, teachers used illustrations based on how other teachers had dealt with comparable events to illuminate how they had dealt with the children who had talked to them. They compared their own difficulties or progress to what others did, or might do, in similar situations. Some teachers told stories that indicated that survivors' or mothers' stories or reactions had affected not only their professional lives but also their personal lives.

Family and school life

In telling their stories, teachers referred both to their own experiences of home and school life and to that of their pupils. Sometimes, there was an overt awareness of their own inexperience of the lives some of their pupils were living. Sometimes, experiences from dealing with abused children in the school context spilled over into their home lives. In one case, a teacher had been badly shaken by having to accept that she could not assume that her pupils had shared her own supportive childhood. Another teacher told of a young colleague losing faith in the educational system and its purpose after being faced by a child's disclosure of abuse by a teacher in the same school, which had later been proven. One young teacher's first case of child sexual abuse involved her in attending a case conference at which the father's extreme violence was discussed. She admitted to having had nightmares about this violence for some months and had been forced to acknowledge that in comparison to many of her pupils she had, at one level, been privileged and was, at another, innocent and ignorant of this aspect of life.

There were instances in which, despite their concern for the well-being of pupils, teachers were judgemental about what constituted a suitable family background. It may be that where, as in New's (1991) case, abuse occurs within the sort of background which teachers have adjudged as 'good', it creates a greater impact on the teacher than when it occurs in a situation that is more noticeably different from their own experience. Several teachers qualified their descriptions of their professional lives by reference to the type of catchment area of the schools in which they worked. Whilst many acknowledged that children from a wide range of family backgrounds might be victims of abuse, there seemed, in the cases described, to be a preponderance of those who were in some way disadvantaged. And on some occasions, the cases which had affected teachers most had involved 'a really nice girl' or someone from 'quite a good family'. This sense of the problem being more prevalent in some social classes than others was increased by additional stories told by teachers, as when they told of colleagues who saw no value in being trained about abuse as 'it doesn't happen in schools like this'. Further affirmation of this tendency came whilst writing this chapter when a colleague relayed his wife's experience in a prestigious school. A colleague of hers, remarking on the irrelevance of such training, had been amazed to hear that the school had had six reported cases that year. Speaking of child protection and teachers' response, McCann (1995) suggests that 'surely the most appropriate response is to consider that there will always be children who are being abused who will not disclose that to their teacher and may never tell anyone' (p.141). It would seem that before that stage can be reached there are a number of teachers who need to be convinced that child protection is an issue for every school, not just those in certain catchment areas.

As a corollary to this, it may be that where schools are not alert to the possibility of some pupils being abuse victims, they may reinforce a code of secrecy by not appreciating the necessity to discuss certain subjects or certain emotions – even amongst the staff.

Furniss (1991) has described conflict avoidance and conflict regulation as polarities in terms of dealing with abuse issues in families. Similarly, I would argue that different teachers, and indeed different schools, may be more open or closed to perceiving the need to be aware of, or to discuss, the kind of issues which surround child abuse. O'Hara (1988) links the need to develop policies which allow support for children and openness in the discussion of such issues to equal opportunities, claiming that until such issues are addressed, inequality of opportunity will continue for many children. She does note that support by senior staff and interest from teachers are prerequisites for such schemes.

At an organisational level, Legge (1995) has noted the 'role of social institutions in patterning behaviour and privileging some discourses above others' (p.307). She addresses how individuals can become enmeshed in the systems they create and argues the need to be more reflexive and to deconstruct, as well as construct, systems. Organisations, including schools, that restrict the opportunities for such reflection restrict opportunities to develop new understandings or promote growth. Bolton (1993) notes the importance of sharing information and awareness between those involved in school management, noting that sometimes those in positions of responsibility within schools themselves abuse, and that greater openness is in itself a protective measure.

McLeod (1996) states that in the counselling sense, stories represent a way of knowing, or of sharing knowledge. This study further implies that just as some families may silence certain stories, so the exercising of authority in broader contexts may provide a silencing threat. I would argue that this is an important issue in schools. Teachers in my study had varying experiences of both family and school life and brought these experiences to their current situations and to their coping strategies. There was a sense in which their perceptions of the organisations in which they worked affected their expectations of the issues with which they would have to deal, and perhaps affected how they carried out their roles. This book does not seek to suggest prescriptive ways of tackling the issues involved in handling child sexual abuse, it seeks only to broaden the context of awareness.

The problems of handling sensitive issues within the school setting are legion. It has been suggested, in an anonymous letter to the *Times Educational Supplement* in 1997, that the revelation of family secrets within the classroom environment is not always a cathartic process, although on some occasions this has been a successful device.

Some teachers referred to the support given by pupils to their peers, others described problems caused by inappropriate disclosures or sexualised behaviour in terms of classroom management issues. Others mentioned the potential for further victimisation of a child at the hands of school bullies, or complaints from parents for inappropriate information being given to children.

It seemed that some schools sought to protect younger teachers from problems which children might present them with. One of the sample said that she had been given a particular form group because 'they came from good families and they didn't think I'd have any problems with that group'. When a child in her group was the subject of a case conference, she was requested to attend. She admitted that she had no understanding of the procedure, and when asked to vote about whether the child should be registered 'at risk' she did not know what this meant.

Other teachers spoke of knowing of staff who would not be able to cope with this sort of situation. There was some sense that certain people should be involved in dealing with these issues, and others who should not. However, there was no hint, in the comments made, that these 'less suitable' people had discussed the issues involved with those who were making the judgements. It was less open than that. If certain teachers are excluded from this process, thus finding themselves and pupils who confide in them less supported, what is the implication for child protection in that school? It may be that the teacher who had been told that those in authority knew about the pupil concerned (p.150) had been deemed less able to cope and hence was thrust into personal anxiety about outcomes for the pupil concerned. How ready would such a teacher be to report the next issue confided in her?

There were justifications for protecting certain members of staff built into the stories of some of the participants. One teacher told of a colleague who had approached him after a child had disclosed to him. He said this colleague was 'ashen white and shaking'. The teacher had reassured his colleague that the situation was known and claimed that this child took pleasure in identifying those teachers who would be most affected by his story. In another school situation an eleven-year-old boy had the ability to disturb female members of staff by leering at them in an overtly sexual way. Such incidents demonstrate something of the horror stories which form the basis of the justification for those teachers playing certain roles to protect their colleagues from such incidents. However, they are reminiscent of the finding (Wattam *et al.* 1989) that the more damaged children are, the more 'bad' they may be perceived to be, and the more they become dealt with in a punitive way rather than provided with therapy or support to enable healing. If the more experienced teachers deal with children who are perceived to be those with the problems, does this make the position of the quiet, perhaps middle-class, child, who is not perceived to be a problem and therefore given to a less experienced teacher, even less visible and hence more difficult to bear?

The view of abuse, and the understandings of abuse, held by those in schools are likely to be varied, and without training or opportunities for discussion hidden assumptions may remain unchallenged. In those schools where, for the best of intentions, certain teachers assume roles which exclude other staff from dealing with known cases, the opportunities for less experienced teachers to further their own understanding of, and response to, abuse may be limited. It may also unintentionally reinforce an assumption that abused children cause problems in the school context, which further weakens the support for those children who are more adept at hiding their problems.

Table 6.2 shows the problems that teachers in the sample have identified in dealing with sexual abuse survivors in the school context. It reveals that in a variety of situations staff have sought to involve other people – sometimes those from official bodies like the police, social services, or the school psychological service; sometimes other teachers within the school, or counterparts from secondary schools if the child is to be transferred.

Table 6.1 Situations faced by teachers in dealing with abuse*

Type of situation	Number of those in sample facing this type of situation	Number who felt need to involve further people
Initial disclosure in private by survivor	3	3
Disclosure in private by survivor	10	10
Disclosure during class by survivor	2	2
Information given about child by official source	5	5
Information given by family	4	3
Innappropriate behaviour towards teacher	6	4
Innappropriate behaviour towards pupil	4	4

Table 6.1 continued		
Type of situation	*Number of those in sample facing this type of situation*	*Number who felt need to involve further people*
Inappropriate behaviour in class	7	4
Inappropriate language	10	5
Acting out/sexualised behaviour	3	3
Survivor being victimised	4	2
Survivor being supported by pupils	2	0
Other pupils reporting suspicions	3	1
Attendance at case conference	3	2
Visiting family	4	2
Attendance at court	2	2
Support to other staff member	3	0
Support from other member	4	4
Discussion of suspicions with other staff member	8	8
Difficulties from other staff member	2	2
Difficulties from family	4	4
Problems from other siblings in school	3	3
Report of concerns by family	3	3
Involvement with family	9	9
Threats or violence from child	2	2
Threats or violence from family	3	3
Ongoing contact with child or family	8	6
Ongoing support for child or family	4	0
Maintenance of contact after child goes to secondary school	3	3
Ongoing problems after conclusion of professional involvement	2	2

* Teachers may have dealt with more than one child.

However, alongside this need to have someone in whom to confide, or with whom to discuss suspicions, there was a secondary theme which occurred in the stories of many of the staff when discussing the school context. It was generally felt by more senior staff that information of this nature should not be made widely available to teachers, but should only be accessible to those who might be involved in a pastoral role towards a child. What was almost being said here was that certain members of staff should not be involved as they might not understand.

This was an area that I tended to probe and, although the statements made in response were guarded, there was a sense that certain teachers might be regarded by those in the sample as potentially damaging to the child involved – owing to their perceived lack of understanding. Comments ranged from 'you've got to be careful who knows, it doesn't do if they're too sympathetic' to 'some teachers don't understand this sort of thing – they might make assumptions about the child or the family, I've seen that sort of thing happen'. The responsibility towards the children and the intention that their business should not become trivial conversation was admirable. But any admiration I had coexisted with an uneasy awareness that those who held what were deemed to be unsuitable views or responses had neither opportunity to broaden these views nor information to extend their perceptions.

The case of the youngest survivor linked with this point, in that she had had a supportive relationship with her head of year, yet had been told in a personal and social education class that abused children tended to come from poor families where parents were either unmarried or had married too young. This was in direct contrast to her own experience, causing her both to doubt other things this teacher said and to question whether her head of year meant what she said.

If, as McCann (1995) has argued, there may be abused children in any and every school, then there must be a case for ongoing opportunities for teachers to acquire new understandings of what is involved. This links with Chamberlain's (1993) concern that the texts which teachers use to learn about child abuse may affect their perceptions of who is involved, potentially making some cases invisible.

Within the sample there were differences in how the organisation involved viewed the problem of child abuse and the support implications for those dealing with it. Those in the tertiary and higher sectors did not have the same legal responsibility to report suspicions as schools did, since they were dealing with students who were above the age of consent. This tended to diminish one aspect of the dilemma which could be faced by those in other sectors who, in taking the decision to report, had to assess factors such as the veracity of the account and the potential severity of allegations. However, there was no formal mechanism for dealing with concerns in these sectors, and in some instances teachers had concerns about younger children who may be facing a continuing situation. Their strategy tended to be to persuade survivors to disclose to the authorities for the benefit of these other siblings. Within the school sector, policies were more defined because of legislation, although there were issues in terms of the knowledge owned by different teachers and of the responsibility delegated in different settings. Whilst often staff would be aware of 'a section in the staff handbook', or know that there was information available 'somewhere amongst all the paperwork you get as a head', the importance or immediacy of this knowledge for individuals was not a prime concern until a situation arose – at which point searching for information on procedure did not form the most immediate response.

It did not seem in all schools that the choice of confidant(e) made by the child was always respected, and some staff felt demeaned by this. One termed her experience 'Judas-like'. Her statement had direct resonances to the category of 'betrayal' in Finkelhor and Browne's (1988) model. She felt she had passed on concerns about a child in her class only to be excluded from further discussions and decisions about outcomes when she felt that she knew the child better than those subsequently involved in the case.

Some respondents spoke of practice which supported the teacher to whom the child had spoken, in a relationship likened to that between a counsellor and supervisor. This gave the impression of schools that aimed to deal with the child, rather than simply with the problem, whilst ensuring support and guidance for the staff member. This would link with the suggestions Porter (1989) made, which suggested that since children often choose the teacher they can trust with secret information, schools should maintain conditions which allow this particular teacher to support the child.

Teachers spoke of how a change of head could mean a change of system in this respect, and two noted the importance of linkages to known people in the other professions that may become involved in cases of this sort. Several teachers had experienced cases which went wrong in some way. Two mentioned cases concerning other members of the teaching profession, which, as Sloan (1989) suggests, produce situations where it is very difficult for other teachers who become involved to strike a balance that is 'neither over- nor under-reactive' (p.11). One of the factors both of these respondents mentioned in this context was the difficulties of the children concerned whilst opinions were divided about where 'the truth' lay. A head who according to one respondent, 'jumped into action with all guns blazing' had damaged both the child and the relationships between staff in her opinion, and had caused increases to her own anxiety when dealing with subsequent cases of this type.

Whilst a majority of the sample agreed that if faced with a similar situation again they would probably still try to work for the benefit of the child, one member of the sample said that he had no wish to be involved again. He hinted that he would not report suspicions in a future situation because of the difficulties and personal stress involved. His comments, not directly echoed by other members of the sample, were perhaps at the furthest end of a continuum. Certainly, teachers were aware of the difficulties of confirming suspicions and were uncertain about when, in the murkiness of hints and possibilities, they should take action or report concerns. Several spoke of how they had conversations with other members of staff, or the school nurse, before moving on to report concerns to the nominated person. Nominated people spoke of their system of recording hints and suspicions before a concern turned into action. In the larger schools, this could be a more formal process. Whilst one teacher from a large school spoke of having to deal with an angry parent after she had reported her concerns to social services, several of those from primary schools had had difficult encounters with parents – on some occasions involving threats of personal violence.

Often, the more senior teachers in the staff had been involved in ongoing work with, or support for, families as well as individual pupils. If siblings attended the same school, this could be one area of involvement; but for some of the sample there was contact with parents, and some had links with others involved in welfare, legal or therapeutic contexts. Often, descriptions of this sort of activity were overlaid with rationality. The teacher was talking of a role function which was being carried out as part of the job. Occasionally, however, this persona slipped and the uncertainties inherent in the tasks involved within this role surfaced.

Morrison (1992), speaking of the emotional impact of working with sexual abuse cases on social workers, notes the linkages between what happens to them and Summit's child sexual abuse accommodation syndrome. This model, briefly, includes:

- *Secrecy* – in which the child does not talk about what is happening and maintains the secret of the abuse. Morrison extends this to workers failing to talk about the personal abuses of the work they do. Teachers spoke of some of the personal costs of dealing with survivors and their families, but often claimed they had not been able to talk, in an organisational or professional context, about these concerns.

- *Helplessness* – where the child is unable to do anything about the predicament or has no ready means of help. Again, Morrison extends this to the social worker and the organisational myths which suggest that professionalism is linked to the ability to help oneself, to stay detached and to maintain a logical, rational response. Here, teachers talked of their own doubts, of their lack of knowledge and of the lack of concrete evidence. There seemed to be a divide between the practices and strategies which were laid down and the impact of 'the real thing' on the teacher who became involved in it. One teacher said that she had had to deal with abuse twice in her career and felt 'no better prepared to cope on the second occasion than on the first'.

- *Entrapment and accommodation* – where a survivor sees the way in which the situation is progressing or being dealt with as normal or the right way to deal with it. Morrison suggests that workers perceive the strategies and structures to which they have to conform in the same way. The anger that they feel may produce a distortion of perception of how others, or the organisation, are dealing with events. Teachers spoke both of taking individual action which might be misconstrued and of how they were annoyed by what they perceived to be either precipitate action or inaction of others.

- *Delayed or unconvincing disclosure* – just as survivors may hint at problems without any real substance to their stories, or act out (displaying challenging behaviours such as self-harming or sexualised behaviours) with no definable reason for behaviour, so Morrison argues workers may use such devices as working harder or resigning. Three teachers spoke of similar processes when they spent periods of time working out strategies to deal with the problems certain children were causing them, when they were desperate for help from others who knew more about the situation but seemed unwilling to provide sufficient help.

- *Retraction* – when children commonly withdraw their disclosure of abuse. Morrison sees that workers can likewise retract their disclosure of difficulties or stress because it contradicts the professional image. Teachers in the sample did not describe this process in terms of their own response, although personal experience within the teaching profession would lead me to believe that many teachers have a tendency to minimise or deny personal problems to fulfil organisational demands.

Morrison argues, on the basis of her extension of this model, that social work agencies need to have an awareness of the organisational impacts on workers' ability to deal with the situations they are asked to face. Similarly, my study would suggest that teachers often face situations which would benefit from wider understanding, better support mechanisms and greater opportunities for discussion of both the personal feelings and the emotional effects of being involved with these difficulties within an organisational framework.

Disclosure and its impact on teachers

Just as in the cases of the survivors and mothers in the study, it would be easy to be judgemental about what teachers did or did not do, or how they handled incidents. The purpose of this study was not to take such a stance, but rather to explore how teachers did respond.

The teachers described situations which they had to face and the organisational contexts in which they had to operate. As has been argued, there is a sense in which they are being asked to react in a prescribed way in situations that are often less easy to define than the guidelines might suggest.

Teachers brought different experiences, perceptions and understandings to what confronted them. Some had experienced recent or regular training; others had undergone no training at all. Comments ranged from 'I think we had one lecture when I was doing my teacher training' or 'I went on a course, I think it would be about ten years ago' to 'The authority runs a sort of network of support for teachers where we can meet and discuss new developments. It really is very useful and very supportive.' Only two of the sample had been trained about the likely impact on themselves of dealing with child abuse issues. For one, this had been because a colleague on a course had asked a question about this issue; and for the other, because her counselling course had dealt with this area. The teacher who felt well supported by his authority was able to talk about concerns or issues but had not had specific training about how issues might impact on those involved with them. He did, however, feel this need was important and covered by the existing provision in his authority.

As has been mentioned, these teachers had dealt with children who had been abused over some 20 years, during which time perceptions and understandings of abuse had changed. One teacher, who I interviewed very near the beginning of the teacher interviews, had dealt with abuse in the early stages of the Cleveland affair, before the introduction of the Children Act 1989 and the concurrent increase in awareness by government. Initially, I thought that her comment about the lack of knowledge she and her colleagues possessed was a product of the lesser degree of awareness of such issues at that time. When a similar lack of preparation for how to respond was present in the stories of two other teachers, with much more recent experiences of dealing with abused children, I was forced to revise that assumption.

Teachers who were nominated people tended, as might be expected, to have the best levels of training about the signs and procedures relating to child sexual abuse. One of these teachers had also had useful opportunities for discussion and networking about the personal issues of those involved in dealing with child sexual abuse. (Personal issues that arose for teachers are summarised in Table 6.2.)

Table 6.2 Personal issues that had an effect on teachers		
Type of personal effect on teacher	Number of teachers describing effect	Type of situations mentioned
Nightmares	2	Dreaming about events a child has described (1) Dreaming about threatened violence by parents (1)
Inability to sleep	4	Worrying about how to deal with a child or family member
Effect on family or sex life	2	Worries about safety of own children (1) Difficulty with sexual relationship after hearing about abuse suffered by child (1)
Unpleasant memories	3	Thinking about what child was going through (2) Flashbacks to own experience of violence (1)
Anxiety	10	Worrying about decisions, actions or response

Table 6.2 continued		
Type of personal effect on teacher	*Number of teachers describing effect*	*Type of situations mentioned*
Difficulties about what action to take	5	Uncertainty about right support for child or about own ability to make judgements within the situation
Feeling of powerlessness	5	Feeling of being insufficient for the task (2) Feeling of losing control of handling of case (1) Feeling of inability to make a difference for the child (2)
Conflict with colleague(s)	3	Disagreement with procedures implemented (1) Feeling of betrayal because of lack of support (2)
Sense of helplessness	7	Frustration at court procedure (3) Lack of ability to communicate with child (2) Lack of support from colleagues and others (2)
Feeling of isolation	7	Lack of support from other agencies (2) No one within organisation able to provide support (3) Feeling alone when dealing with a situation (2)
Increased stress	14	Dealing with child or family or peers or other class members
Uncertainty about where to seek help or advice	6	Lack of availability of professional help (3) Lack of sharing of knowledge or advice by other professionals involved (3)
Dissatisfaction with outcome	3	Frustration at cases that were poorly handled (2) Perceived lack of follow-up after child changed school (1)
Role conflict	4	Differences between own abilities and perceptions other bodies had of them (2) Desire to support and comfort versus professional role (2)

The other nominated teacher had incorporated the realities of the role into a perception of such aspects as 'part of the job'. The catchment area of her school included a large, troublesome council estate, and a good number of the cases which came to her attention were from this population. Many of her descriptions of the cases she had dealt with drew on images of the difference between these families and 'what we do for our [own] children'. Her training had involved some home visits with social services and she described neglected and squalid homes as the backdrop against which abuse was being perpetrated. Without negating the excellent and caring work she did for the children with whom she came into contact, I wondered whether she would be able to employ the same strategies if she was coping with the same role in a less overtly different environment. Deblinger *et al.* (1994) conducted a study which explored the differences in female social workers' perceptions of their response to abusers and the families involved, when these were hypothesised as their own lovers or spouses. This mechanism caused the workers involved to re-examine some of their own responses. It may be that such mechanisms would widen teachers' perceptions of abuse if applied as part of their training.

Teachers described a variety of ways in which they had divided responsibilities. Although they might be aware of the problems an individual child was experiencing, they had also to assess the needs of other members of a class and ensure discipline was maintained. Teachers described incidents that had the potential to disturb the balance they were attempting to maintain. Disclosure in front of a group of children was a difficult area to handle, as were incidents of sexualised behaviour or attention-seeking devices. Two teachers spoke of how they sought to apply discipline in public but often tried to allow pupils opportunities to discuss their behaviour in private after the lesson.

Teachers could feel personally threatened by pupils' behaviour or unsure of how to handle it. One teacher spoke of how she always wore loose-fitting clothes if she knew she would have to teach a certain pupil because of how he looked at female members of staff; another of how a child in the class was emotionally volatile and could not handle even the mildest criticism – her attempts to use positive reinforcement had only served to produce a dependency on her which was difficult to handle.

There were differences in the responses of teachers to disclosure when a child was younger. Unfortunately, older children may have developed the reputation for being liars or manipulators, and hence the longer reasons for their behaviour remain unknown, the less likely they are to be believed if they do disclose. A child without such a reputation may be more readily helped. Teachers seemed more likely to believe what a primary school child said than some older children whom they knew to be liars or manipulators.

Teachers here described very much the same day-to-day issues of dealing with problem behaviour that some of the mothers had to face. They sometimes used similar descriptions in terms of the lack of information they received from those with social work or therapeutic responsibilities towards the child. They could be similarly distressed by sexualised behaviours or unpredictability.

One teacher spoke of the difficulties of getting through the medical barriers of confidentiality and perceived a need for agencies to work together for the benefit of children. Whilst not advocating that cases become subjects for casual conversation, it does seem to me that a climate in which secrets were preserved in the name of confidentiality could only serve to diminish opportunities for the sharing of understanding. I could envisage benefits in allowing less experienced or less well-trained staff to benefit from a sharing of multi-professional insights that could aid in the development of new strategies and understanding. Teachers' sense of isolation or powerlessness might also be diminished if they could become part of a professional support network. As with the other groups studied, it seemed that teachers' experiences of support were patchy – at best they could experience real sources of support, at worst these were non-existent, despite the lessons and legislation since the 1980s.

Interactions with others

All of the teachers had been involved in dealing with others as a result of the disclosure to them of sexual abuse. Often, the sector within which they were working seemed to have an impact both on who was told and on the potential repercussions of this action.

Part of the problem for teachers dealing with younger children involved their interpretations either of what was said to them or of behaviour. There seemed to be dilemmas for these teachers about the meaning of signs or behavioural changes, and, as has been said earlier, more likelihood of close contact with the parents involved. One teacher who had dealt with nursery school children spoke of working with some families and never finding the evidence to validate her fears, thus having to trust that the support she and social workers gave families did something to ameliorate children's situations.

Those in secondary education had perhaps similar issues around interpreting behaviour, but were often in organisational cultures that were not predisposed to believe children's stories. The primary teachers worried about a child's problems being overlooked in the larger secondary school environment. The secondary teachers generally spoke of children who exhibited obvious behavioural problems or who sought out help for themselves, either because they had built up trust in a certain teacher or because there was a forum available to them where they could obtain help if necessary. One school, for example, had a drop-in arrangement where pupils could socialise and discuss problems with a teacher should they require to do so. This teacher told of how a number of pupils built up confidence in this system over a period of time before they made a more major disclosure.

Teachers in both types of establishment spoke of the point at which they felt they had to involve others and formalise concerns. There were barriers to taking this next step, which came from a variety of sources. The first level of concern was a personal one. Teachers often were unsure of whether their concerns were justified, and several described the devices they used to acquire more confidence in what they were beginning to suspect. It was unlikely at this stage that they would involve those at a different level in the hierarchy or the named person, unless the school was very small and the lines of communication simple. It seemed that at this level a child's case could be dismissed if the hints were small, they had not been picked up by a peer of the teacher concerned, or the child did not elaborate or confirm them if questioned further. Included in this category was the fact that teachers might often dwell on aspects of a case at home, thinking about it at night or discussing it with a spouse or friend, particularly if this person was also involved in teaching. Whereas a named person who had these suspicions might make a written note of the small hints, it is unlikely that the ordinary teacher would do so. Although hints could act in a cumulative way so that a series of smaller incidents could eventually prompt a teacher to proceed to further action. Children who drew little attention to themselves, or who were less willing or able to articulate their concerns, would seem to be disadvantaged by this tendency.

A second and related area which provided a barrier for teachers was the issue of confidentiality. One teacher commented specifically about her personal dilemma about confidentiality when she said that she made a practice of prefacing conversations, which might result in a child confiding sensitive information, with a statement that she would have to pass information on to others if it involved anything which it was her legal duty to report. Confidentiality, it seemed, could work in two ways. The teacher who mentioned it worried that it might prevent a child who needed help from making the disclosure which would trigger that help. She felt that, in her experience, her promise of support which went alongside her disclaimer on confidentiality had been enough to prompt children to continue in their disclosures, although she worried that this would not always be the case. It seems possible that others could use a similar disclaimer to distance themselves from the difficult information which they felt might pursue a request to talk about this sort of issue. Still other teachers saw the whole area of confidentiality and breaching confidentiality as problematical, especially when disclosures were ambiguous.

A third barrier was identified by teachers in terms of the organisational response. Passing information to those in more official positions in relation to child protection could prompt a variety of responses, ranging from perceived inaction and seeming unconcern, to precipitate or over-hasty reactions that invoked procedural measures without regard for the readiness of the child to be involved in them. Two secondary school teachers spoke of their concerns that children had been labelled as 'liars' or 'manipulators' and worried that this sort of behaviour was what was being judged rather than its cause. One teacher, indeed, was given the impression by a senior colleague that she was being too quick to report concerns, many of which would probably turn out to be trivial. Here, perhaps, the normally co-operative child who makes a coherent disclosure is more likely to be supported than a known troublemaker.

A fourth barrier could exist in terms of teachers' knowledge and perception of what constituted suitable cause for concern. Hallett and Gorman (1994) suggest that it is essential that all teachers should in a school be made aware of 'the boundaries between acceptable and unacceptable behaviour' (p.52). Similarly, teachers need to be aware of the mechanisms for dealing with such cases. Wurtele and Schmitt (1992) have drawn attention to delays and problems caused by teachers' or childcare workers' lack of knowledge regarding their responsibilities in connection with abuse. They see increased knowledge as essential in providing those at risk with the necessary support. Whilst this barrier was a specific cause of concern for those in smaller schools, it is also possible that teachers who have little, or no, training about abuse could be in a comparable position in many schools.

A further barrier may exist in terms of the catchment area of the school and the perception of the types of family being dealt with. This may still prevent an individual teacher from whistle-blowing, especially if the family concerned has particular status within a community.

Teachers spoke of interaction with a variety of others after disclosures prompted action. Disclosures which moved beyond the vagaries of hints were usually reported to the named person. This could bring teachers into contact with families, police or social workers. Four teachers spoke of their feelings of powerlessness, or lack of control, once other agencies became involved. They regretted the lack of co-operation between agencies, which they argued should be in place to benefit the child. Certainly, the one teacher who was involved in a system which embraced such multi-agency co-operation spoke highly of its benefits and the progress which could be made with, and for, children under the auspices of such involvement. Whether survivors or parents would perceive this level of co-operation in the same way is not clear.

A related area, raised as a concern by three teachers, was the lack of feedback they were given by psychiatrists or psychologists who became involved in the case. One teacher spoke of a child whose behaviour gave real cause for concern and of the lack of detail about both cause and likely effect with which she was furnished. Another teacher spoke of children joining her school from a variety of places with very little information forwarded from their previous schools, so that unexpected problems could manifest themselves without warning. A child who subsequently perpetrated against younger boys in her school was one such case that could have been differently handled if a previous school had communicated what it held on record. Not only did this lack of information cause difficulties for the school, it also provided a source of further problems for the child, emotional stress for the teachers and complaints and dissatisfaction from parents of the other children involved.

The sense of teachers wanting to help children, but not knowing what to do or how to help when behaviour became this difficult, was strong. In this sense, teachers experienced some of the same dilemmas as mothers when they were unsure about how to handle aspects of a child's behaviour. Just as Hooper (1992) suggests that the demands put upon mothers of survivors may be too high, so it would seem that the expectation that teachers will know how to deal with a child may be open to question. Some teachers spoke of schools involving auxiliary help for these children – although one respondent saw this as being of little real value as the woman brought in to help had no specialist training. Several teachers tended to be cynical about the will to do anything of real value for such children because of the costs involved. They saw the most damaged children as being shifted from one establishment to another without any real hope of healing available for them. In one teacher's words: 'All we can really do is supply a holding operation – we've no real knowledge of what to do or what to look for.'

The teacher who was a trained counsellor spoke of how she had counselled children and sometimes other members of their families within the school situation, but she had not had any time or monetary recognition for this work and doubted that this service would be continued if she left the school.

As with so many other areas of this study, there were no clear patterns of how interaction with others might affect teachers. What was regarded as useful was the existence of a network of support which could be tapped into when problems arose. It seemed that teachers wanted to preserve confidentiality as much as was possible for the child, but to have the benefit of being able to discuss case issues as widely as necessary to further their own understanding and maximise the support they could offer. This seems paradoxical when coupled with the suspicion which seemed to exist about how some of the people who might become involved might handle aspects of the situation. Where teachers felt that support that was compatible with their own beliefs existed, they were comparatively happy with provision; where they felt powerless or excluded, they felt unsure that the best was being done for a child. It was not simply what had happened to the child that could disturb teachers; how a case was handled, the verdict if it went to court and the aftercare of the child involved could also have an emotional impact on them.

Not all of the teachers had had to deal directly with the families of those involved in abusive situations. There was some tendency, as has been said, to perceive the families involved as, generally, less able to support a child than other families. Perhaps in many of the cases described there was justification in this view, but just as social worker interventions have tended to be more common in poorer, less functional families (e.g. Glaser and Frosh 1988), so a system which relies heavily on teachers noticing 'signs' is weighted towards identifying those who are less successful at keeping the 'secret'. Certainly, where teachers have specifically commented on the child as being 'quite a nice girl' or 'from quite a good family', there are hints of an expectation that this might not generally be the case and often of a greater effect on the teacher concerned.

Teachers, who may have described considerable problems with a particular child, could make comments implying that they thought the family was having difficulty in dealing with the situation or the child. Whilst this was not stated in overtly 'mother-blaming' terms, it did seem that there was an expectation of how a family should handle such issues, and teachers were less likely to empathise with the effects on other family members than on children. Boushel and Noakes (1988) note the importance for the child's recovery of strengthening the relationship with the mother and of sensitivity to the issues which the mother may be facing. The teacher who commented that these parents were unlikely to come into school perceived that as being indicative of lack of support for a child, rather than possibly being either an effect of personal trauma connected with the abuse (Manion *et al.* 1996) or an avoidance of potentially threatening or judgemental situations, as suggested in the chapter on mothers.

It is possible that if teachers had been given training before the 1990s a perception of mothers as culpable might have been incorporated into it – the strength of this stereotype has been demonstrated in the literature review. If teachers come into contact with families, this may constitute an area of their own values and beliefs that would be necessary for them to explore, as Parry (1991) has suggested is important for therapists.

The teachers as they are now

In some cases, the abuse teachers described had happened several years ago; for others, the cases they spoke of were current. Whilst issues from cases they have been involved with have continued to affect the teachers' views and feelings towards child sexual abuse, I will deal here with their views about how schools might be able to affect outcomes in this area.

At the end of the teachers' interviews I included questions on whether preventive education, and education for parenting, had a place in the school curriculum. Since these interviews, the government has stressed the importance of education for parenting. The majority of the sample saw this as crucial, although one expressed doubts about how it could be incorporated into the timetable – there was, in fact, some tendency for the National Curriculum to be seen as discouraging of initiatives to address issues not directly compatible with its points of focus. Teachers were also asked to comment on what else, if anything, schools could do to support children who had experienced sexual abuse.

Often teachers felt that current procedures and practices within their schools were not the most appropriate way of dealing with this issue. In terms of their current feelings, a number mentioned that, despite problems which had arisen on previous occasions, they would probably act in a similar way should such a situation arise again. For two people this might include saying things to, or acting towards, survivors, or their families, in a way which might not be compatible with current policies. Those teachers, who had responded by procrastinating in order to work through issues with a child before reporting the problem, or who had reported a case despite later difficulties with a family member, felt that they would have responded in a similar way again. The teacher who had not wanted to hear details of what her pupils had suffered maintained that she was better able to help children when she was not aware of the nature of their difficulties – although it has to be said that had she been working in a mainstream school rather than a school which specialised in those with emotional disorders this may not have been the case. Two teachers said that they would push harder for action, or make more fuss, if they had to deal with comparable situations again. Only one said that he would try to avoid such issues completely in future.

Teachers were less convinced about the benefits of preventive education than they were about the value of education for parenthood. I was somewhat disappointed by the number who equated preventive education only with such initiatives as 'Stranger Danger', although I accepted the reticence expressed by those who were more aware of the percentage of abusers who are known contacts of a child about the implications of making young children more aware of the risk from those they know. Part of preventive education was perceived, by some, as providing a safe environment in school where children could discuss concerns and problems, although more than one mentioned the cynicism of colleagues about whether anything can be done to protect children by this means.

Education for parenting was seen as being potentially more useful and was perceived as an element in PSE (Personal and Social Education) by several secondary teachers. Though it was felt that this was a valuable area, there seemed to be some tendency to ascribe any taught intervention as belonging to another educational sector, or to another subject area's ambit. One secondary teacher was involved in a new project that sought to identify potential family and relationship difficulties as part of a religious studies module. She reasoned that, as a number of children had discussed personal worries after a comparable module on drug abuse, there might now be an upsurge of discussion about personal abuses. One teacher mentioned the teacher–pupil relationship as a possible role model for parenting. She was from a forces' school and was concerned by the large number of disturbed children she encountered, who she felt lacked stability in either their home or their school lives. She feared they would move on into relationships which, in turn, lacked the stability that had never been their experience.

This transience had resonances with some of the other teachers' stories of the most damaged children being moved from school to school, without longer-term strategies for therapy or healing. Such a process is directly contrary to Wyatt and Mickey's (1987) finding, which links the uncoupling of abuse from its potential effects to parental, or other, support. The perceived lack of consistent support, for some children, was a particular concern of primary or special needs teachers.

However, teachers did have other ideas about what could be done in schools to improve the current levels of understanding about sexual abuse and provision for dealing with survivors. Teachers from a variety of sectors expressed the view that part of teacher education should be involved with raising awareness about abuse issues in general. It was also felt by the majority of the sample that counselling skills should form part of this training – if only to ensure that teachers were more aware of when to pass issues on to others. This links with the work of McLaughlin (1995), who suggests that whilst there are different levels of skill within counselling, all teachers should have first level skills to allow them to respond to any issues which arise. Teachers were aware that some of their colleagues may not be willing to deal with sexual abuse specifically, and there was disagreement within the sample as to whether training about this should be compulsory. Those who felt it should be the subject of wider training provision outweighed those who wanted to protect some colleagues from it. But it was generally accepted that whilst knowledge and awareness should be raised, not everyone would be willing or able to deal with all the issues it might arouse. One teacher mentioned that whilst the subject was included in the staff handbook, it should also be addressed on at least one training day each year so that new staff were made aware of practice and procedures.

Teachers also felt that a wider network of contacts with those in other areas of the systems dealing with child protection was a beneficial aim. One spoke of his school's attempts to 'penetrate the medical mafia with its oaths and secrecy'. Another teacher felt that a system based on known contacts with police and social services, such as had existed in the past, would be beneficial. Its demise she connected to an increase in demand for social services and an overdependency on procedures, which she worried biased concerns away from the child's needs towards procedural considerations.

Despite procedures being in place to deal with immediate issues surrounding an initial disclosure, a number of the teachers felt isolated by a lack of knowledge of how best to assist children after the system had run its course. This could be exacerbated by two types of situation mentioned by respondents. The first was where a court case had been unsatisfactory – the perpetrator had been found guilty but not sentenced because of his age and health. The teacher concerned had supported the family and was left dealing with both a personal sense of disappointment at the outcome and a continuing need to support the child and the family, but with no focal point towards which to channel their hopes or expectations. A second, and potentially more complex, situation was when a child had moved schools after being involved in an abusive situation, but where no records had been forwarded. After problems had arisen at school, parts of the story had emerged but the teacher had insufficient knowledge of the child, or the situation, to know how best to proceed or what agencies to involve.

There were hints from the teacher in further education that there might be some tendency for those who had been abused to seek educational courses connected to the caring sector. I tested this finding on three colleagues who confirmed their own experiences of this. Some survivors seem to feel that such courses will provide them with access to people who can provide personal support and assistance. Teachers were worried by this.

The university lecturers who had dealt with survivors suspected that because students had left home they were, for the first time in their lives, faced by the possibility that they need not return to a situation they had perhaps kept secret for years. One spoke of how a girl had stayed with her in her own home over part of the Christmas holidays as she had nowhere else to go, wryly adding that she did not know how her colleagues would view this sort of arrangement. In common with the other samples in the study, often, it seemed, the outcomes depended very much upon the individuals involved in the assistance or support sought, rather than on the processes which were in place.

Teachers were aware of difficulties in combining a timetable with the needs of individual children. One spoke of colleagues who paid lip service to counselling help 'as long as you don't do it in my lesson'. Another spoke of withdrawing children under the guise of special needs, although that had the potential for repercussions on the child if other children labelled them as 'remmy'. A paper commissioned by the Bishops' Conference of England and Wales (O'Keefe *et al.* 1992) recommends that 'the education sector needs to acknowledge the special need for children who have been abused to experience some kind of teaching style which offers experience of success, however humble' (p.4).

Some schools were providing counselling support, some were supporting the teachers to whom a child had disclosed. In others, there was no apparent provision for this to be conducted either officially or unofficially, and teachers could feel vulnerable both if their help was sought and if a child was being dealt with elsewhere and they were not sure of what behaviour or reaction to expect. It seemed that provision was *ad hoc* at every level, including higher education, and that teachers or lecturers who had little or no training could be perceived as suitable recipients of a disclosure – it seemed that what happened subsequently was similarly *ad hoc.*

Summary of issues for the teachers

It appeared to me that the teachers acknowledged that discovering that a child in their care had been sexually abused had an emotional impact upon themselves. Despite the fact that this was their belief, several of them, during the interview, moved into the role of discussing this emotion in a logical way. Often, it was not until they had detailed the 'facts' of what had happened that they began to discuss the emotion. However, what interested me in the telling of their stories was how often the emotion was still welded to the facts. This was demonstrated by changes in tone and pace in the story as it was told. There was, it seemed to me, a level at which certain emotions were relived in the telling of the tale in however sequenced or logical a fashion they were attempting to do this. Often, teachers' own values had a bearing on their perceptions of who was at risk, and where perceptions had been challenged there was a sense of guilt or responsibility for other children who might have gone unnoticed.

My impression is that just as Finkelhor and Browne's (1988) model can be applied to mothers (Dempster 1993) (pp.130–131), so it also has applicability to teachers. The four factors of this model have echoes in the comments of teachers within this study:

- *Stigmatisation* – feelings of guilt, shame or badness related to the abuse. Teachers could suffer guilt about a variety of factors, ranging from their own easy childhood to their initial disbelief of a survivor. There were hints that one teacher had been made to feel guilty about reporting concerns of this nature.

- *Powerlessness* – where a survivor feels invaded against his or her will and has a perception of increased threat if attempts at disclosure fail. This has links to the teachers who experienced inaction by those in authority in a school, or felt out of control when the process initiated by their action moved in ways they perceived as being detrimental to the child.

- *Betrayal* – where a survivor feels cheated or manipulated by a trusted adult. This has links to the teacher who promises support or confidentiality to a child and is subsequently let down or excluded from the provision of that support – or, as in one case in this study, promised anonymity if concerns are formalised, then left to face a violent parent on the same day.

- *Traumatic sexualisation* – how sexual behaviour is viewed: perhaps as a way to gain affection, perhaps as something to avoid. Teachers may be repulsed by aspects of sexuality or disturbed by the overt sexualised behaviour of children.

An issue which I found important, and which linked to my initial concerns about the teacher cast in this role, was that one of the teachers mentioned that she had had counselling herself for some six months after dealing with her first survivor. The levels of training the sample had received to prepare them for any potential personal effects of dealing with abuse victims was minimal. Yet almost ten years ago, Braun (1988) recommended that teachers need the opportunity to explore their own values and feelings in this context to broaden their awareness of abuse and 'to recognise the way these feelings might influence their actions' (p.11). My suspicions about teachers' lack of opportunity to explore their feelings and values, and my sense of the importance of Chamberlain's (1993) concern about the restrictions of teachers' understanding of abuse as a result of the texts they read, were not diminished by respondents' stories.

Teachers, though recognised widely as a first line of defence against abuse (e.g. Braun 1988; Hallett 1995; Porter 1989), were often ill-equipped to recognise or deal with it. Indeed, Hallett has commented that it is not only teachers who are unsure of their role: other professionals, whilst believing that teachers play a valuable role, are unsure of how they fit into the child protection framework. Although writers often advocate that teachers use their intuition in dealing with children's problems (e.g. Braun 1988, in relation to abuse; Jewett 1982, in relation to loss), there was a strong feeling among respondents that they did not want to make mistakes or, in three cases, to hand over aspects of caring for the child to those who might make mistakes. Such sentiments can be explored in different ways. Teachers may express a laudable aim in wishing to do no further damage, but inaction may do more harm than taking action. Teachers may find that trusting their intuition places them in a position that does not always produce the expected results – but this may also be true of other interventions, be they by family, friends or professionals. Perhaps more opportunities for training and support would provide teachers with a better ability to assess both the value and the limitations of their contribution, and give them more permission to make mistakes and to learn from them – as Morrison (1992) has suggested in relation to social workers.

Research would indicate that a supportive relationship with the survivor is the important thing (e.g. Gilgun 1991; New 1993; Wyatt and Mickey 1987). Research on bereavement indicates that those affected do not always perceive the actions of those helping them as being as valuable as the helpers intend, but interventions which are less valued by the helpers may be crucially important to the bereaved (Rosenblatt *et al.* 1991). The importance of support may similarly be linked to attachment theory. If survivors have formed a bond with a particular teacher, it may be the security of this attachment that allows healing to take place rather than any specific actions which the individual concerned performs or omits. Sage (1993) notes the likelihood of a child confiding in a trusted teacher, and the importance of that teacher's subsequent action in reporting concerns. It would seem that schools which ignore the child's choice of confidant(e) when handling disclosure may be doing that child a disservice by sending the message that this is not a suitable attachment figure. If such a child lacks secure attachment elsewhere, this disservice may be magnified. Gibson and Hartshorne (1996) note mistrust of, and isolation from, others as a potential long-term result of child sexual abuse. The handling of disclosure in school and the maintenance of support by someone the child has chosen may improve long-term outcomes. As one teacher stated:

> The child must come first and help must be fitted to the child's needs, not the child fitted into the rest of the thing. I don't think there is a particular profession for it, but we need help, we need training, we need input from people and it shouldn't be a question of bumping along doing the best we can. There needs to be a network with the child as the centre of the thing, and we are all around with different skills that we can help with.

And as Orr (1995) has concluded, there is no right way to deal with sexual abuse – each survivor and each family is different; all have different needs. The teachers in the sample had different skills and different reactions; with the backing of a network of support and opportunities for training, it would seem that both their own needs and those of the children they sought to help could be better served.

CHAPTER 7

Compatibilities
and Tensions

This chapter will explore how the experiences of those in the different samples illuminate some of the complexities of dealing with child sexual abuse by juxtaposing some of the issues they have raised. It is very much the thrust of the argument that individual strategies and response are central to actual relationships and that by their dynamic nature they will differ from case to case.

The study in itself posed a number of tensions when it came to relating the experiences of the individuals concerned to existing theories. Whilst some of the theories had obvious resonances with the experience of those interviewed, there were other areas which were far less compatible. From the standpoint of the factors involved in making meaning of the events and reactions associated with child sexual abuse, I wanted to produce a model which could be applied to all three groups I had studied. I wanted a model that allowed for individual differences. The model by Spaccarelli (1994) moved in the direction I was seeking. It permitted a variety of factors to be involved and acknowledged individual differences in coping and outcomes. That model, I felt, had applicability for others involved in assisting a survivor, but did not move into exploring how interaction between participants might also exert an effect upon outcomes.

Another strong influence on my thinking was the strand suggested by Laing and Esterson (1964) concerning the need to study not only the individuals within a group, but also the relationships within a group, and the group as a system. This focus on relationships and systems became linked with the whole notion of storytelling and the ways in which reality is constructed. The notion of the co-construction of reality, as evidenced in some of the methodological literature (e.g. Jorgenson 1991), is operating within the developing awarenesses of any who seek to understand a situation.

Despite both research findings and media coverage over the last decade, which have increased the stock of knowledge about this area, some of the stereotypes, debunked by such research, were still apparent within the understandings of abuse encountered by those in my study. It seemed that an experience which challenged an individual's existing stereotypes was a catalyst to understand more, or to challenge practice. Hence the final strand to my thinking was the narrative technique advocated by those such as Parry (1991) who suggest that meaning is dynamic and capable of being reframed.

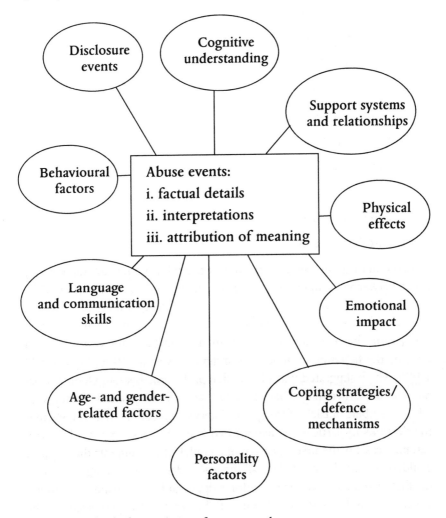

Figure 7.1 Individual construction of response to abuse

I wanted to produce a model which could indicate how the factors involved in any individual's understanding might be linked to, and influenced by, the reactions and understanding of others. The first diagram (Figure 7.1) demonstrates some of the areas that may influence both understanding and the making of meaning of events for an individual, be they survivor, mother, teacher or indeed any other who becomes involved in dealing with the situation. The factors are listed here, and later in the chapter are explored and used in different scenarios to demonstrate their relevance. Whilst these factors are isolated in this list, they do not exist in isolation and are essentially interactional. They are:

1. Cognitive understanding

2. Support systems and relationships

3. Physical effects

4. Emotional impact

5. Coping strategies and defence mechanisms

6. Personality factors

7. Age- and gender-related factors

8. Language and communication skills

9. Behavioural factors

10. Disclosure events.

The second diagram (Figure 7.2) moves into exploring how interaction may occur between the individuals involved in responding to the abuse. The notion that support and understanding could exist at a variety of levels was an attractive one, but it very quickly became apparent that such a situation could easily become idealistic rather than attainable. This was confirmed both by the literature on mother blaming (e.g. Caplan 1990; Sommerfeld 1989), which suggested that all too often professionals should look at what mothers do rather than where they fail, and by the research findings, in which members of each of the groups interviewed could reflect on whether their actions in particular situations had been the 'best way' to deal with certain areas. So, the first limitation of a model which suggests that support could, or should, be available at all the levels identified as being affected in the first diagram is that it may reinforce opportunities for blame and guilt – which, as has been shown, is one of the reactions experienced by the different groups in response to abuse. In terms of this study, if, as has been

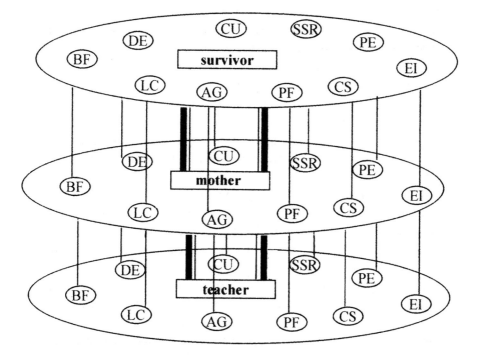

Figure 7.2 Idealised construction of meaning

argued earlier, some survivors are searching for the 'perfect' mother, such a model implies that ideal support can exist. This prescriptive model could serve to undermine what some of the mothers in the study have achieved, and it could reinforce the teachers' feelings of anxiety about 'doing the wrong thing'.

The second area which is not encompassed by this diagram is the dynamic nature of relationships and understanding. If this diagram is seen as a cake stand, it implies that there is potential for lasting understandings within certain areas, both for the individuals concerned and interpersonally.

This is open to doubt. Members of the different groups spoke of changing relationships and changes to understanding. Rosenhead (1990), dealing with problem solving, speaks of how participants within a system can be 'customers, actors and problem owners' (p.15). In the current model, it would seem that this might be a useful distinction. If a customer is defined as one who receives something, an actor one who does something and a problem owner one who wrestles with something, it can be seen that this balance might shift between participants when dealing with abuse. One survivor (taking a customer role) talks of how her first counsellor (actor role) was sympathetic and very understanding, but how a subsequent counsellor (problem owner) was firmer and moved the survivor away from dependency (customer) towards autonomy (actor or problem owner). A mother (actor) talks of 'the sticking plaster approach' to her child's (customer) problems and her realisation that there were other ways to respond (problem owner). A teacher describes her positive rewarding response (actor) to a survivor (customer role), which produced unacceptable dependency on her. A model based on fixed areas of understanding may produce a tendency to maintain roles rather than move towards change. There is hence a danger in stasis.

If the diagram in Figure 7.2 is seen as a carousel, which allows for movement in which understandings change, there is perhaps still too rigid a structure. Understandings may not correspond in the way that this aspect of the model would suggest and yet, as Rosenblatt *et al.* (1991) argue in relation to bereavement, support not perceived as useful by helpers may be interpreted positively by those affected. Hence the model needs to have cognisance of areas of interaction without predicting linear linkages, or the need for them. One of the factors revealed by recent studies, according to an internet source (Redwood 1997), suggests that sexual abuse is too often medicalised and treated as a condition, rather than acknowledged as an experience which can lead to a wide variety of differing outcomes.

The idealised construction of understanding does not allow for problematical interactions, or a range of differing needs, and it is argued that how these affect those involved needs to be acknowledged. It would seem therefore that the third diagram (Figure 7.3) allows for the more dynamic nature of interaction between factors by limiting predictability. This model is based on the assumption that aspects of the construction of meaning of abuse, both personally and interpersonally, affect outcomes. The model is based on the notion of the juggler balancing plates on sticks. The plates depend on equilibrium, however precarious, with the different factors weighted in some way to achieve this. Such weighting may exist in any, or all, of the areas but a change in one area may necessitate an adjustment in others before equilibrium is regained. In the worst case, the plate may topple and have to be rebalanced before it is able to spin again.

This model allows for the fact that plates may be able to spin for long periods with bizarre or distorted forms of equilibrium – very far from perfect or ideal – and apparently function normally. The catalyst to change comes from a variety of sources. It may be triggered by one of the players, by all of them or by external factors. The box in the diagram, which exerts momentum on the spinning plates, can operate from any subsequent event, action or reflection. This can include failure to act, a non-event or an apparently unconnected situation that forms some sort of trigger.

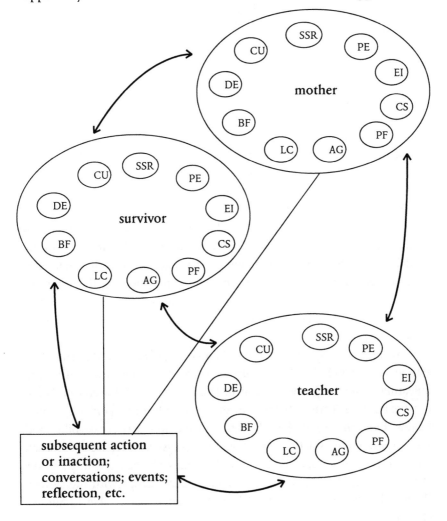

Figure 7.3 Interactional construction of response to abuse

Hence, in my study a survivor believing that all fathers behaved to their children as hers did continued to function accordingly (no action, no challenge, equilibrium maintained). A later realisation that this was not the case, prompted by recurrent dreams and flashbacks (subsequent event, challenge, disturbance of equilibrium), caused a revisiting of the assumptions of normality (cognitive understanding) built over years, and a shedding of the denial (defence mechanism) that had allowed her to dissociate the daytime father from his night-time practices.

A mother knew her husband was a drunkard (cognitive understanding) and rationalised (defence mechanism) much of his violence, including his children's fear of him, as related to that. A subsequent incident (challenge, disturbance of equilibrium) that challenged this belief and led to a disclosure from her daughter caused her to revisit aspects of her construction of her family's reality.

A teacher had never questioned that some children did not share her happy, supportive childhood (cognitive understanding) until she was party to a case conference (subsequent event – challenge, disturbance of equilibrium). Whilst she had read of underprivileged children, this event provided a connection between her understanding and her emotions. Each of these three cases will be explored in greater detail in the next section to demonstrate the workings of the model.

The model is intended to be neither judgemental nor prescriptive. It does not suggest that certain factors will be dealt with before others, neither does it imply that all factors will affect all of those involved. The ten areas of the model are not intended to be definitive; it is likely that in different cases different areas may be involved. Even if this is not the case, the argument centres on the fact that meanings have to be negotiated and constructed within each of the areas concerned and that this is a dynamic rather than a static process.

Lewin (1952) argued for a cyclical process of change, in that change is effected by an individual or group learning something new, and thence unlearning something already learned. This is followed by the consolidation of what has been learned, before a further cycle of learning (and unlearning) begins. Berg and Smith (1988) note a distinction between stability and resilience. Stability is defined as the ability of a system to regain equilibrium after a disturbance; resilience is seen as the means whereby an entity absorbs change or disturbance, whilst maintaining relationships with the system. Potentially, the entity becomes less stable, but is better able to survive changes.

It is here that the notion of cycles of abuse may be criticised. If a victim is seen as damaged, and hence likely to inflict damage, this reduces the opportunity to value the strengths and resilience of many of those affected. Those who never face problems may never have the opportunity to learn from those events. It is not the fact of being abused which should produce stigma, it is the lack of understanding or support from wider communities that is often culpable.

It became apparent when talking to those involved in the different samples that their thinking and reactions to abuse were subject to change, or the possibility of change. However, such change could be risky and painful, and, on occasion, it was likely that they would revert to earlier forms of coping. It seemed that change could operate in any one of a number of areas and that the need for change could be triggered by a variety of factors which could be either intrapersonal or interpersonal. The model, therefore, needed to reflect this dynamic frame, whilst allowing for the possibility that change might happen in some areas of its ambit but not in others. It is also possible, using this sort of layout, to visualise the way in which other clusters of interaction may impact on each of those involved – so that the model would more easily accommodate networks of support for any of the parties involved and could reflect how wider interactions might impact upon the relationships of those regarded by this study as its central core. To demonstrate the model in action, I will now deal with three cases in the light of the factors identified.

Three stories

Though the research did not deal with connected cases, three unconnected stories will be juxtaposed to demonstrate the operation of the model in different instances taken from the study. The survivor was one of a family of ten children. She had been sexually abused by her father since the age of two and subsequently by her brothers and other men brought into the house. Her brothers and sisters alike were abused by her parents, and she had had an under-age pregnancy to a member of her family. Her mother had delivered and disposed of the baby. She alleged that the baby was left out on a cold night either before or after it had been killed; the body was found by the police years later. At the time of the interviews, she had received four years of counselling. She was also currently involved in police investigations, as she was concerned about the possibilities of her nieces being abused by members of her family.

The mother was aware that other families could be, and were, different from her marital base. She rationalised many of the problems she experienced as resulting from her husband's alcoholism and violent temper. She was aware that her husband's sexuality involved violence and that he was interested in pornography, but did not connect any of these understandings with the possibility that this could extend to her children. At the time of the interviews, her family had been through the process of police investigations, her ex-husband had pleaded guilty to offences against her children, and she had undergone counselling herself.

The teacher was in her first teaching job. Although she had some textbook knowledge of disadvantaged children, she had no experience of dealing with children in this sort of situation. Her family was middle class, caring and supportive, and the tutor group she had been given were perceived to be similar. Her discovery of a sexually abused child in her group led to her needing counselling herself to deal with the issues it raised for her.

The initial categories juxtapose these three cases and explore them using the areas of the model. The following analysis demonstrates that some interesting possibilities and potential problem areas emerge if the three cases are explored in terms of the compatibilities and tensions that might have been present had the three individuals been connected.

Cognitive understanding (Table 7.1)

This area of the model is concerned with the knowledge the person has about the subject. This may be theoretical knowledge, or information acquired from stereotypes or myths surrounding the area, or may be the perceptions gained by previous experience. It provides the knowledge base against which a person makes sense of the events involved and which allows them to be defined for the individual. Whilst, for some potential players in an interaction, such knowledge may remain relatively unchallenged until a specific incident demands a re-evaluation, for others the knowledge itself is constantly evolving. Such 'knowledge' may be flawed, as in Briere's (1989) abuse continuum, but it forms the base on which the individual is currently operating. Indeed, Himelein and McElrath (1996) argue that healthy functioning can coexist with distorted cognitions of reality and that this is sometimes a factor in resilience.

Table 7.1 Cognitive understanding	
Survivor experience	There was no memory of ever being warned not to mention what happened at home. Sexual abuse was normal, not something which could be changed or stopped – simply what happened to everyone.
Mother experience	Sexual abuse was something which happens to some people, but not in her experience. Her husband was alcoholic and violent, and often sexually cruel to her but she had no conception that this could be happening to her children.
Teacher experience	Middle-class families are supportive, loving and caring. Some children who do not come from families like this are treated differently. Sexual abuse causes a certain package of symptoms; it is linked to cycles of abuse.
Survivor–mother views	Mother would expect survivor to be aware of norm of sexual behaviour and be able to differentiate. Survivor saw abusive events as unwanted but normal.
Survivor–teacher views	Teacher would be aware that sexual abuse might happen to this child as she is from a disorganised family. Survivor would see teacher as an authority figure to be avoided.
Mother–teacher views	Mother and teacher might agree on the type of child likely to be abused. Teacher unlikely to assume this mother's child might be abused.
Problem areas	Assumptions of who is, or is not, abused. Expectations of child's knowledge of 'normality'.

Support systems and relationships (Table 7.2)

This area involves those with whom any player can discuss or not discuss events. It encompasses the nature of the assistance which is, or is not, on offer to an individual and includes their ability to relate to others. The nature of this support may vary from personal, family or community relationships to organisational or professional support. This includes not only the physical resources, or lack of resources, an individual can use, but is linked to their perceptions of the motives and role of such people. For example, if an individual has a damaged pattern of attachment (e.g. Alexander 1992), not only may support relationships be lacking, but they may also be perceived as unlikely to be beneficial should they exist.

Table 7.2 Support systems and relationships	
Survivor experience	Family relationships are close and predictable. Sexual matters not discussed. The Catholic influence is strong and there is fear of authority. Survivor has no awareness of other possibilities. Teachers, priests and police are all regarded as authorities to be avoided.
Mother experience	Mother has and expects little support from her husband. She was distanced from friends before marriage both by moving from area and by her husband's behaviour towards them. At work she has support from colleagues. She lives in a geographically isolated home. She supported and defended her children.
Teacher experience	Teacher was in the first month of a new job. She had contact by phone with her family and was living with her fiancé. Some colleagues were supportive, some unknown – but she believed in the possibility of finding support. Her family was caring and supportive.
Survivor–mother views	Mother would assume her child felt supported and able to confide in her. Survivor unaware of possibilities for support. Belief that her parents cared for her.
Survivor–teacher views	Teacher would assume child was supported by parents. May have some concerns about this family. Survivor would not see teacher as possible source of support.
Mother–teacher views	Mother and teacher might agree on likelihood of support by parents as the norm. Teacher likely to identify with this mother and assume similarities with own experience.
Problem areas	Interpretation of support. Assumptions about who needs or gives support.

Physical effects (Table 7.3)

This area involves the physical effects that may have been caused by the abuse, or by having to deal with it. The physical effects upon a survivor may be short-term, long-term or linked to psychological symptoms. Such symptoms may also become linked to judgements about the relative severity of the abuse. Likewise, the physical appearance of a survivor may produce assumptions about their responsibility for events or the veracity of what they allege. Draucker (1992) and Hall and Lloyd (1993) note the importance of allowing survivors physical space and of appreciating how such actions as sudden movements might affect them. The area can likewise be closely linked to behaviour.

Table 7.3 Physical effects	
Survivor experience	Pain, occasional marks of physical violence on face – particularly when one brother involved. Pregnancy and morning sickness at age 12.
Mother experience	Violence towards self, children suffered from stomach upsets and exhibited signs of fear of father.
Teacher experience	More affected by hearing of a child who had been treated violently in addition to sexual abuse. Physical revulsion at details in case conference.
Survivor–mother views	Survivor often dirty and ill-kempt, some signs of violence on face, under-age pregnancy. Mother likely to act in this situation – mother affected by physical signs.
Survivor–teacher views	Survivor attended school during under-age pregnancy. Teacher likely to act in this situation. Teacher repulsed by violence.
Mother–teacher views	Mother and teacher would both seek to protect a child who showed physical signs of abuse or neglect.
Problem areas	Likelihood that action will be dependent on physical signs – invisibility of some survivors.

Emotional impact (Table 7.4)

The emotional impact of the abuse may produce differing reactions at different times and in different people. The emotions involved may vary and range from anxiety to anger. In some instances, there may be no apparent emotion – perhaps where emotional deadness has been used as a defence mechanism. Emotional reactions, or the lack of them, may be differently constructed by different parties. Herman (1992) notes that trauma can disconnect normal function. The range of survivor reactions can be from highly emotional with little memory of events, to detailed memories with no emotional reaction.

Table 7.4 Emotional impact	
Survivor experience	Portrayed very little emotion in recounting events – linked to earlier defence mechanism. Described how her mind was currently revealing further details to her – some anxiety about the unpredictability of this.
Mother experience	Afraid of husband in some moods, belief in her ability to protect children from his violence shattered by the subsequent disclosure. Described not knowing how to feel about an experience like this.
Teacher experience	Nightmares and sense of inability to accept what had happened to a known child. Frightened by own feelings, guilty about lack of understanding of case conference and the procedures. Intimidated by those in authority at school.
Survivor–mother views	Survivor unemotional in describing events. Emotion suppressed in order to cope. Mother has emotional reponse to abuse of children.
Survivor–teacher views	Survivor unemotional about abuse but often problematical at school. Teacher likely to probe disruptive behaviour.
Mother–teacher views	Mother and teacher both likely to exhibit emotional response to abuse as response to effect on child and on self.
Problem areas	Potential for misinterpreting lack of, or excessive, emotions in connection with abuse.

Coping strategies and defence mechanisms (Table 7.5)

This concerns how those involved deal with the information or experiences they have had. A wide range of possibilities is identified in the literature (e.g. Draucker 1992; Hall and Lloyd 1993; Herman 1992). Again, different strategies may be perceived differently by survivors, or by other people involved. For example, promiscuity may be perceived less sympathetically than minimisation (where a survivor plays down what has happened). A child who is well behaved or a high achiever may not be perceived as having this sort of problem. Varia, Abidin and Dass (1996) suggest that survivors who use minimisation may be less able to protect their self-esteem than those who are more open about what has happened. Ironically, minimisation may also lead other people to perceive such survivors as coping more effectively. Perrott *et al.* (1998) note linkages between coping style and both mental health and subsequent relationships with others – another area in which factors in this model interact.

Personality factors (Table 7.6)

The individual characteristics of those involved may again affect how they deal with events, or respond to others who become involved. This may have links to the type of symptoms exhibited or to the defence mechanisms employed. It may have an impact on disclosure and on the degree of support made available. Both the characteristics of resilient survivors (e.g. Wolin and Wolin 1995) and the conditions which might foster resilience (e.g. Esparza 1993; Gilgun 1991) are debated in the literature.

Age- and gender-related factors (Table 7.7)

When a survivor is very young, or very old, there will be different interpretations formed by those involved about the meaning of the event. There is a possibility that some age groups attract less sympathetic treatment than others (e.g. Hooper 1992) and that some groups are perceived to be at greater risk than others (e.g. Glaser and Frosh 1988). The literature suggests that male survivors are less likely to be identified (e.g. Mendel 1995). Feiring *et al.* (1999) also note that adolescents are likely to both feel more shame and report less support than younger children.

Table 7.5 Coping strategies and defence mechanisms

Survivor experience	Denial, dissociation of daytime and night-time perceptions of father. Rationalising her experience as normal. Eventual quest for help when flashbacks became severe.
Mother experience	Minimising of own experiences, compartmentalising of events in order to continue with relationship and combine belief in sanctity of marriage with events. Belief in her ability to protect her children. Eventually her realisation of some aspects of her children's situation caused her to leave her husband to improve this. She reported disclosure to the police as soon as it occurred. She asked for counselling support after the conclusion of the court case.
Teacher experience	Her response was to seek for more information, and to gain support from teacher at school. She undertook personal counselling followed by counselling course in order to be better equipped to deal with subsequent cases should they arise.
Survivor–mother views	The survivor practised denial, was disruptive and challenging. Mother tended to be shy and reserved.
Survivor–teacher views	Survivor was truanting, disruptive and challenging. Teacher would be likely to challenge and probe such behaviour.
Mother–teacher views	Mother likely to be embarrassed by child's behaviour. Teacher likely to challenge it.
Problem areas	Potential for difficulties or alliances in this area. Child may be seen as a problem, rather than as a person with a problem.

Table 7.6 Personality factors	
Survivor experience	Bubbly extrovert, tended to question as an adult. Regarded as the challenger within the family. Badly behaved at school.
Mother experience	Fairly shy and private person, loyal.
Teacher experience	Extrovert and practical, a preference for action rather than reflection.
Survivor–mother views	Loud, rebellious, extrovert. Mother quiet, introverted.
Survivor–teacher views	Both extrovert – potential for alliance or clash.
Mother–teacher views	May be differences in style. Mother may not find it easy to confide in this teacher.
Problem areas	Possibility for better understanding between survivor and this teacher than teacher and this mother.

Table 7.7 Age- and gender-related factors	
Survivor experience	Female from disorganised family. Very young at age of onset.
Mother experience	Middle-class family, one male, three females. Children between 6 and 13 at times of disclosure.
Teacher experience	Child involved female and middle class – existing beliefs unlikely to locate abuse within this group.
Survivor–mother views	This female survivor was abused from age 2. This mother would be unlikely to believe abuse a possibility at this age.
Survivor–teacher views	The teacher, young and female, may hold views about age or gender of likely victims.
Mother–teacher views	Teacher and mother are both likely to be shocked by age of survivor. This mother was older than this teacher, hence may be unlikely to talk to her.
Problem areas	Perceptions of likely victims, or of potential sources of support. Babies, males or older girls perhaps less likely to be seen as victims.

Language and communication skills (Table 7.8)

The ability of a survivor to communicate the nature of the problem may influence outcomes, as may the ability of an individual to demonstrate understanding and comprehension (e.g. Hooper 1992). In my study, a survivor claimed that there may be assumptions about the veracity of a story if emotions are not apparent, and a mother spoke of assumptions made about her motives because her ability to communicate was of a high standard.

Table 7.8 Language and communication skills

Survivor experience	The standard of education of this family was low. There was no discussion of sexuality to provide vocabulary for this area, bodies were regarded as 'filthy' and not discussed. There was scope for misunderstanding if an attempt at disclosure had been made.
Mother experience	High awareness of vocabulary, her children were taught anatomical names for parts of the body. She believed in answering their questions about sexual matters. She was aware of her children's fear but not in tune with reasons.
Teacher experience	Awareness of vocabulary hampered by stereotypes about victims.
Survivor–mother views	Survivor has poor vocabulary for emotional or sexual matters. Mother likely to expect own child to have vocabulary – likely to listen and be aware of a problem.
Survivor–teacher views	Differences in vocabulary. Teacher likely to talk to child and to listen. Different styles used with groups and individuals.
Mother–teacher views	Mother and teacher likely to be able to communicate in comparable language.
Problem areas	Interpretation of what is being said. Need for acute communication skills and plenty of opportunities to talk or listen.

Behavioural factors (Table 7.9)

Behaviour may be affected by abuse events (e.g. Hooper 1992), or by having information about such events (Johnson 1992). The behaviour may apparently be directed against people other than those responsible (e.g. Hall and Lloyd 1993) – or may be very different in different contexts (e.g. Herman 1992).

Table 7.9 Behavioural factors	
Survivor experience	Often dirty and ill-kempt, likely to truant from school, regarded as a liar.
Mother experience	Children produced no problems at school, tendency to be compliant, average to high levels of achievement.
Teacher experience	Revised views of victim behaviour after case – resulting in change of tactics when dealing with disruptive children.
Survivor–mother views	Survivor rebellious and challenging, truancy, attention seeking. Mother likely to attend to symptoms and seek help but to become anxious.
Survivor–teacher views	Teacher likely to spend time with this pupil but problems with discipline likely.
Mother–teacher views	Mother and teacher likely to equate problems with overt behavioural problems.
Problem areas	The quiet, or compliant, child is less likely to be noticed by either.

Disclosure events (Table 7.10)

The willingness or ability of those concerned to believe and act upon a disclosure may have an impact on other factors in the model. The degree of support or consultation afforded to the person concerned may affect subsequent interactions in this connection (e.g. Wyatt and Mickey 1987).

Table 7.10 Disclosure events

Survivor experience	Memory of talking to mother about father and being met with incomprehension. Regarded as liar by family but social services, counsellors and police listened.
Mother experience	Believed own children at disclosure, though very upset by detail and own perceived lack of awareness.
Teacher experience	Disturbed by details, uncertain of how to respond – this was at case conference, not with survivor.
Survivor–mother views	Survivor unlikely to disclose. Mother likely to believe child if disclosure made.
Survivor–teacher views	Teacher likely to suspect, may probe to obtain disclosure. Survivor may not disclose.
Mother–teacher views	Mother and teacher likely to be supportive of disclosure but unlikely to involve each other.
Problem areas	Children who disclose in veiled ways or who do not fit expected patterns.

This sort of analysis would yield different results for each change which was made in terms of the cases used. It is just this complexity and difference which the model seeks to address. Whereas Orr (1995) has argued there is no right way to address these issues, there are improvements that can be incorporated into general levels of understanding.

Areas of tension for the groups involved

The model has attempted to demonstrate the variety of areas of intrapersonal and interpersonal operation that may be involved in those dealing with child sexual abuse. The areas have been defined and have been expanded through exploring cases.

The following analysis (Table 7.11) is based around a case incident which happened since the conclusion of the original study. This involved a small school that became involved in a sexual abuse case. The perpetrator was in a position of authority in the school. When the incidents for which he was responsible came to court, it was found that he had been abusing children in his care for more than 15 years. Clapton, Lonne and Theunissen (1999), commenting on a similar case in Australia, note that the needs of those involved can be diverse and that small communities can often be particularly resistant to help.

I have analysed the case and the potential responses of some of those affected by it through applying the model suggested in this chapter. My information is based on newspaper reports and a discussion with only one teacher from the school. Although this does not provide the actual personal insights of those involved, it does draw upon a real incident and the reported repercussions it had. Within this scenario, I also propose to pose questions to enable the reader to assess their possible reaction within the given situation.

Table 7.11 Analysis of small school case study

1. Cognitive understanding

Pupil	Aware that what was happening was wrong but aware of potential consequences of telling. Aware of the power of this man both within the school and with parents.
Parent	'Knows' this teacher. Regards him as a 'good' teacher. Aware of his professional standing and its implications for status. Aware of own status in relation to his man. Aware that sexual abuse happens (this may be linked to stereotypical views of who abuses or who is abused) – unlikely to suspect it in this situation as the teacher has been in post for 20 years. Knows what child has alleged.
Teacher	Knows and respects this colleague. Aware that this man has some 'idiosyncrasies'. Possibly feels that this man sometimes is more familiar with children than he would be – but could this man do this? Knows this colleague is in a senior position. Aware that an allegation has been made. Knows the child. Has had some training about the procedures for dealing with an allegation.
You	What do you know about abuse and abusers? What do you assume about your colleagues? Would you know how to deal with an allegation about a colleague?

Table 7.11 continued

2. Support systems and relationships	
Pupil	The pupil is experiencing abuse by this man. He is frightened and confused. Because of the role this man holds within the school and its community, the pupil is isolated from sources of support as he is likely to be aware of some of the impacts of disclosure – perhaps by the way he has been groomed – and may feel that he would not be believed.
Parent	The parent may believe that the support systems within the school would prevent any risk of abuse – after disclosure is unlikely to trust his or her own judgement about support again. If a single parent, may be very unsure of where to turn.
Teacher	The teacher may have difficulty accepting that this has happened, and may find it difficult to talk about this issue as it involves failure to protect the child, a concept enshrined within the career of which he is part – what has happened to 'in loco parentis' here? May be caused to rethink safeguards and procedures within the school context.
You	Could you ask for help when something went wrong personally or professionally? Would this be perceived as inefficiency or not coping? Would you perceive others in this way? Alternatively, could you have voiced concerns or would this have been seen as ridiculous or paranoid? Who could you approach with this sort of problem? What would happen if someone approached you?

Table 7.11 continued

3. Physical effects

Pupil	This child has been overeating and bed-wetting and has been acting aggressively towards both parents and teachers.
Parent	There is quite a degree of stress about the child and why he should be behaving like this, and a number of angry outbursts at the child before disclosure. The disclosure makes the parent feel as if things are not real. Sleep becomes broken and headaches are frequent.
Teacher	The teacher was physically sick when details of the abuse were discussed in the press. He found it difficult to sleep, was subject to nightmares and found that the physical side of a personal relationship was difficult because of the associations some of the behaviour carried.
You	How might you be affected? How might you perceive these symptoms in others, in the child, the parent? How might you be affected when others respond differently from you? Does this happen to a 'nice', clean, shy, well-dressed boy?

4. Emotional impact

Pupil	Frightened, confused and isolated from potential sources of support. The child may believe he has been bad, or is responsible. He may have some feeling of being specially chosen by the teacher and this may have made him feel superior to other children at the same time as being guilty about what he is doing. He may also have enjoyed aspects of what was done to him.
Parent	Disbelief that this teacher could have been doing what was alleged. As awareness that the allegation may be true grows, the parent is likely to feel anger, self-doubt and responsible that this has been done to his or her child without it being noticed.

Table 7.11 continued	
Teacher	Disbelief that this person could be involved. This may be replaced by a feeling of being duped and the accompanying guilt alongside the question of how everyone was duped. Lack of trust can generalise to others, did others; in authority know? This may impact on the school and wider community.
You	What would be the effect on you of discovering that a spouse, relative or colleague was an abuser? How might the emotional impacts of a discovery such as this affect your family, organisation or community?

5. Coping strategies and defence mechanisms	
Pupil	Frequent bouts of feeling 'unwell' leading to absences from school. Avoidance of certain areas in the school. In this case does disclose – a number of other pupils over the years had not disclosed, or had not been believed.
Parent	May be able to rationalise the causes for this behaviour without imagining that this was possible. After disclosure could assume that the child was fantasising, or lying. May attempt to minimise, or may channel anger into action. May need to talk when the child does not, or may not want to confront aspects when the child is ready to do so.
Teacher	May be able to rationalise the causes for this behaviour without imagining that this was possible. After disclosure could assume that the child was fantasising, or lying. May continue to try to believe that colleague could not do such a thing and that everything will be shown to be a mistake. May use denial to protect self against a feeling that he 'should have known'. May channel energies into learning more about this issue and push for more opportunities to talk amongst staff about suspicions, concerns or practice.
You	How would you cope? Would your tendency be to talk and act, or to mull over issues and bury them? If these two potential responses can be seen as two ends of a continuum ranging from denial and inaction to obsessional discussion of the subject and ill-considered action, where might you fall on this spectrum, and how might your method of response affect someone who responded differently?

Table 7.11 continued

6. Personality factors

Pupil	The child is badly behaved, noisy and has a tendency to be aggressive towards his peers and moody towards his teachers. He is regarded as difficult – this has sometimes been attributed to the fact that he is of mixed race.
Parent	The parent is comparatively quiet, regarded as a pleasant person. He or she shows interest in the child's education and is responsive to the concerns expressed by the school.
Teacher	The teacher is outgoing and intelligent, with a good sense of humour. He relates well to colleagues and is regarded as a capable member of staff.
You	How do you see others? How do you attribute personality characteristics to them? How do others see you? What would you expect from an abuser? How do you classify a 'bad' child? How might labels such as this prevent people from seeing other characteristics?

7. Age- and gender-related factors

Pupil	The pupil is male and under ten years of age. He is old enough to perceive that he is doing something 'wrong' and may feel some responsibility. Believes that this senior teacher knows what is right and what is good for him – aware of his power and authority. Is less likely than a girl to be perceived as a victim.
Parent	May regard the pupil as unlikely to be a potential victim. The abusing teacher may be perceived by parent as an authority figure within the community, who is unlikely to be seen as a potential abuser. Parent may think that girls are more at risk from abuse and may hold stereotype about likely abusers – even if there is cognitive awareness that men who work with children can abuse this is a step away from linking that possibility to this individual.
Teacher	May assume an older child would be able to seek support or disclose, or know how to handle the situation, especially if a programme such as 'Stranger Danger' had been used. Potentially similar responses to the parent.

Table 7.11 continued	
You	How do age and gender factors affect your thinking about who abuses and is abused? Would knowledge of the age or gender of a victim make you perceive abuse differently?

8. Language and communication skills

Pupil	The pupil may not have adequate language to describe what is being asked of him or done to him. The concepts of good and bad touch may be there but the abuser may have imposed another construction on these. The pupil may be too embarrassed to talk about aspects of what has been involved. There may be taboos on talking about bodily functions at home or at school.
Parent	There may be an adequate vocabulary but this may be perceived as a risqué subject, or not one which is openly dealt with at home.
Teacher	There may be no forum in school to discuss concerns, and sex education may not be on this school's curriculum – particularly difficult to remedy where a powerful player in such decisions is also a perpetrator. Teacher may not know how to facilitate a child who needs to talk about such issues or may prevent discussion which moves into this area. Hence a child may not be able to discriminate between what is salacious and what is not.
You	How can this area be made more open? What aspects of it do you find difficult? How could children be provided with opportunities to communicate problems connected with sensitive issues?

9. Behavioural factors

Pupil	Moody, sullen. This child can suddenly lash out and sometimes is quiet and 'sullen'.
Parent	Unsure of how to deal with child's outbursts. Has brought problems to the notice of the school – discussions may have excluded the child's perspectives or input.

Table 7.11 continued	
Teacher	Sees the child as a challenge. Tries to be fair to the child. Aware that child causes problems for other members of the class. Will be glad when child moves on to next class.
You	How do you interpret behaviour? Do you evaluate causes as well as courses of action? What sort of balance do you have to maintain between the demands of your role and an individual's needs? Could you handle behaviour differently? What alternatives do you have? What are your options for support in this connection?

10. Disclosure events	
Pupil	Pupil discloses during a lesson when being disciplined for hitting another child. Pupil is regarded as having 'a chip on his shoulder' and having the tendency to lie.
Parent	Unsure of what to believe as child has lied about things and been difficult before. Forced to revisit own knowledge and own construction of events and of the man involved. Understands the need to support the child.
Teacher	Forced to weigh word of difficult child against knowledge of colleague. Aware that children lie, but about *this*?
You	What would you do/feel/believe/set in motion? What would be of most help to you or any of the others involved in this situation?

Tensions and issues

This use of the model illustrates how the situation is dynamic and how it is evolving – it does depend not only on the characteristics of the individuals within it but also on what they know and think, and how they react. This is why procedures and structures are important, but why they can never be regarded as infallible. A theoretical knowledge of trends, procedures and likely outcomes can never sufficiently respond to the particular needs of an individual who is affected by a unique combination of circumstances.

The model points to cognitive understanding, and it is at this level that the differing levels of knowledge of those involved is addressed. Survivors pointed to the difficulties of dealing with others who had limited understanding of their situation despite, on occasion, having greater theoretical knowledge. In situations where theoretical knowledge was offered contrary to a respondent's own experience, it could have negative effects. Examples are the cases where a teacher had spoken of the sort of child who might be abused, and where a psychiatrist had suggested to a mother that her child would have permanent problems in connection with sexuality.

A number of survivors mentioned specifically that they did not realise that teachers might be able to help with their problems; such knowledge or awareness might have been beneficial. Teachers who were nominated people in connection with child protection tended to have recent training, but the likelihood of training for the other teachers in the sample, or how recent it might have been, was questionable.

Though the subject area is more regularly publicised than it was even ten years ago, many of the teachers in the sample were concerned about their own limited knowledge and worried that they might do the wrong thing. Several of this sample had possession of, or knew of, codes of practice for dealing with disclosure. They had less knowledge either of how to handle ongoing situations or of the effects of such situations on themselves or, in some cases, on other pupils in the school. Greater knowledge is available now than it was when many of the cases covered by the study occurred, but it would seem that myths and stereotypes still abound in this area. Survivors spoke of how this could impact on their lives and of their need to hide this aspect of their experience. Mothers anticipated blame for their perceived shortcomings and teachers spoke of colleagues who did not see that there was likely to be any incidence of child sexual abuse in their school. Some survivors felt that their knowledge could be better used than it was, and felt that they might be able to detect abuse more quickly than some of those responsible for this. Knowledge was an area which, for differing reasons, had provided challenges for all of the groups. The extent to which their knowledge was used, extended or valued is perhaps linked to another important issue, that of power.

Power issues can be seen to have had relevance at all levels within the study. Often, survivors had suffered from those in positions of power taking advantage of them. Subsequently, some of them associated power with the possibility of abuse and failed to acknowledge that power could be used positively, or in order to support them. Often, survivors perceived their mothers as powerless to assist them or to change situations, especially where the mothers were in difficult relationships of which the child was aware.

Sometimes this perceived powerlessness resulted in blame for the mother, sometimes it meant that survivors tried to protect mothers by failing to disclose their own problems. In some cases, teachers were seen as authority figures and thus not trusted; in another case, a school did not value a child's choice of confidante, thus disempowering both teacher and child. Teachers, likewise, could feel disempowered by lack of support or lack of knowledge when dealing with abused children, or could perceive that they had lost control of the situation and its potential outcome when others became involved. The medical and legal professions were seen as powerful in this context, although not all of those in the study believed that these bodies had the best interests of those involved as their primary concern.

Power could also link with roles and boundaries. Teachers who were in certain roles within a school could attempt to protect others from contact with difficult situations. Whilst survivors might disclose, or otherwise seek attention, in the school situation, teachers may need to balance the needs of other children, tasks or roles. There may be a tendency in all sections of the sample to associate certain behaviours with certain roles and to ascribe blame if these functions were not perceived to be carried out, sometimes leading to judgement rather than support.

The final area where tensions might occur was that of emotions. Again, this has a link to knowledge and stereotypes. Disruptive children might be noticed and helped or punished, whereas quieter ones might remain unobserved. Action may be taken more quickly on behalf of a disclosure by a normally compliant child than by one assumed to be a liar. The lack of emotion when describing horrific experiences may be seen as unconvincing by some. Survivors may choose to disclose to someone who responds inappropriately for their needs. Mothers may choose not to relay concerns to the school because of something a school official has said about this area. Teachers may not be thought as needing support because they seem to be coping, or not perceived as able to help a child because they might be too sympathetic or too emotional.

It would seem that any of these areas can contribute to children's needs not being met, or those involved being inappropriately supported. Those in the study had all learnt from their experiences. It seemed to me that these experiences, which could have formed a basis for improving practice, were often insufficiently valued. Some of what the respondents themselves recommended is included in the following chapter.

CHAPTER 8

Concerns, Issues, Recommendations and Conclusions

In this final chapter, I will explore various perspectives on how those dealing with child sexual abuse can be supported. Respondents' suggestions were conceptualised differently, both in terms of the perspective of the individual involved and of their role within the situations they describe. As has been established already, there are complexities and confusions which operate at a variety of levels when dealing with such an issue. The model developed in the previous chapter demonstrates how differing dimensions might impact upon those involved.

Concerns and issues identified by those in the sample

The search for answers and understanding was a theme mentioned by several of those I interviewed. Both survivors and mothers described a search for answers and outlined how they had attempted to solve the problems the abuse had caused them. Teachers were less likely to conceptualise the effects on them as a search for answers. Their response seemed rather to involve a revisiting of assumptions. The search for answers, for survivors and mothers, frequently involved long periods of reflection on issues of personal responsibility and feelings of guilt or blame. Indeed, in my sample several people had not completely resolved these issues.

It seemed that, if a teacher was fortunate enough to have well-structured mechanisms for support, such issues would be resolved comparatively quickly. It was where teachers were unsupported, or let down by existing provision, that they seemed to internalise some of the responsibility for the shortfalls of the system. Where this was the case, there was the potential for a sense of isolation which could mirror the experience of survivors and mothers and leave the individual involved with uncertainties about suitable sources of support for future purposes.

Various strategies were used to acquire understanding of the events which had taken place. These included consulting others – friends, family, colleagues or agencies ranging from counsellors and healthcare professionals to the church. Whilst support was possible from any, or all, of these sources, it rarely resolved the needs of the person concerned.

Support, whilst generally considered by those in the sample to be essential, was not in itself perceived as sufficient to resolve issues. Mothers and teachers could find themselves concurrently required to provide support and be in need of support. In either of these roles, they could experience difficulties or feel inadequate. Indeed, within the teacher sample, in particular, there was a sense in which teachers worried that their support may be inappropriate, or in some way damaging, if it was based on insufficient knowledge. Tsoukas (1994), writing of organisational behaviour, suggests that a distinction should be made between the concepts of ambiguity and uncertainty. He perceives that uncertainty can be reduced if knowledge and information about a problem are increased. Ambiguity, where meanings are open to alternative interpretations, is not subject to resolution in this way. I would argue that those coping with abuse issues often face both uncertainty and ambiguity. Support or training could reduce the uncertainty, although it seems that every individual will deal with the ambiguities differently.

Frequently, though for differing reasons, respondents eventually acknowledged that some sort of personal learning was central to rectifying issues in this connection. One strategy mentioned, by both mothers and survivors, was writing. Three survivors specifically said how by writing poetry, prose or diaries they had been able to reflect on their situations differently. In one instance, a survivor had commenced writing a book spurred on by her father's own success at publication, which she believed had denied large elements of her own story – her writing became an attempt to redress this balance. Mothers spoke both of writing letters to their children and of using diaries or prose to re-examine their perceptions of what had taken place. One mother, in particular, had been asked by her solicitor to write down her family problems. She describes how as she wrote...

> it seemed as if all the pieces started to link together and I realised what we'd been putting up with. I didn't know what he'd been doing with the kids at that point but I'd compartmentalised everything and not connected how he'd been treating me. I'd survived by keeping every incident separate and not thinking about them together.

The need to reflect upon and change strategies was mentioned by those in all areas of the sample. Several survivors spoke of the need to take charge of their own lives. Three mothers described the need to move beyond thinking that the abuse had permanently blighted the family or irreparably damaged the child. With few exceptions, teachers perceived that reliance on existing systems, or training, was often insufficient and in some instances, particularly where they had been let down, viewed such dependence as potentially harmful to both teacher and child. So, whilst support was regarded as important by all groups, it had to be support which addressed their current needs.

One area, mentioned by members of all sample groups, was how official procedures once implemented often seemed to assume a momentum of their own and move beyond the control of the initiator. This could result in making people who were already distressed feel increasingly powerless. Hence, a survivor spoke of the procedures which were actioned after she disclosed to the police and social services because she worried about what her abuser might be doing to his own children. This led both to problems with her own family and to explorations of her own situation, which she felt unready to examine at that juncture. Three mothers spoke of how elements of their previous relationships had been offered up for professional debate when they had acted upon information given by their children. Teachers mentioned procedures which neglected the needs of the child, or promises of anonymity which were not honoured.

Often, different areas of professional involvement with this problem were seen to be in conflict. The requirements of the legal, or social work, processes involved were not always regarded as aligned to the needs of others involved. Teachers, who could provide an interface between families and these groups, could suffer particularly from a dilemma in this connection, especially if they had had previous experience. Table 8.1 will examine the types of issues which arose for members of the different sample groups linked to the model devised in the previous chapter.

Table 8.1 Issues discussed by the sample groups

Area of the model concerned	Survivor	Mother	Teacher
Cognitive understanding	Why me? Beliefs about why abuse happened. Perception of self and others. Awareness of possibility of change.	Attributions of responsibility for abuse. Beliefs about effects of abuse. Knowledge of events. Expectations of the reactions of others.	Beliefs about abuse and abusers. Training about abuse. Knowledge of self and own family. Knowledge of family concerned.
Support systems and relationships	Awareness of existence of support. Awareness of need for support. Expectations of support. Perceptions of purpose of support.	Awareness of range of support available or of need for support for self or child. Expectations of support. Experience of support. Beliefs about potential of support. Beliefs about self as a source of support	Awareness of range of support available. Awareness of need for support for self or child. Expectations or experience of support. Beliefs about potential of support. Beliefs about self as a source of support or constraints on support.

Table 8.1 continued

Area of the model concerned	Survivor	Mother	Teacher
Physical effects	Awareness of impact of physical signs – perhaps unwilling to take PE lessons. Embarrassment about medicals. Poor standards of care in some survivors, no physical signs in others. Perhaps illness and absence from school. Perhaps signs of physical violence.	Interpretation of child's physical state, impact of own physical condition on awareness of others. Standards of care and awareness – degree of communication about perceived changes.	Awareness of possible signs and symptoms, and of possibility that these may not be present. Level of communication with child concerned. Opportunities for proximity to child, opportunities for discussion.
Emotional impact	Availability of range of emotional response – ability to convey emotion. Control of emotion versus control by emotion.	Own emotional awareness and range. Ability to detect emotion or convey emotional response. Difficulties of showing 'right' emotion to child at different times. Understanding of range of emotional responses to this area. Need to deal with positive and negative emotions from others.	Understanding of emotional response of self and others. Awareness of range of emotional response and ways in which own emotions may be involved. Need to be able to deal with emotional disturbance within a group of people.

Table 8.1 continued

Area of the model concerned	Survivor	Mother	Teacher
Coping strategies and defence mechanisms	Need to be able to employ range of coping strategies and to be able to change and progress.	May be difficulties where a mother needs to talk and a child does not, or vice versa. Difficulties when coping becomes shared.	Events may trigger personal issues for teachers. Survivors may need more support than one teacher can give. Problems of families within a school and coping with varying needs.
Personality factors	Likely to be differing effects on children of differing personality types.	May be difficulties where child's behaviour is unacceptable to parent. Likely to exacerbate existing difficulties.	Need for knowledge about likely effects. Behaviours may cause difficulties or offend. Teacher may need range of strategies.
Age- and gender-related factors	May not know that abuse is abusive. May believe/be told that this is normal. May be too embarrassed to reveal what has happened if it contravenes notions of what is right.	May not believe child is old enough to be a victim or may believe child seduced abuser. May be led to conclusions through behaviour.	May suspect abuse in very young children, e.g. sexualised behaviour – but proof is difficult. Assumption of promiscuity with older child. May have little knowledge of effects on certain groups, e.g. males or quiet middle-class children. Knowledge of stereotypes may be dated.

Table 8.1 continued

Area of the model concerned	Survivor	Mother	Teacher
Language and communication skills	May not have vocabulary or understanding to describe events, or name abuse for what it is. May have little knowledge of physical terminology or emotional vocabulary.	May have problems in discussing sexuality or may misinterpret message from child. May misinterpret child's meaning.	May have problems in discussing sexuality, may not share child's vocabulary in this area. May have to control subject matter when with other children. Little time to listen to obscure hints.
Behavioural factors	May alienate potential sources of help by 'bad' behaviour. May be shy and introverted and may not communicate readily. May misinterpret adults' motives.	May respond to behaviour rather than cause. May be the respondent of hurt and anger when experiencing personal difficulties. May not know how to respond.	May respond to behaviour rather than cause. May not have support mechanisms in school. May misinterpret behaviour, may not know how to respond.
Disclosure events	Fear of reprisals or blame. Anticipation or experience of response of others. Perceived or actual consequences.	Response to child and by child. Source of information. Ability to believe and act.	Response to child and by child or family. Ability to believe and act. Personal consequences. Previous experience may affect response.

As has been indicated earlier, only one of the survivors involved in the study had disclosed anything of her experiences to a teacher, although all seven had been abused during their school years. Mothers in the sample had in some cases sought help from teachers, and teachers had been involved in reporting their concerns, or dealing with parents as well as with survivors. Hughes (1993) found that mothers and teachers formed the principal groups responsible for reporting concerns about child abuse. Since the literature has noted the importance of mothers and teachers in supporting survivors and reporting abuse, it would seem important to examine what could be done to support them within these roles.

How might existing provision be improved?

A number of differing suggestions were made as to how provision might be improved. Since a school setting provides a potential meeting place for the three groups involved in this study, the ways in which schools might provide help will be the starting point of this discussion. Indeed, American research (Beasley and Christenbury 1991) suggests that school-based interventions are important and should be developed.

Survivors, in my study, had differing perceptions of how school might have supported them. The two oldest survivors did not perceive their own schools as a suitable forum for disclosure or help, although both felt that currently schools might be a good source of support. The younger survivors had mixed responses about the question of disclosing at school. One comments:

> When I look back at those school years from when I was 4 to when I was 12, I know, without any doubt, that I did everything to catch their attention. I cried out for help all the way through those school years and not one person ever said to me, 'What's wrong [X], why are you the way you are?' They just never did say – all they would say was, 'Well we're not surprised because you're just like your brother and your sisters before you.'

Those who mention school indicate that they feel it would not have taken much in the way of understanding from a teacher for them to have unburdened themselves of their problems. Whilst this is an adult reflection upon the situation and there may have been additional barriers present at the time of the abuse, the younger survivors' comments, like the one quoted above, are reminiscent of Blagg's point that the most damaged children are often the most naughty in adult terms (Wattam *et al.* 1989). Conversely, another survivor's description of her introversion at school indicates that it is not only the 'naughty' child who risks being misinterpreted. There seems to be some suggestion that teachers may construct certain explanations for a child's behaviour based on the meaning of a particular family within the school. One of the teachers in the sample indicated that some of her colleagues expected certain families to provide problems.

The degree of support available from schools depended very much on a variety of factors. At one level, a survivor or mother had to perceive that a teacher would respond to what was being said. The teacher concerned would probably have had to demonstrate a certain type of awareness, or an ability to listen, over some period of time. Such concern may have been demonstrated by the teacher asking a child a direct question about a change in mood or behaviour – it is worth noting that a single enquiry might be insufficient to prompt a child to talk. One teacher noted that children often presented problems to her in the guise that they were concerned about 'a friend'. A mother may test out a teacher's views by asking guarded questions and may proceed, or otherwise, after a number of such encounters. As has been suggested earlier, there is a considerable degree of risk involved in any disclosure. Those who have been poorly received in the past may have huge barriers to overcome in this connection. Two mothers discussed their experiences with teachers and the different ways in which behaviour was constructed by different teachers.

School counsellors were mentioned by two survivors. One did not know what they were for: 'I thought they were meant to be for if you were having problems with your work or something like that. I didn't know you could talk to them about personal problems or anything like that.' The other was unsure about wanting their involvement: 'At first I didn't want Miss [X] to know and thought I might be treated differently, but it wasn't like that, and in the end I thought she understood me more because she knew.' Not all of the survivors had felt supported by school, although, interestingly, the survivor who described her experiences at school in the most overtly damning language realised schools' potential for supporting children from families such as hers. She said:

> I felt like I was being 70 per cent abused at home and then I went to school for a second helping and it didn't help at all. Obviously, there was no hiding place, there was no sanctuary, there was nowhere to get away from it all, you know. So to be quite honest with you it was quite hard. It was making something that was quite hard to handle even more hard to handle.

She saw that school could provide a sanctuary and be a source of information to children that there were alternatives to what they were experiencing. She envisaged a scenario where trained survivors from a local community could talk to children and provide them with opportunities to talk. Mothers and survivors felt that more could be done to provide children with opportunities to talk over personal issues, although there was an awareness that this would need to be handled with sensitivity.

Practice in the educational organisations represented in the study varied considerably. In some, it seemed, there was no specific provision for children with problems to talk: form tutors or class teachers were the point of contact for pastoral issues – sometimes these people had little or no relevant training about either child sexual abuse or counselling skills. In others, there were counsellors, support groups organised through the auspices of remedial education, or networked linkages to support agencies within the community. The levels of support for all involved varied accordingly. Nevertheless, a common factor in each situation was the question of whether a child would feel sufficiently comfortable to be able to disclose, or to take advantage of whatever support was on offer. It seemed from what one teacher said that even other teachers within her school were not aware of all that took place under the guise of remedial education. If *they* did not know, did the pupils? Survivors often felt that there was no forum for them to discuss their feelings. Was it possible that others, like the three survivors who mentioned the difficulty of concentrating on school subjects when there were more pressing concerns or worries, could have made use of a forum for discussing these problems had they been aware of it?

Several survivors felt acutely disadvantaged by the way in which abuse had damaged their education. Their self-image had not only been damaged by the abuse, but the abuse had often perpetuated underachievement in terms of career opportunities. It seemed that opportunities for support needed to be suitably promoted by schools. One survivor spoke of how she had begged the school to let her return to sit her GCEs, only to be told that unless she was living at home she could not be considered.

Sex education was perceived to be a forum for introducing issues related to abuse by some mothers and survivors. It was commented on by most of the survivors. It could be double-edged, as comments from two survivors indicate:

Probably a teacher just thought that it was an embarrassing subject but I thought that they might know what had happened to me from the way I looked.

It was useful 'cos I got told about periods and stuff like that. Stuff my mother didn't talk about.

Some teachers tended to have worries about abuse being disclosed in a lesson if there were not facilities available to remove a child to talk in more privacy. One was actively planning a series of lessons around family issues which she hoped would prompt children to seek her out and talk. Experiences varied between one teacher who had been amazed by the level of support a junior school class had given to a survivor, and another's concerns about the pressures which hearing about a peer's abuse could put on other children.

Interestingly, survivors were more likely than teachers to mention the need for emotional education. Some felt that if people either had more education about how to relate to each other without resort to force or bullying, or were helped towards a better command of a vocabulary for resolving issues, there might be long-term improvements in how people treated each other. This may have been raised by this group for a number of reasons. Their personal experience may have sensitised them to the potential for improvement, whereas teachers' current workloads may have restricted their desire for further areas of responsibility. Indeed, one teacher expressed her view that preventive or parenting education would be useful but added that she had 'no idea how it could be fitted into the timetable'.

The final area through which the school environment could be improved for survivors was seen to be by the creation of better linkages to other agencies dealing with abused children. Some teachers perceived schools as a centre where families might be supported – often siblings were at the same school and the setting was more familiar to them than a specialist centre might be. Teachers wanted more active contacts with social services, the police and medical professionals involved in treating abused children. They wanted to feel that the process was child centred and less surrounded by secrecy. A 'known' social worker, with regular links to the school, was regarded as a valuable ally in this connection. Unless such linkages were in place, a child could come from treatment by a psychiatrist and proceed to behave badly in school – teachers felt that more information and more opportunity to help to prepare such a child would be useful to them.

Unfortunately, if the sort of provisions requested by those in the study were implemented, it is unlikely that the minimal costs suggested by

Hancock (DES Circular No. 4/88) would continue to be applicable. There is a certain irony in the message sent out by a great deal of research which suggests that teachers should trust their intuition (e.g. New 1993), or understand the limitations of their role (e.g. Oxley and Sanderson 1993). This would seem to partly mirror the role assigned to mothers, in that their support is expected but the facilities which might enhance such support are often lacking. It is worth noting that Redwood (1997) found no correlation between therapy for survivors and improved functioning the single most important factor in improvement was support for mothers. A school- or community-based support system may provide the most appropriate location for this. Local and accessible systems may furnish more effective support, even if they are largely self-help groups, than more distant professional organisations which often have long waiting lists.

The teachers, especially in primary education, spoke of the way in which they made relationships with the children concerned and worried about the fate of these children once they went to secondary schools or elsewhere. If the understandings of attachment theory (e.g. Bowlby 1988) and the need for bonding with a supportive adult are pursued in this connection, it may be that, in some cases, a teacher, or other school worker, could provide at least some measure of the support which is lacking for some children. If this is the case, there appears to be a real need for continued mechanisms for support by a trusted person after a child has moved to secondary school.

The message from those who had encountered the problem, either personally or professionally, was that there needed to be more openness, more people, more involvement and more opportunities for support.

Ideas for further support

> No person or group operates entirely out of a single view of reality ... Nothing happens 'where one is'; there is no action within a single reality for one's actions come from the interface of one view of reality with another. (McWhinney 1992, p.29)

McWhinney points to the intrinsic paradox of a world view which has at its polarities determinism and freedom. Such polarities would seem to be inherent in this research. There is a sense in which all of the participants want answers, want to do 'the right thing' and find 'the solution'. When dealing with a subject such as child sexual abuse, the desire for answers and solutions is seemingly paramount. This contains a weighty potential for failure and disappointment. It is difficult to argue against the need for procedures to protect children who are at risk, just as it is difficult not to look for blame when existing procedures are less than successful. Theorists want to isolate 'the causes' and 'the right treatment'. If the notion of multiple realities is pursued, the safeties of determinism are reduced. If prognosis is determined, choice is restricted. Or as May (1975) puts it: '...freedom and determinism give birth to each other. Every advance in freedom gives birth to a new determinism, and every advance in determinism gives birth to a new freedom.' (p.84.)

Dealing with the issues covered by this study involved many of the respondents in a realisation both of the limitations of existing provision and of the importance of individual response. My model, which provides for individual reactions and response, does not dismiss existing provision, it merely questions how it interfaces with individuals who become involved in the situation. The survivors who have realised that healing involves them in taking control of their own lives have attributed that element of meaning to the variety of devices or situations which they have encountered; others are still searching for the external which might contain the magical solution. Current legal and procedural measures provide a means of paying attention to protecting children, but it seems that those who have experienced these procedures feel that often individual needs are sacrificed to the demands of systems, and that frequently such individual needs remain unmet when procedures have been completed.

The consensus would seem to be that there is a need for better training. Education is seen by some in the sample as a potential route for change. One area which straddles the divide between longer-term education and current practice is the provision of a better understanding for survivors of how schools may be able to support them. This has implications for the degree of training which teachers get. A large number of the teacher sample felt that more information about how to handle difficult or sensitive personal issues should be included in teacher training provision. Since they were convinced that children would not inevitably seek out the best qualified person to help them, this may point to the need, as McLaughlin (1995) suggests, for counselling training to be incorporated for all teachers – as implied, the officially appointed people may not be those whom survivors choose to tell. The teachers who had access to professional networks of expertise were in the minority in this study, and it was certainly my reaction that the sort of practice available in some areas of the country should be made more generally available. This would have the dual purpose of supporting survivors and the teachers who deal with them.

The level of general training received by those in education was found to be low, or non-existent, and this could provide discomfort for survivors and mothers. The child who was supported at home might be able to cope with the effects of abuse without any additional support from school, but the child whose family was either not supportive or was unsure of how to obtain additional help could be disadvantaged if the school was unable to provide or suggest alternative sources of support. As mentioned earlier, how a teacher responds to tentative requests for support might colour the decision of a child or mother to confide further. Manion *et al.* (1996) suggest that the nature of support and its impact on survivors and their families should warrant further study.

According to Hooper (1992), the responsibilities placed upon a mother, consequent to the discovery of abuse, may be too great. A television documentary has hinted that current expectations on schools include roles previously played by family, social workers and church.[1] Similarly, I would argue that the burdens put upon teachers are often unacceptable in this connection. A system which is closely networked and which recognises the strengths of different parties in providing support may be the most appropriate way forward. Survivors have suggested that they themselves can be a resource. Similarly, it has been shown that mothers' groups can often provide the best support for other mothers. One of the most common grouses by those who attempted to gain support from professionals was that they 'did not know' what it was like to experience the event. The practice of using people with real-life experience, to support others similarly affected, has formed the basis of organisations like Cruse, which trains those who have suffered bereavement to counsel and assist others in a similar position.

The shroud of confidentiality which surrounds child abuse can be as detrimental as it is valuable. Survivors spoke of having to deny aspects of their existence to conform to expected norms; but, paradoxically, most were grateful that they did have this privacy. In a comparable context, Jamison (1995) speaks of how, as a professor of psychiatry, she had had to hide her own schizophrenia from her peers. One member of her own profession had received her disclosure, of her own illness, with a statement of his disappointment in her – she was not the person he had thought she was. She knew that publishing her story was a massive professional risk for her. Similarly, those in the sample had felt obliged to protect elements of their realities from those whose tendency was to judge them guilty by association. In this connection, education to broaden public awareness of who might be affected by abuse would be beneficial. Such education could diminish some

1   'A lesson for us all' – documentary about Banbury School. BBC2, 23 March 1997.

of the sensationalism that can result from the media coverage of abuse, and would be valuable so long as it did not minimise or trivialise the real and continuing concerns of those affected.

My research has indicated that it is not only those in the compulsory sector of education who would benefit from training to equip them to deal with disclosure or the task of supporting survivors. There is the suggestion that for some survivors leaving home may be a catalyst for disclosure. Hence teachers in the further and higher education sectors, to who disclosures might be made, would also benefit from support and training.

As has been mentioned by other studies, it is not only training which is involved – it is often the provision of opportunities for attitudes to change. Such changes in attitudes may have an impact on process issues and hence on practice. It would seem that there is a need for a greater sharing of knowledge about dealing with child sexual abuse, both in valuing and respecting the insights of those who have experienced abuse, and in providing an extended system of networking with those who have expertise in particular aspects of the problem. Such a network could form the basis of empowering others to deal with the issues they face.

The need for standardised procedures and individual requirements for support could best be combined through employing the sort of 'simultaneous loose–tight properties' advocated by Peters and Waterman (1982) in their description of factors contributing to excellence in organisations. Here, certain central core values were tightly controlled and individual decentralised units dealt with day-to-day issues. However, this freedom would only be effective if it was properly resourced. Whilst tight control can be argued to be important to protect a child from risk and to deal with documentation or legal process, flexibility could be incorporated to provide individual support for those involved.

It would seem that greater availability of information is an essential. There is a growing body of international information available on the internet concerning child sexual abuse. Since there is currently a political impetus to give all schools access to the internet, this is one potential means of acquiring expert information, and facilitating support-group networking. Practice across the small number of organisations covered by this study varies massively. The internet could be a useful means of connectivity and a means of informing and improving practice.

The notion of providing community-based homework clubs may provide an alternative location where survivors could continue to meet with those who had supported them in earlier education. If teachers' roles were changed, in line with changing labour practices, to include a casework element, coupled with some flexibility in hours, recognition might be able to be given to an element of support or counselling work as part of their role. Certainly, if this were the case, it might be possible to involve survivors and their families more actively in the provision of ongoing support. My study reveals a need for support to continue, or at least be available on request, after legal or social work investigations have been completed. The all too common perception that need for support stems from weakness or culpability needs to be challenged by organisations as well as individuals.

As education, in all sectors, moves towards more regional- or community-based provision, it is possible that there may be scope for better linkages between institutions and hence the creation of local centres of support. The interagency co-operation required by such legislation as the Crime and Disorder Act 1998 is one potential starting point for this. A further development which offers promise, in terms of both empowerment and recognition of the needs of individuals, is the development of Family Group Conferences where families are encouraged to assess their own mechanisms for support and to evolve their own solutions (Lupton 1998).

It has been argued that Finkelhor and Browne's (1988) model of traumagenic dynamics can be applied to members of each of the groups concerned. The applicability of this model seems to relate to the degree of help, training or support available in the case of teachers in the current study. It has been argued elsewhere that adverse effects on survivors and mothers can be limited by the provision of individual support (e.g. Hooper 1993) or mothers' support groups (Priest *et al.* 1993). It would seem that support networks for professionals are equally important here. As has been argued, organisational cultures can often disempower professionals working in this difficult area by perceiving their concerns, or their requirements for support, as misplaced.

Whilst the experiences of those in the study were all different, there were ways in which what happened to them had resonances with existing theory. Vestiges of the myths identified by those such as Kelly (1988) or Driver and Droisen (1989) had coloured their experiences. Herman's (1992) recognition of the existence of judgemental attitudes even in friends or family was evident for several of them. Teachers could, as Chamberlain (1993) feared, be restricted by their own perceptions of who might be affected by abuse, and such perceptions could prevent survivors from speaking out. This had the potential for restricting sources of support. As trust has been shown to be both difficult for survivors to achieve and important in recovery, this is an important issue and one which is worthy of further research.

There were specific areas which, though applicable to each of the groups, in some measure seemed to have especial importance for one of the groups. Survivors, it appeared, could be particularly affected in the area of their emotional response to situations. As has been noted earlier, there could be problems in gaining sympathy or even being believed if their emotional response was perceived to be 'wrong' by others. It may be that further research on how emotions are perceived and handled might be appropriate in this connection. As argued earlier, there may also be differences in emotional literacy which can affect outcomes. Not only might an improved linguistic base assist survivors, it may be that schools could also allow more opportunities for the exploration of emotional responses to situations. Mothers have been noted in the existing literature as being likely to be faced by enormous stress when the abuse of their child is disclosed or discovered. It is felt that current descriptors of stress can fail to acknowledge how traumatic such an experience can be. More discussion of the problems a mother may face and greater opportunities for support would help to reduce the isolation and sense of blame that can exacerbate a mother's situation at such a time. This would support the mother as an individual. It has also been demonstrated that a supportive mother–child relationship is a very important factor in recovery, though a further suggestion in this connection will be made later in this conclusion. Finally, teachers – particularly those in small schools – expressed a need for better training and support. Generally, teachers had not been prepared for the personal effects of dealing with abuse. It was felt that better training and support would have reduced their uncertainties while allowing them to cope more easily with the ambiguities inherent in identifying or dealing with abuse.

In several areas, there was an element of contradiction to existing theoretical expectations. Two of the survivors continued to have what they described as close relationships with their mothers. As mentioned earlier, this is generally perceived to contribute to healing (Esparza 1993; Gilgun 1991). However, in one family the actual abuse had been discussed and in the other it had not. Although no generalisation can be drawn from only two cases, it seems from this that the development of shared meaning about the abuse and how it has affected those involved might be important ingredients in the healing process. This links with the claims made for storytelling as part of therapy (Parry 1991; Shepherd 1990). Further research on mother and survivor pairs who had successfully dealt with abuse could be valuable to explore this possibility.

The research drew attention to the ongoing nature of relationships, be they with mothers or with teachers, and this sense of dynamism, with its attendant questions of the making of meaning from events or behaviour, led to the construction of the model described in Chapter 7. The ongoing aspect of relationships is one which is seen as important, especially in relation to attachment theory. If a survivor forms a trusting relationship with a teacher and such a relationship has the potential to assist recovery, the current practice of severing connections with primary teachers may exacerbate difficulties for some survivors. If, as has also been suggested by the literature, secure attachment reduces the likelihood for abusive relationships in general, an educational system which provided a role model for this might contribute to effective preventive education. Once again, further research would be warranted to assess the feasibility or value of alternative strategies for support.

The discussion of the model involved a suggestion that respondents play different roles in the situations they handle. The discussion used the terms 'customer', 'actor' and 'problem owner' after Rosenhead (1990). It is felt that these terms could be explored further in connection with the way in which any of those involved deal with abuse issues. Just as transactional analysis has argued that in healthy functioning the adult, parent and child roles are all available to the individual, so it may be that part of dealing with abuse calls upon those involved to develop their understanding of when the customer, actor and problem owner roles are most appropriate – not only for themselves, but also for others involved in situations. This can partially link with McLaughlin's (1995) discussion on counselling skills in school, but also has resonances with the mother in the study who reached the awareness that her child had to make mistakes in order to learn rather than be protected and hence restricted.

Another issue that I had identified as being important was that I wanted to explore respondents' thoughts on what more could have been done to help and support them, and how they thought provision could be improved for others. An area warranting further exploration in this connection, I feel, is how survival or support issues are affected by organisational cultures and beliefs. This study has pointed to differing practice, understanding and levels of training in schools or colleges; survivors have also mentioned their experiences in relation to work or to the provision of healthcare services. All three groups have noted difficulties with how official interventions have been handled. Some of these difficulties stem from ambiguities encapsulated within the disparate aims of official bodies, but others are based on uncertainties. Such uncertainties (for example, in the case of the teacher who did not know the purpose of the 'at risk' register) could be reduced by a more consistent programme of training for teachers.

Important issues from this study include:

- the role and responsibilities of parents and the assumptions which may lead to blame

- the perceptions of which children are at risk from abuse and the behaviours which might suggest this

- a fresh consideration of needs for support in the aftermath of abuse and a reassessment of how various agencies might contribute to such support

- an assessment of how policies and practices interact and how systems impact on the uncertainties inherent in the situations people face.

Theoretical perspectives have broadened considerably in the past decade; what seems to be important now is to find a means of extending the awareness and understanding of those who are most likely to have to deal with day-to-day issues in connection with surviving and survivors. The model has proposed that interactions and interpretations should be explored in terms of a wider base than the more usual knowledge- or skills-based methods. It would be interesting, and potentially valuable, to explore its applicability with a wider group of people. I hope that this book may allow that to happen.

The debate moves on; the whole issue has become more visible, though, sadly, stereotypes remain in the consciousness of many who may be faced with coping with abuse. Whatever the future makes of the issue, I feel that for everyone who is abused there needs to be a fresh awareness, from all who become involved, of the impacts, difficulties and issues being experienced by that individual.

References

AACAP (1996) 'Responding to child sexual abuse.' American Academy of Child and Adolescent Psychiatry, <http://www.psych.med.umich.edu/web/aacap/>.

Abrahams, N., Casey, K. and Daro, D. (1992) 'Teachers' knowledge, attitudes and beliefs about child abuse and its prevention.' *Child Abuse and Neglect 16*, 229–238.

Adamakos, H., Ryan, K., Ullman, D.G., Pascoe, J., Diaz, R. and Chessare, J. (1986) 'Maternal social support as a predictor of mother–child stress and stimulation.' *Child Abuse and Neglect 10*, 463–470.

Agyeman, S. (1996) 'Of fingers and crosses out of Calgary – Readings and mis-readings of (symbolic) con(texts)(tacts).' Paper presented at the 14th International Conference of the Standing Conference on Organisational Symbolism, University of California, Los Angeles, July.

Ainsworth, M.D. (1962) 'The effects of maternal deprivation: A review of findings and controversy in the context of research strategy.' *Deprivation of Maternal Care: A Reassessment of Its Effects*. Public Health Papers 14. Geneva: World Health Organization.

Ainsworth, M.D., Bell, S.M. and Stayton, D.J. (1971) 'Individual differences in strange situation behavior of one-year-olds.' In H.R. Schaffer (ed) *The Origins of Human Social Relations*. London: Academic Press.

Alexander, P.C. (1992) 'Application of attachment theory to the study of sexual abuse.' *Journal of Consulting and Clinical Psychology 60*, 2, 185–195.

Alexander, P.C. (1993) 'The differential effects of abuse characteristics and attachment in the prediction of long-term effects of sexual abuse.' *Journal of Interpersonal Violence 8*, 3, 346–362.

Alexander, P.C., Anderson, C.L., Brand, B., Schaeffer, C.M., Grelling, B.Z. and Kretz, L. (1998) 'Adult attachment and longterm effects in survivors of incest.' *Child Abuse and Neglect 22*, 1, 45–61.

Arcana, J. (1981) *Our Mothers' Daughters*. London: The Women's Press.

Archard, D. (1993) *Children: Rights and Childhood*. London: Routledge.

Arnold, R.P., Rogers, D. and Cook, D.A.G. (1990) 'Medical problems of adults who were sexually abused in childhood.' *British Medical Journal 300*, 6726, 705–709.

Askham, J. (1984) *Identity and Stability in Marriage*. Cambridge: Cambridge University Press.

Back, S. (1998) 'Child sexual abuse: Victim age, victim gender, and observer gender as factors contributing to attributions of responsibility.' *Child Abuse and Neglect 22*, 12, 1239–1252.

Baker, A.W. and Duncan, S.P. (1985) 'Child sexual abuse: A study of prevalence in Great Britain.' *Child Abuse and Neglect 9*, 4, 457–467.

Barber, B.K. (1996) 'Parental psychological control: Revisiting a neglected construct.' *Child Development 67*, 3296–3319.

Barker, P. (1992) *Basic Family Therapy*, 3rd edition. Oxford: Blackwell Science.

Barrett, M.J. (1993) 'Mothers' role in incest: Neither dysfunctional women nor dysfunctional theories when both are explored in their entirety.' *Journal of Child Sexual Abuse 2*, 3, 141–143.

Bauman, Z. (1993) *Postmodern Ethics*. Oxford: Blackwell.

Beasley, C. and Christenbury, N.J. (1991) 'School-based interventions with child and adolescent victims of sexual abuse.' Paper presented at the Annual Meeting of the Mid-South Educational Research Association, Lexington, KY, November.

de Beauvoir, S. (1958) *Memoirs of a Dutiful Daughter*. New York: Harper Torchbooks.

Beitchman, J.H., Zucker, K.J., Hood, J.E., Da Costa, G.A., Akman, D. and Cassavia, E. (1992) 'A review of the long-term effects of child sexual abuse.' *Child Abuse and Neglect 16*, 1, 101–118.

Benishek, L.A. and Morrow, S.L. (1995) 'Positive coping strategies developed by survivors of childhood sexual abuse.' *Directions in Mental Health Counselling 5*, 234–239.

Benoit, D. and Parker, K.C.H. (1994) 'Stablility and transmission of attachment across three generations.' *Child Development 65*, 1444–1456.

Bentovim, A., Elton, A., Hildebrand, J., Tranter, M. and Vizard, E. (1988) *Child Sexual Abuse within the Family: Assessment and Treatment*. London: Wright.

Berg, D.N. and Smith, K.K. (1988) *The Self in Social Enquiry*. London: Sage.

Berne, E. (1964) *The Structure and Dynamics of Organisations and Groups*. New York: The Free Press.

Berne, E. (1983) *Games People Play*. Harmondsworth: Penguin.

Besharov, D.J. (1990) *Recognising Child Abuse*. New York: The Free Press.

Birns, B. and Meyer, S.L. (1993) 'Mothers' role in incest: Dysfunctional women or dysfunctional theories?' *Journal of Child Sexual Abuse 2*, 3, 127–135.

Bloom, B.S., Engelhart, M.D., Furst, E.J., Hill, W.H. and Krathwohl, D.R. (1956) *Taxonomy of Educational Objectives*. London: Longman.

Bogat, G.A. and McGrath, M.P. (1993) 'Preschoolers' cognitions of authority, and its relationship to sexual abuse education.' *Child Abuse and Neglect 17*, 5, 651–662.

Bolton, J. (1993) 'Child abuse.' Paper presented to the Middlesbrough Diocese Conference, 6 April.

Borduin, C.M. and Henggeler, S.W. (1987) 'Post-divorce mother–son relations of delinquent and well-adjusted adolescents.' *Journal of Applied Developmental Psychology 8*, 273–288.

Boulton, M.G. (1983) *On Being a Mother*. London: Tavistock.

Boushel, M. and Noakes, S. (1988) 'Islington Social Services: Developing a policy on child sexual abuse.' *Feminist Review 28*, 150–157.

Bowlby, J. (1951) *Maternal Care and Mental Health*. London: HMSO.

Bowlby, J. (1965) *Child Care and the Growth of Love*. Harmondsworth: Penguin.

Bowlby, J. (1987) 'Attachment.' In R.L. Gregory (ed) *The Oxford Companion to the Mind*. Oxford: Oxford University Press.

Bowlby, J. (1988) *A Secure Base*. London: Routledge.

Brannen, J. (1988) 'The study of sensitive subjects.' *Sociological Review 36*, 552–563.

Braun, D. (1988) *Responding to Child Abuse: Action and Planning for Teachers and Other Professionals*. London: Community Education Development Centre in association with Bedford Square Press.

Braun, M.J. and Berg, D.H. (1994) 'Meaning reconstruction in the experience of parental bereavement.' *Death Studies 18*, 105–129.

Bray, M. (1991) *Poppies on the Rubbish Heap: Sexual Abuse, the Child's Voice*. London: Canongate.

Breckenridge, J. and Baldry, E. (1997) 'Workers dealing with mother blame in child sexual assault cases.' *Journal of Child Sexual Abuse 6*, 1, 65–80.

Briere, J.N. (1989) *Therapy for Adults Molested as Children*. New York: Springer.

Briere, J.N. (1992) *Child Abuse Trauma*. London: Sage.

Briggs, F. and Hawkins-Russell, M.F. (1994) 'Follow up study of children 5–8 years using child protection programmes in Australia and New Zealand.' *Early Child Development and Care 100*, 111–117.

Briner, R.B. (1997) 'Feeling for the facts.' *People Management 3*, 1, 34–37.

Brown, J.A.C. (1969) *Freud and the Post-Freudians*. London: Penguin.

Butler-Sloss, Dame E. (1988) *Report of the Inquiry into Child Abuse in Cleveland 1987*. London: HMSO.

Campbell, B. (1993) 'Families the minister did not see.' *The Independent*, p.28, 29 September.

Caplan, P.J. (1990) 'Making mother blaming visible: The emperor's new clothes.' *Women and Therapy 10*, 1–2, 61–70.

Carroll, L., Miltenberger, R.G. and O'Neill, H.K. (1992) 'A review and critique of research evaluating child sexual abuse prevention programs.' *Education and Treatment of Children 15*, 4, 335–354.

Carter, B. (1993) 'Child sexual abuse: Impact on mothers.' *Affilia 8*, 1, 72–90.

Chamberlain, R. (1993) 'Critique of the definitions and ideologies of child sexual abuse that underpin current educational texts for teachers.' *Pastoral Care in Education 11*, 2, 29–34.

Christiansen, J.R. and Blake, R.H. (1990) 'The grooming process in father–daughter incest.' In A.L. Horton, B.L. Johnson, L.M. Roundy and D. Williams (eds) *The Incest Perpetrator – A Family Member No One Wants to Treat*. London: Sage.

Christo, G. (1997) 'Child sexual abuse: Psychological consequences.' *The Psychologist 10*, 5, 205–209.

Christopoulos, C. and Dell, S.B. (1989) 'Dimensions of the mother–child relationship as predictors of social competence.' Paper presented at the biennial meeting of the Society for Research for Child Development, Kansas City, April.

Clapton, S., Lonne, R. and Theunissen, C.A.G. (1999) 'Multi-victim sexual assault: A case study in rural Australia.' *Child Abuse and Neglect 23*, 4, 395–404.

Collins, M. (1992) 'The mind as combat zone.' *The Guardian*, p.2, 4 November.

Conte, J. (1990) 'The incest offender: An overview and introduction.' In A.L. Horton, B.L. Johnson, L.M. Roundy and D. Williams (eds) *The Incest Perpetrator – A Family Member No One Wants to Treat.* London: Sage.

Courtois, C. and Sprei, J. (1988) 'Retrospective incest therapy for women.' In L. Walker (ed) *Handbook on Sexual Abuse of Children.* New York: Springer.

Crase, D.R. and Crase, D. (1996) 'Responding to a bereaved child in the school setting.' Unpublished paper, University of Memphis.

Cullingford, C. (1997) 'Parents from the point of view of their children.' *Educational Review 49*, 1, 47–55.

Dally, A. (1982) *Inventing Motherhood.* London: Burnett Books.

Danica, E. (1989) *Don't – A Woman's Word.* London: The Women's Press.

David, T. (1993) *Child Protection and Early Years Teachers: Coping with Child Abuse.* Buckingham: Open University Press.

Deblinger, E., Hathaway, C.R., Lippmann, J. and Steer, R. (1993) 'Psychosocial characteristics and corelates of symptom distress in nonoffending mothers of sexually abused children.' *Journal of Interpersonal Violence 8*, 2, 155–168.

Deblinger, E., Lippmann, J., Stauffer, L. and Finkel, M. (1994) 'Personal versus professional responses to child sexual abuse.' *Child Abuse and Neglect 18*, 8, 679–683.

Dempster, H.L. (1993) 'The aftermath of child sexual abuse: Women's perspectives.' In L. Waterhouse (ed) *Child Abuse and Child Abusers: Protection and Prevention.* London: Jessica Kingsley Publishers.

Department of Health (1991) *Working Together under the Children Act 1989.* London: HMSO.

Draucker, C.B. (1992) *Counselling Survivors of Child Sexual Abuse.* London: Sage.

Driver, E. and Droisen, A. (eds) (1989) *Child Sexual Abuse: Feminist Perspectives.* London: Macmillan.

Duane, E.A. and Bridgeland, W.M. (1992) 'Child abuse: Social Services faces the schools in Michigan and Ontario.' *Education 112*, 3, 352–359.

Dziuba-Leatherman, J. and Finkelhor, D. (1994) 'How does receiving information about sexual abuse influence boys' perceptions of their risk?' *Child Abuse and Neglect 18*, 7, 557–568.

Easton, S. and Van Laar, D. (1995) 'Experiences of lecturers helping distressed students in higher education.' *British Journal of Guidance and Counselling 23*, 23, 173–178.

Eckenrode, J., Laird, M. and Doris, J. (1993) 'School performance and disciplinary problems among abused and neglected children.' *Developmental Psychology 29*, 1, 53–62.

Elliott, M. (n.d.) *Why My Child?* Leaflet produced by Kidscape.

Elrod, J.M. and Rubin, R.H. (1993) 'Parental involvement in sexual abuse prevention education.' *Child Abuse and Neglect 17*, 4, 527–538.

Ennew, J. (1986) *The Sexual Exploitation of Children.* Cambridge: Polity.

Erooga, M. and Masson, H. (1989) 'The silent volcano: Groupwork with mothers of sexually abused children.' *Practice 1*, 24–41.

Esparza, D. (1993) 'Maternal support and stress response in sexually abused girls ages 6–12.' *Issues in Mental Health Nursing 14*, 85–107.

Faller, K.C. (1988) *Child Sexual Abuse: An Interdisciplinary Manual for Diagnosis, Case Management and Treatment.* London: Macmillan.

Faller, K.C. (1990) *Understanding Child Sexual Maltreatment.* London: Sage.

Famularo, R., Fenton, T., Kinscherff, R., Ayoub, C. and Barnum, R. (1994) 'Maternal and child posttraumatic stress disorder in cases of child maltreatment.' *Child Abuse and Neglect 18*, 1, 27–37.

Farmer, E. and Owen, M. (1995) *Child Protection Practice: Private Risks and Public Remedies, Decision-Making, Intervention and Outcome in Child Protection Work.* London: HMSO.

Faulkner, N. (1996) 'The sexual abuse recognition and non-disclosure inventory (Sarandi) for young adolescents – ages 12–15.' <http://www.cs.utk.edu/~bartley/faulkner/sarandi.html>.

Featherstone, B. and Fawcett, B. (1994/95) 'Feminism and child abuse: Opening up some possibilities.' *Critical Social Policy 42*, Winter, 61–80.

Feinauer, L.L., Callahan, E.H. and Hilton, H.G. (1996) 'Positive intimate relationships decrease depression in sexually abused women.' *American Journal of Family Therapy 24*, 2, 99–106.

Feiring, C., Taska, L. and Lewis, M. (1999) 'Age and gender differences in children's and adolescents' adaptation to sexual abuse.' *Child Abuse and Neglect 23*, 2, 115–128.

Fineman, S. (ed) (1993) *Emotion in Organizations.* London: Sage.

Finkelhor, D. (1984) *Child Sexual Abuse: New Theory and Research.* New York: The Free Press.

Finkelhor, D. (1986) *A Sourcebook on Child Sexual Abuse.* London: Sage.

Finkelhor, D. (1988) 'The trauma of child sexual abuse: Two models.' In G.E. Wyatt and G.J. Powell (eds) *Lasting Effects of Child Sexual Abuse.* London: Sage.

Finkelhor, D. and Browne, A. (1988) 'Assessing the long-term impact of child sexual abuse: A review and conceptualisation.' In L. Walker (ed) *Handbook on Sexual Abuse of Children.* New York: Springer.

Fivush, R. (1989) 'Exploring sex differences in the emotional content of mother–child conversations about the past.' *Sex Roles 20*, 11–12, 675–691.

Flaskas, C. and Humphreys, C. (1993) 'Theorizing about power: Intersecting the ideas of Foucault with the "problem" of power in family therapy.' *Family Process 32*, 35–47.

Foucault, M. (1981) *The History of Sexuality Volume 1: An Introduction.* Harmondsworth: Penguin.

Francis, J. (1992) 'Safe and sound.' *Community Care*, 946, 24–25.

Frost, L. (1987) 'Teaching children to say no.' *The Guardian*, 6 January.

Furniss, T. (1984) 'Conflict-avoiding and conflict-regulating patterns in incest and child sexual abuse.' *Acta Paedopsychiat 50*, 299–313.

Furniss, T. (1991) *The Multi-professional Handbook of Child Sexual Abuse.* London: Routledge.

George, C. (1996) 'A representational perspective of child abuse and prevention: Internal working models of attachment and caregiving.' *Child Abuse and Neglect 20*, 5, 411–424.

Gerwert, U., Thurn, C. and Fegert, J. (1993) 'Wie erleben und bewältigen Mütter den sexuellen Missbrauch an ihren Töchtern?' *Praxis der Kinderpsychologie und Kinderpsychiatrie 42*, 8, 273–278.

Giarretto, H. (1982) 'A comprehensive child sexual abuse treatment program.' *Child Abuse and Neglect 6*, 263–278.

Gibbons, J., Gallagher, B., Bell, C. and Gordon, D. (1995) *Development after Physical Abuse in Early Childhood: A Follow-up Study of Children on Protection Registers.* London: HMSO.

Gibson, R.L. and Hartshorne, T.S. (1996) 'Child sexual abuse and adult loneliness and network orientation.' *Child Abuse and Neglect 20*, 11, 1087–1093.

Gil, E. (1983) *Outgrowing the Pain.* California: Lauch Press.

Gilgun, J.F. (1991) 'Resilience and the intergenerational transmission of child sexual abuse.' In M. Quinn Patton (ed) *Family Sexual Abuse: Frontline Research and Evaluation.* London: Sage.

Gill, M. and Tutty, L.M. (1997) 'Sexual identity issues for male survivors of childhood sexual abuse: A qualitative study.' *Journal of Child Sexual Abuse 6*, 3, 31–47.

Gillham, B. and Thomson, J.A. (1996) *Child Safety: Problem and Prevention from Preschool to Adolescence.* London: Routledge.

Glaser, B.G. and Strauss, A.L. (1964) 'Awareness contexts and social interaction.' *American Sociological Review 29*, 5, 669–679.

Glaser, D. and Frosh, S. (1988) *Child Sexual Abuse.* London: Macmillan Education.

Goddard, C. and Hiller, P. (1993) 'Child sexual abuse: Assault in a violent context.' *Australian Journal of Social Issues 28*, 1, 20–33.

Goffman, E. (1959) *The Presentation of Self in Everyday Life.* London: Penguin.

Goldner, V. (1985) 'Feminism and family therapy.' *Family Process 24*, 31–47.

Goldstein, E. (1992) 'Sexual abuse in families: The mother–daughter relationship.' *Issues in Ego Psychology 15*, 1, 63–64.

Goleman, D. (1996) *Emotional Intelligence.* London: Bloomsbury.

Golombok, S. and Fivush, R. (1994) *Gender Development.* Cambridge: Cambridge University Press.

Gomes-Schwartz, B., Horowitz, J. and Cardarelli, A. (1990) *Child Sexual Abuse: The Initial Effects.* London: Sage.

Gordon, L. (1989) *Heroes of Their Own Lives: The Politics and History of Family Violence.* London: Virago.

Grant, L. (1994) *Sexing the Millennium: A Political History of the Sexual Revolution.* London: HarperCollins.

Greene, R.M. and Leslie, L.A. (1989) 'Mothers' behavior and sons' adjustment following divorce.' *Journal of Divorce 12,* 2–3, 235–251.

Grice, E. (1994) 'Shere Hite blames men for failings in the family.' *The Daily Telegraph,* 19 February.

Gudykunst, W.B. (1994) *Bridging Differences: Effective Intergroup Communication.* London: Sage.

Hall, L. and Lloyd, S. (1993) *Surviving Child Sexual Abuse,* 2nd edition. London: Falmer.

Hallett, C. (1995) *Interagency Coordination in Child Protection.* London: HMSO.

Hallett, N. and Gorman, P. (1994) 'The secret crime.' *The Executive-Educator 16,* 3, 52–53 and 63.

Hancock, D.J.S. (1988) 'Working together for the protection of children from abuse: Procedures within the education service.' DES Circular No. 4/88.

Harris, A.B. and Harris, T.A. (1985) *Staying OK.* London: Pan.

Harris, T. (1978) *I'm OK, You're OK.* London: Pan.

Hawkins, N.G., Davis, R. and Holmes, T. (1957) 'Evidence of psychosomatic factors in the development of pulmonary tuberculosis.' *American Review of Tubercular Pulmonary Disease 75,* 5, 768–780.

Hendessi, M. (1992) *4 in 10: Report on Young Women Who Become Homeless as a Result of Sexual Abuse.* London: CHAR (now the National Homeless Alliance).

Herbert, M. (1993) *Working with Children and the Children Act.* Leicester: BPS Books.

Herman, J.L. (1992) *Trauma and Recovery: From Domestic Abuse to Political Terror.* London: Pandora.

Herman, J.L. and Hirschman, L. (1981) *Father–Daughter Incest.* Cambridge, MA: Harvard University Press.

Hetherton, J. (1999) 'The idealization of women: Its role in the minimization of child sexual abuse by females.' *Child Abuse and Neglect 23,* 21, 161–175.

Himelein, M.J. and McElrath, J.A.V. (1996) 'Resilient child sexual abuse survivors: Cognitive coping and illusion.' *Child Abuse and Neglect 20,* 8, 747–758.

Hinde, R.A. and Stevenson-Hinde, J. (1987) 'Implications of a relationships approach for the study of gender differences.' *Infant Mental Health Journal 8,* 3, 221–236.

Hoffman, L. (1988) 'A constructivist position for family therapy.' *The Irish Journal of Psychology 9,* 1, 110–129.

Hollows, A. (1992) 'Staying on course.' *Community Care,* 921, i.

Honess, T.M. and Lintern, F. (1990) 'Relational and systems methodologies for analysing parent–child relationships: An exploration of conflict, support and independence in adolescence and post-adolescence.' *British Journal of Social Psychology 29*, 331–347.

Honig, A.S. (1998) 'Attachment and relationships: Beyond parenting.' Paper presented at the Head Start Quality Network Research Satellite Conference, East Lansing, MI, August.

Hooper, C.A. (1992) *Mothers Surviving Child Sexual Abuse.* London: Tavistock/Routledge.

Hooper, C.A. (1993) 'An overview of current research.' Paper presented at NCH Conference, 19 November.

Hooper, C.A. and Humphreys, C. (1998) 'Women whose children have been sexually abused: Reflections on a debate.' *British Journal of Social Work 28*, 4, 565–580.

Hopson, B. (1981) 'Transition: Understanding and managing personal change.' In C.L. Cooper and P. Makin (eds) *Psychology for Managers.* London: The British Psychological Society and Macmillan.

Horsfall, J. (1991) *The Presence of the Past: Male Violence in the Family.* Sydney: Allen and Unwin.

Horton, A.L., Johnson, B.L., Roundy, L.M and Williams, D. (eds) (1990) *The Incest Perpetrator – A Family Member No One Wants to Treat.* London: Sage.

Hughes, S. (1993) *Study of Referrals of Child Sexual Abuse in the Hereford Area.* Report of the Hereford and Worcester Social Services Department.

Humberside County Council (1992) *Child Protection What You Can Do: Guide for Those Working in Educational Establishments.* Beverley: Humberside County Council.

Humphreys, C. (1997) 'Child sexual abuse allegations in the context of divorce: Issues for mothers.' *British Journal of Social Work 27*, 4, 529–544.

Hunt, M. (1993) *The Story of Psychology.* London: Doubleday.

Jackson, G. (1991) 'The rise of post-traumatic stress disorders: More disasters and more awareness of their consequences.' *British Medical Journal 303*, 6802, 533.

Jacobs, J.L. (1990) 'Reassessing mother blame in incest.' *Signs*, Spring, 500–514.

Jacobs, J.L. (1994) *Victimized Daughters: Incest and the Development of the Female Self.* London: Routledge.

Jamison, K.R. (1995) *An Unquiet Mind: A Memoir of Moods and Madness.* London: Picador.

Jewett, C. (1982) *Helping Children Cope with Separation and Loss.* London: Batsford Academic and Educational.

Johnson, J.T. (1992) *Mothers of Incest Survivors: Another Side of the Story.* Indianapolis: Indiana University Press.

Johnstone, H. (1993) 'Judge frees two men who had sex with 13-year-old.' *The Times*, p.7, 30 October.

Jorgenson, J. (1991) 'Co-constructing the interviewer/co-constructing "family".' In F. Steier (ed) *Research and Reflexivity.* London: Sage.

Kahn, T. (1994) 'Back to school for practical parenting.' *The Observer*, p.42, 30 January.

Kaufman, K.L., Harbeck-Weber, C. and Rudy, L. (1994) 'Re-examining the efficacy of child sexual abuse prevention strategies: Victims' and offenders' attitudes.' *Child Abuse and Neglect 18*, 4, 349–356.

Kelly, L. (1988) *Surviving Sexual Violence*. Cambridge: Polity.

Kelly, L. (1992) 'Outrageous injustice.' *Community Care*, 921, ii–iii.

Kelly, L., Regan, L. and Burton, S. (1991) *An Exploratory Study of the Prevalence of Sexual Abuse in a Sample of 16–21 Year Olds*. Child Abuse Studies Unit, Polytechnic of North London.

Kempe, R.S. and Kempe, C.H. (1978) *Child Abuse*. London: Fontana/Open Books.

Kenward, H. (1988) 'Child sexual abuse.' In P. Maher (ed) *Child Abuse: The Educational Perspective*. Oxford: Blackwell.

Kenway, J. and Fitzclarence, L. (1997) 'Masculinity, violence and schooling: Challenging "poisonous pedagogies".' *Gender and Education 9*, 1, 117–133.

Kirkwood, C. (1991) 'From the scars of survival to wisdom for change.' Unpublished doctoral thesis, University of York.

Kirkwood, C. (1993) *Leaving Abusive Partners*. London: Sage.

Kitzinger, S. (1978) *Women as Mothers*. Oxford: Martin Robertson in association with Fontana.

Klein, I. and Janoff-Bulman, R. (1996) 'Trauma history and personal narratives: Some clues to coping among survivors of child abuse.' *Child Abuse and Neglect 20*, 1, 45–54.

Knight, C. (1997) 'Therapists' affective reactions to working with adult survivors of child sexual abuse: An exploratory study.' *Journal of Child Sexual Abuse 6*, 2, 17–41.

Knut, S. (1997) 'Child-care personnel's failure to report child maltreatment: Some Swedish evidence.' *Child Abuse and Neglect 21*, 1, 93–105.

Kohler Riessman, C. (1993) *Narrative Analysis*. London: Sage.

Laing, R.D. and Esterson, A. (1964) *Sanity, Madness and the Family*. Harmondsworth: Penguin.

Lambeth Women and Children's Health Project (1993) *A Booklet for Mothers of Children Who Have Been Sexually Abused*. London: Oval Printshop.

Lee, R.M. (1993) *Doing Research on Sensitive Topics*. London: Sage.

Legge, K. (1995) *Human Resource Management: Rhetorics and Realities*. London: Macmillan Business.

Legge, K. (1996) 'Is HRM ethical? Can HRM be ethical?' Alec Rodger Memorial Lecture given at Birkbeck College, London, June.

Levy, G.D. and Carter, D.B. (1989) 'Gender schema, gender constancy and gender role knowledge: The roles of cognitive factors in pre-schoolers' gender-role stereotypic attitudes.' *Developmental Psychology 25*, 444–449.

Lewin, K. (1952) 'Group decision and social change.' In G.E. Swanson, T.N. Newcomb and E.L. Hartley (eds) *Reading in Social Psychology*. New York: Holt.

Liddle, A.M. (1993) 'Gender, desire and child sexual abuse: Accounting for the male majority.' *Theory, Culture and Society 10*, 103–126.

Lovett, B.B. (1995) 'Child sexual abuse: The female victim's relationship with her non-offending mother.' *Child Abuse and Neglect 19*, 6, 729–737.

Lupton, C. (1998) 'User empowerment of family self-reliance? The family group conference model.' *British Journal of Social Work 28*, 107–128.

Mac an Ghaill, M. (1994) *The Making of Men: Masculinities, Sexualities and Schooling.* Milton Keynes: Open University Press.

MacLeod, M. and Saraga, E. (1988) 'Challenging the orthodoxy: Towards a feminist theory and practice.' *Feminist Review 28*, 16–55.

MacLeod, M. and Saraga, E. (1991) 'Clearing a path through the undergrowth: A feminist reading of recent literature on child sexual abuse.' In P. Carter (ed) *Social Work and Social Welfare Yearbook 3*. Milton Keynes: Open University Press.

Maher, P. (ed) (1988) *Child Abuse: The Educational Perspective.* Oxford: Blackwell.

Main, M. and Weston, D. (1981) 'Quality of attachment to mother and to father: Related to conflict behaviour and the readiness for establishing new relationships.' *Child Development 52*, 932–940.

Manion, I.G., Mcintyre, J., Firestone, P., Ligezinska, M., Ensom, R. and Wells, G. (1996) 'Secondary traumatization in parents following the disclosure of extrafamilial child sexual abuse: Initial effects.' *Child Abuse and Neglect 20*, 11, 1095–1109.

Marks, J. (1994) *The Hidden Children: Secret Survivors of the Holocaust.* London: Book Club Associates.

Marris, P. (1986) *Loss and Change.* London: Routledge and Kegan Paul.

Mason, B. (1993) 'Towards positions of safe uncertainty.' *Human Systems: The Journal of Systematic Consultation and Management 4*, 189–200.

Massat, C.R. and Lundy, M. (1998) 'Reporting costs to nonoffending parents in cases of intrafamilial child sexual abuse.' *Child Welfare 77*, 4, 371–388.

Masson, H. and O'Byrne, P. (1990) 'The family systems approach: A help or a hindrance?' In The Violence Against Children Study Group (eds) *Taking Child Abuse Seriously*. London: Unwin Hyman.

May, R. (1975) *The Courage to Create.* New York: Bantam.

Maynard, C. and Wiederman, M. (1997) 'Undergraduate students' perceptions of child sexual abuse: Effects of age, sex and gender-role attitudes.' *Child Abuse and Neglect 21*, 9, 833–845.

Mazur, E. and Wolchik, S. (1992) 'The mother–child relationship and children's appraisals of negative divorce events.' Paper presented at the biennial meeting of the Southwerken Society for Research in Human Development, Tempe, AZ, March.

McCann, A.O. (1995) 'Changing attitudes: Child protection and abuse prevention in Cleveland primary schools.' Unpublished thesis, University of York.

McGuiness, J. (1995) 'Personal and social education: Pupil behaviour.' In R. Best, P. Lang, C. Lodge and C. Watkins (eds) *Pastoral Care and Personal-Social Education: Entitlement and Provision.* London: Cassell.

McLaughlin, C. (1995) 'Counselling in schools: Its place and purpose.' In R. Best, P. Lang, C. Lodge and C. Watkins (eds) *Pastoral Care and Personal-Social Education: Entitlement and Provision.* London: Cassell.

McLeod, J. (1996) 'The emerging narrative approach to counselling and psychotherapy.' *British Journal of Guidance and Counselling 24,* 2, 173–184.

McWhinney, W. (1992) *Paths of Change: Strategic Choices for Organisations and Society.* London: Sage.

Mendel, M.P. (1995) *The Male Survivor: The Impact of Sexual Abuse.* London: Sage.

Miller, A. (1990) *Banished Knowledge: Facing Childhood Injuries.* London: Virago.

Miller, A.C. (1990) 'The mother–daughter relationship and the distortion of reality in childhood sexual abuse.' In R.J. Perelberg and A.C. Miller (eds) *Gender and Power in Families.* London: Routledge.

Mills, J.C. (1988) 'Putting ideas into their heads: Advising the young.' *Feminist Review 28,* 163–174.

Minuchin, S. (1991) 'The seductions of constructivism.' *Networker,* September/October, 47–50.

Mitchell, J. (1974) *Psychoanalysis and Feminism.* Harmondsworth: Penguin.

Monck, E. (1991) 'Patterns of confiding relationships among adolescent girls.' *Journal of Child Psychology and Psychiatry and Allied Disciplines 32,* 2, 333–345.

Morrison, T. (1992) 'The emotional effects of child protection work on the worker.' *Practice 4,* 4, 253–271.

Muram, D., Rosenthal, T.L. and Beck, K.L. (1994) 'Personality profiles of mothers of sexual abuse victims and their daughters.' *Child Abuse and Neglect 18,* 5, 419–424.

Murray, K. and Gough, D.A. (eds) (1991) *Intervening in Child Sexual Abuse.* Edinburgh: Scottish Academic Press.

Nakashima, I. and Zakus, G. (1977) 'Incest review and clinical experience.' *Pediatrics 60,* 696–701.

Neate, P. (1992) 'Family circle.' *Community Care,* 954, 16.

Nelson, A. and Oliver, P. (1998) 'Gender and the construction of consent in child–adult sexual contact: Beyond gender neutrality and male monopoly.' *Gender and Society 12,* 5, 554–577.

Nelson, S. (1987) *Incest – Fact and Myth.* Edinburgh: Stramullion Press.

New, A. (1991) 'The school's role in supporting sexually abused children.' Unpublished thesis, University of Bristol.

New, A. (1993) 'Sexually abused children: The importance of the school's role in providing on-going support.' *Pastoral Care in Education 11,* 2, 21–28.

Newson, J. and Newson, E. (1989) *The Extent of Parental Physical Punishment in the UK.* London: Approach.

Norwich Consultants On Sexual Violence (1988) 'Claiming our status as experts: Community organising.' *Feminist Review 28,* 144–149.

O'Hagan, K. (1989) *Working with Child Sexual Abuse.* Milton Keynes: Open University Press.

O'Hara, M. (1988) 'Developing a feminist policy on child sexual abuse.' *Feminist Review 28,* 158–162.

O'Keefe, J., De San Lazaro, C., McArdle, P.A. and Cullen, J. (1992) 'The sexual abuse of children.' Paper commissioned by the Committee for Social Welfare of the Bishops' Conference of England and Wales.

Oakley, A. (1985) *Sex, Gender and Society* revised edition. Aldershot: Temple Smith/Gower.

Oakley, A. (1986) 'Feminism, motherhood and medicine – Who cares?' In J. Mitchell and A. Oakley (eds) *What is Feminism?* Oxford: Blackwell.

Olson, D.H., McCubbin, H.I., Barnes, H.L., Larsen, A.S., Muxen, M.J. and Wilson, M.A. (1989) *Families: What Makes Them Work.* London: Sage.

Olver, R.R., Aries, E. and Batgos, J. (1989) 'Self–other differentiation and the mother–child relationship: The effects of sex and birth order.' *Journal of Genetic Psychology 150,* 3, 311–321.

Orr, T. (1995) *No Right Way: The Voices of Mothers of Incest Survivors.* London: Scarlet Press.

Osborn, J. (1990) *Psychological Effects of Child Sex Abuse on Women.* Social Work Monograph. Norwich: University of East Anglia.

Oxley, B. and Sanderson, K. (1993) 'Child protection training for teachers.' *Child Abuse Review 2,* 203–206.

Parry, A. (1991) 'A universe of stories.' *Family Process 30,* March, 37–54.

Parton, C. (1990) 'Women, gender oppression and child abuse.' In The Violence Against Children Study Group (eds) *Taking Child Abuse Seriously.* London: Unwin Hyman.

Patten, S.B., Gatz, Y.K., Jones, B. and Thomas, D.L. (1989) 'Posttraumatic stress disorder and the treatment of sexual abuse.' *Social Work 34,* 3, 197.

Pearce, J.W. and Pezzot-Pearce, T.D. (1994) 'Attachment theory and its implications for psychotherapy with maltreated children.' *Child Abuse and Neglect 18,* 5, 425–438.

Pedler, M. (1986) *A Manager's Guide to Self Development.* London: McGraw-Hill.

Perelberg, R.J. and Miller, A.C. (eds) (1990) *Gender and Power in Families.* London: Tavistock/Routledge.

Perrott, K., Morris, E., Martin, J. and Romans, S. (1998) 'Coping styles of women sexually abused in childhood: A qualitative study.' *Child Abuse and Neglect 22,* 11, 1135–1149.

Peters, T.J. and Waterman, R.H. (1982) *In Search of Excellence.* London: Harper and Row.

Phillips, A. (1993) *The Trouble with Boys.* London: Pandora.

Phillips, M. (1993) 'The lost generation.' *The Observer,* 17 October, p.23.

Piachaud, D. (1984) *Around Fifty Hours a Week.* London: Child Poverty Action Group.

Pincus, L. and Dare, C. (1978) *Secrets in the Family.* London: Faber and Faber.

Porter, R. (1989) *Child Sexual Abuse within the Family.* London: Tavistock/Routledge.

Priest, M., Mockridge, L. and Clear, M. (1993) 'Working with mothers: In partnership for protection.' Humberside County Council/NCH Action for Children Evaluation Report.

Print, T.B. and Dey, C. (1992) 'Empowering mothers of sexually abused children – A positive framework.' In A. Bannister (ed) *From Hearing to Healing: Working with the Aftermath of Child Sexual Abuse.* London: Longman/NSPCC.

Quick, J.C. and Quick, J.D. (1984) *Organizational Stress and Preventive Management.* New York: McGraw-Hill.

Quinton, A. (1994) 'Permission to mourn.' *Nursing Times 90*, 12, 31.

Rando, T.A. (1986) 'The unique issues and impact of the death of a child.' In T.A. Rando (ed) *Parental Loss of a Child.* Champaign, IL: Research Press.

Reason, P. (ed) (1988) *Human Inquiry in Action: Developments in New Paradigm Research.* London: Sage.

Reder, P., Duncan, S. and Gray, M. (1993) *Beyond Blame, Child Abuse Tragedies Revisited.* London: Routledge.

Redwood (1997) 'Treating sexually abused children.' <http://redwood.northcoast. com/.~dka/studies.htm>.

Reid, C. (1989) *Mothers of Sexually Abused Girls: A Feminist View.* Social Work Monograph. Norwich: University of East Anglia.

Reidy, T. and Hochstadt, N. (1993) 'Attribution of blame in incest cases: A comparison of mental health professionals.' *Child Abuse and Neglect 17*, 3, 371–381.

Reilly, B.J. and DiAngelo, C. (1990) 'Communication: A cultural system of meaning and value.' *Human Relations 43*, February, 129.

Reis, S.D. and Heppner, P.P. (1993) 'Examination of coping resources and family adaptation in mothers and daughters of incestuous versus non-clinical families.' *Journal of Counseling Psychology 40*, 1, 100–108.

Remer, R. and Elliott, J.E. (1988) 'Management of secondary victims of sexual assault.' *International Journal of Psychiatry 9*, 4, 389–401.

Reynolds, K. (1999) 'The changing child and the evolving picture book.' *Royal Society of Arts Journal 2*, 4, 98–106.

Ribbens, J. (1994) *Mothers and Their Children: A Feminist Sociology of Childrearing.* London: Sage.

Richardson, D. (1993) *Women, Motherhood and Childrearing.* London: Macmillan.

Rogers, C. (1967) *On Becoming a Person: A Therapist's View of Psychotherapy.* London: Constable.

Rosenblatt, P.C., Spoentgen, P., Karis, T.A., Dahl, C., Kaiser T. and Elde, C. (1991) 'Difficulties in supporting the bereaved.' *Omega 23*, 2, 119–128.

Rosenhead, J. (1990) *Rational Analysis for a Problematic World: Problem Structuring Methods for Complexity, Uncertainty and Conflict.* Chichester: Wiley.

Russell, D.E.H. (1986) *The Secret Trauma: Incest in the Lives of Girls and Women.* New York: Basic Books.

Sabatelli, R.M. and Anderson, S.A. (1991) 'Family system dynamics, peer relationships and adolescents' psychological development.' *Family Relations 40*, 363–369.

Sage, G. (1993) *Child Abuse and the Children Act: A Critical Analysis of the Teacher's Role.* London: ATL Publications.

Sanford, L.T. and Donovan, M.E. (1984) *Women and Self-Esteem: Understanding and Improving the Way We Think and Feel about Ourselves.* Harmondsworth: Penguin.

Schein, E.H. (1988) *Organizational Psychology*, 3rd edition. Englewood Cliffs, NJ: Prentice-Hall International.

Schonberg, I.J. (1990) 'A review of the mommy trap in child sexual abuse.' Paper presented at the Children's Center Spring Conference, Detroit, MI, May.

Scott-Peck, M. (1990) *The Road Less Travelled.* London: Arrow.

Sgroi, S.M. (1982) *Handbook of Clinical Intervention in Child Sexual Abuse.* Lexington, MA: Lexington Books.

Sharland, E., Jones, D., Aldgate, J., Seal, H. and Croucher, M. (1995) *Professional Intervention in Child Sexual Abuse.* London: HMSO.

Shepherd, V. (1990) *Language, Variety and the Art of the Everyday.* London: Pinter.

Silverman, D. (1993) *Interpreting Qualitative Data: Methods for Analysing Talk, Text and Action.* London: Sage.

Sirles, E.A. and Franke, P.J. (1989) 'Factors influencing mothers' reactions to intrafamily sexual abuse.' *Child Abuse and Neglect 13*, 1, 131–139.

Skinner, J. (1998) 'Research as a counselling activity? A discussion of some uses of counselling within the context of research on sensitive issues.' *British Journal of Guidance and Counselling 26*, 4, 533–540.

Skinner, J. (1999a) 'Dealing with the aftermath of child sexual abuse: A reflection on three case examples.' *Pastoral Care in Education 17*, 1, 32–36.

Skinner, J. (1999b) 'Teachers coping with sexual abuse issues.' *Educational Research 41*, 3, 329–339.

Sloan, J. (1989) 'Child abuse in schools.' *Educational and Child Psychology 6*, 1, 11–14.

Smith, J. (1989) *Misogynies.* London: Faber and Faber.

Smith, M. and Grocke, M. (1995) *Normal Family Sexuality and Sexual Knowledge in Children.* London: Royal College of Psychiatrists and Gorkill Press.

Smith, R. (1991) 'Child care: Welfare, protection or rights?' *Journal of Social Welfare and Family Law 6*, 469–481.

Sommerfeld, D.P. (1989) 'The origins of mother blaming: Historical perspectives on childhood and motherhood.' *Infant Mental Health Journal 10*, 1, 14–24.

Spaccarelli, S. (1994) 'Stress, appraisal and coping in child sexual abuse: A theoretical and empirical review.' *Psychological Bulletin 116*, 2, 340–362.

Stanko, E.A. (1985) *Intimate Intrusions, Women's Experience of Male Violence.* London: Unwin Hyman.

Stanley, N. (1997) 'Domestic violence and child abuse: Developing social work practice.' *Child and Family Social Work 2*, 135–145.

Steedman, P.H. (1991) 'On the relations between seeing, interpreting and knowing.' In F. Steier (ed) *Research and Reflexivity*. London: Sage.

Stow, J. (1994) *Sexual Abuse, Feminism and Family Therapy*. Social Work Monograph. Norwich: University of East Anglia.

Strand, V.C. (1991) 'Mid-phase treatment with mothers in incest families.' *Clinical Social Work Journal 19*, 4, 377–389.

Strawbridge, S. (1992) 'Roles, rules and relationships.' In J. Walmsley, J. Reynolds, P. Shakespeare and R. Woolfe (eds) *Health, Welfare and Practice*. London: Sage.

Street, H. (ed) (1980) *You and Your Rights*. London: Reader's Digest.

Thompson, K.E. and Range, L.M. (1992) 'Bereavement following suicide and other deaths: Why support attempts fail.' *Omega 26*, 1, 61–70.

Times Educational Supplement (1997) Anonymous letter, 17 January.

Timmons-Mitchell, J. and Gardner, S. (1991) 'Treating sexual victimization: Developing trust-based relating in the mother–daughter dyad.' *Psychotherapy 28*, 2, 333–338.

Todd, I. and Ellis, L. (1992) 'Divided loyalties.' *Social Work Today*, 25 June, 14–15.

Tougas, K., Shandel, T. and Feldmar, A. (1989) *Did You Used to be R.D. Laing?* TV Documentary Transcript. Channel Four, London, and Third Mind Productions Inc. Vancouver.

Trolley, B.C. (1994) 'A bridge between traumatic life events and losses by death.' *Omega 28*, 4, 285–300.

Tsoukas, H. (1994) *New Thinking in Organizational Behaviour*. Oxford: Butterworth Heinemann.

Tsun, O. (1999) 'Sibling incest: A Hong Kong experience.' *Child Abuse and Neglect 23*, 1, 71–79.

Tutty, L.M. (1992) 'The ability of elementary school children to learn child sexual abuse prevention concepts.' *Child Abuse and Neglect 16*, 4, 369–384.

Tutty, L.M. (1994) 'Developmental issues in young children's learning of sexual abuse prevention concepts.' *Child Abuse and Neglect 18*, 2, 179–192.

van den Boom, D. (1994) 'The influence of temperament and mothering on attachment and exploration: An experimental manipulation of sensitive responsiveness among lower-class mothers with irritable infants.' *Child Development 65*, 1457–1477.

Varia, R., Abidin, R.R. and Dass, P. (1996) 'Perceptions of abuse: Effects on adult psychological and social adjustment.' *Child Abuse and Neglect 20*, 6, 511–526.

Viinikka, S. (1989) 'Child sexual abuse and the law.' In E. Driver and A. Droisen (eds) *Child Sexual Abuse: Feminist Perspectives*. London: Macmillan.

Vizard, E. and Tranter, M. (1988) 'Recognition and assessment of child sexual abuse.' In A. Bentovim (ed) *Child Sexual Abuse within the Family: Assessment and Treatment*. London: Wright.

Vulliamy, G. and Webb, R. (1992) *Research and Special Educational Needs*. London: David Fulton.

Walby, C., Clancy, A., Emetchi, J. and Summerfield, C. (1989) 'Theoretical perspectives on father–daughter incest.' In E. Driver and A. Droisen (eds) *Child Sexual Abuse: Feminist Perspectives*. London: Macmillan.

Walker, M. (1992) *Surviving Secrets*. Buckingham: Open University Press.

Wallerstein, J.S. and Kelly, J.B. (1980) *Surviving the Breakup: How Children and Parents Cope with Divorce*. New York: Basic Books.

Ward, E. (1984) *Father–Daughter Rape*. London: The Women's Press.

Waterhouse, L. (ed) (1993) *Child Abuse and Child Abusers: Protection and Prevention*. London: Jessica Kingsley Publishers.

Waterhouse, L., Carnie, J. and Dobash, R. (1993) 'The abuser under the microscope.' *Community Care*, 972, 24.

Watkins, B. and Bentovim, A. (1992) 'The sexual abuse of male children and adolescents: A review of current research.' *Journal of Child Psychology and Psychiatry* 33, 1, 197–248.

Wattam, C., Hughes, J. and Blagg, H. (1989) *Child Sexual Abuse: Listening, Hearing and Validating the Experiences of Children*. London: Longman.

Webb, S. (1997) 'How to manage child protection in your school.' Course delivered to teachers, 9 May.

Weinberg, N. (1995) 'Does apologizing help? The role of self-blame and making amends in recovery from bereavement.' *Health and Social Work 20*, 4, 294–299.

Weissmann-Wind, T. and Silvern, L. (1994) 'Parenting and family stress as mediators of the long-term effects of child abuse.' *Child Abuse and Neglect 18*, 5, 439–453.

Welldon, E.V. (1992) *Mother, Madonna, Whore – The Idealization and Denigration of Motherhood*. London: Guilford Press.

Wells, R.D., McCann, J., Adams, J., Voris, J. and Ensign, J. (1995) 'Emotional, behavioral and physical symptoms reported by parents of sexually abused, nonabused and allegedly abused prepubescent females.' *Child Abuse and Neglect 19*, 2, 155–163.

White, M. (1986) 'Assumptions and therapy.' Dulwich Centre Newletter, Summer, 7.

Wolfe, D.A., Sas, L. and Wekerle, C. (1994) 'Factors associated with the development of posttraumatic stress disorder among child victims of sexual abuse.' *Child Abuse and Neglect 18*, 1, 37.

Wolin, S. and Wolin, S. (1995) 'Resilience among youth growing up in substance abusing families.' *Substance Abuse 42*, 2, 415–429.

Woodcraft, E. (1988) 'Child sexual abuse and the law.' *Feminist Review 28*, January, 122–130.

Worden, J.W. (1983) *Grief Counselling and Grief Therapy*. London: Tavistock.

Wurtele, S.K. and Schmitt, A. (1992) 'Child care workers' knowledge about reporting suspected child sexual abuse.' *Child Abuse and Neglect 16*, 3, 385–390.

Wyatt, G.E. and Mickey, M.R. (1987) 'Ameliorating the effects of child sexual abuse.' *Journal of Interpersonal Violence 2*, 4, 403–414.

Wyatt, G.E. and Newcomb, M. (1990) 'Internal and external mediators of women's sexual abuse in childhood.' *Journal of Consulting and Clinical Psychology 58*, 6, 758–767.

Wyatt, G.E. and Powell, G.L. (eds) (1988) *Lasting Effects of Child Sexual Abuse.* London: Sage.

Young, L. (1992) 'Sexual abuse and the problem of embodiment.' *Child Abuse and Neglect 16*, 1, 89–100.

Subject Index

Author Index